IMAGES
of America

DERRY REVISITED

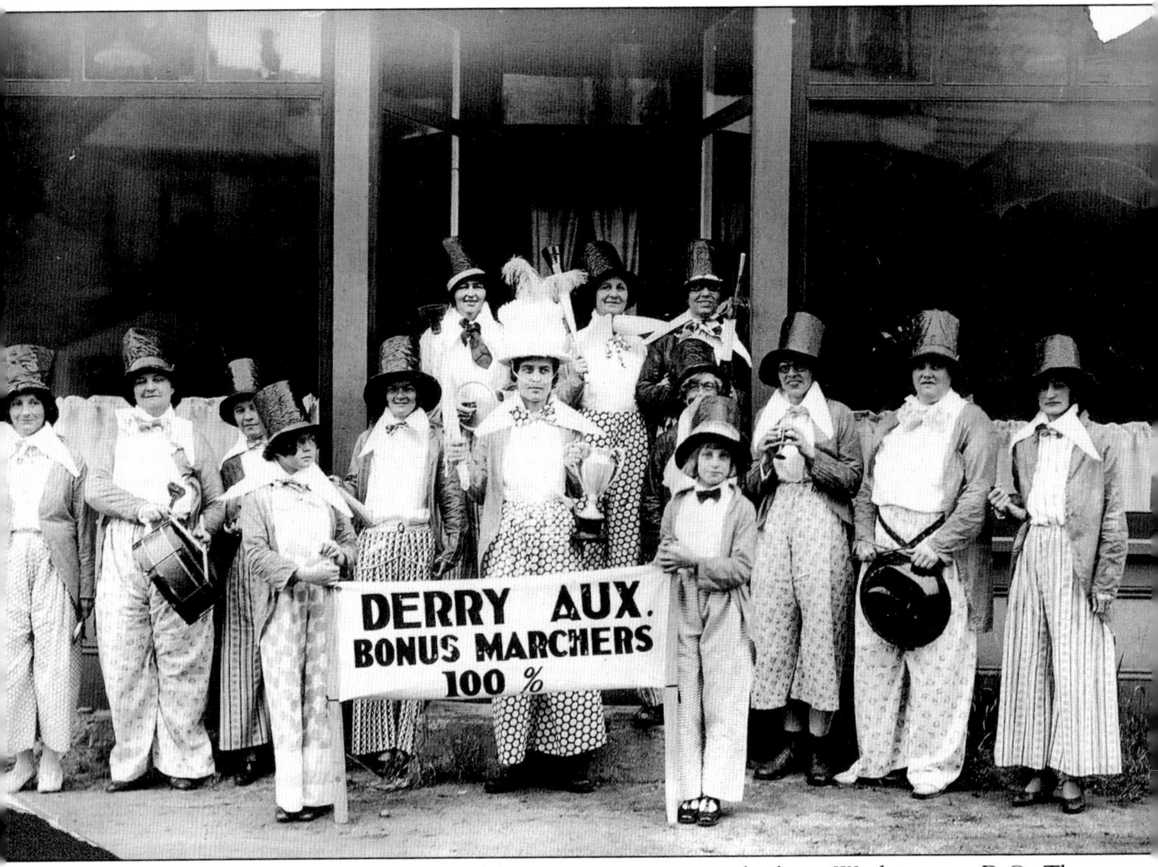

In the spring of 1932, 80,000 World War I veterans marched on Washington, D.C. The government had promised each a $1,000 award (plus interest), but the money would not be paid until 1945; the protesters wanted immediate payment of the bonuses. (President Hoover later called in army troops, who savagely drove the marchers from the nation's capital.) These members of the Derry American Legion Auxiliary marched in the town's George Washington Bicentennial Parade to show support for their veterans.

IMAGES
of America

DERRY REVISITED

Richard Holmes and William Dugan

ARCADIA PUBLISHING

ISBN 978-0-7385-3763-4

Published by Arcadia Publishing
Charleston, South Carolina

Printed in the United States of America

Library of Congress Catalog Card Number: 2004115789

For all general information, contact Arcadia Publishing:
Telephone 843-853-2070
Fax 843-853-0044
E-mail sales@arcadiapublishing.com
For customer service and orders:
Toll-free 1-888-313-2665

Visit us on the Internet at www.arcadiapublishing.com

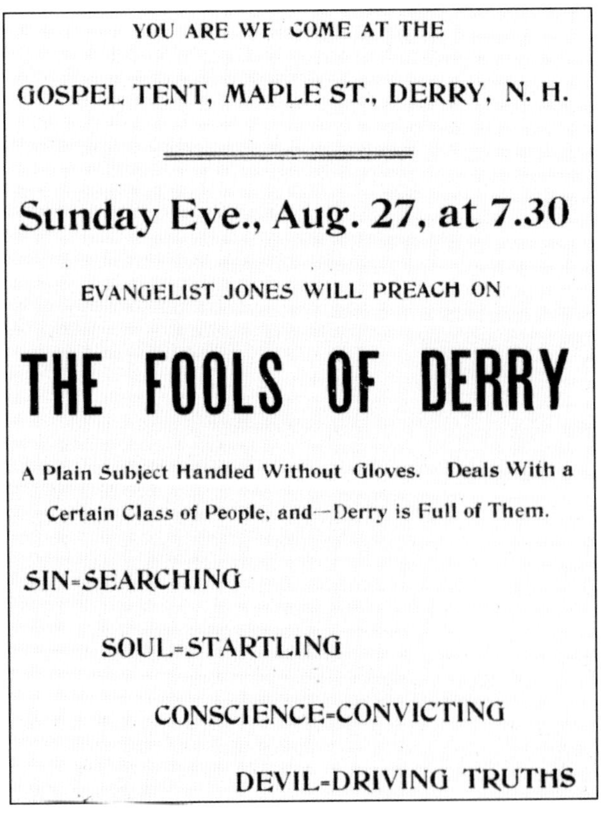

YOU ARE WE COME AT THE

GOSPEL TENT, MAPLE ST., DERRY, N. H.

Sunday Eve., Aug. 27, at 7.30

EVANGELIST JONES WILL PREACH ON

THE FOOLS OF DERRY

A Plain Subject Handled Without Gloves. Deals With a Certain Class of People, and—Derry is Full of Them.

SIN-SEARCHING

SOUL-STARTLING

CONSCIENCE-CONVICTING

DEVIL-DRIVING TRUTHS

An open field on Maple Street was the site of a 1904 visit by evangelist Sam Jones (1847–1906). A reformed alcoholic and lawyer, Jones developed a national following. He was known for using "crude wit and coarse stories" to get sinners saved. There were many conversions during his Derry visit.

Contents

ACKNOWLEDGMENTS

We wish to sincerely thank the following individuals and groups for their help in producing this book. Some loaned treasured family photographs, others gave technical assistance. Without them, the book never would have been completed: Walter Chapman Photo Restorations of Penacook, Derry Museum of History, Paul and Deede Loffler, the *Derry News*, H. P. Hood Inc., Bertha MacDougall, Chantel and Brigette Pion, Walter Borowski, Image Ability, Hercules Pappachristos, Laurie and William Petch, Marilyn Ham, Derry Public Library, the Grant Benson family, Marion Pounder, Jacob Holmes, Christopher Gonzalez, Delaney Paige Dugan Kearns, the Derry Heritage Commission, Derry Historical Society, the families of the late Henry Shepard and Judge George Grinnell, and most importantly we thank our loving, patient, and forgiving wives, Carol Holmes and Lois Dugan.

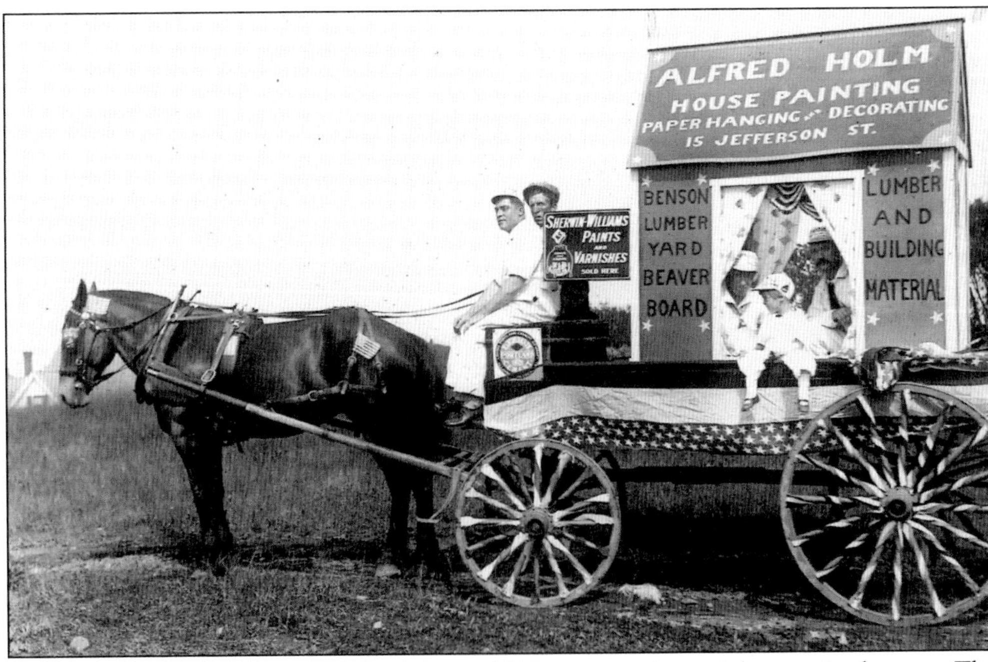

The celebration of Derry's 200th birthday in 1919 was a major social event in the area. The parade had, in addition to the usual marching bands and fire trucks, a number of floats created by local businessmen. This carefully crafted wagon that was used in several parades speaks well of the skill of these two home-improvement companies.

INTRODUCTION

In 1719, a pioneer band of 16 families left Londonderry, Northern Ireland, to seek freedom in America. Led by their Presbyterian pastor Rev. James MacGregor, they founded their colony deep in the untracked wilderness on the crest of East Derry Hill. Originally, the grant of 114 square miles was called Londonderry. The section called Derry was the site of the first settlement and broke away in 1827 to form its own town.

Derry remained primarily an agricultural community until 1849, when the railroad came to town. Soon, shoe factories began to employ the majority of men and women. Derry remained a shoe town for nearly a century. Another large local employer was the H. P. Hood dairy company. The Great Depression hit industrial Derry very hard. By the mid-20th century, most of the shoe factories had closed. The 1960 federal census reported that the town's population was in decline for the first time in memory.

The construction of interstate highway Route 93 in 1963 changed Derry forever. The townspeople suddenly had an easy commute to the factories and office parks in Massachusetts. Thousands of families left the urban life to settle in the suburban green of Derry. Within a decade of the highway's opening, the population of our town doubled, then doubled again. Today, Derry's population is nearly five times what it was only 40 years before. We are now the largest town in the state and are only surpassed in population size by the cities of Manchester, Nashua, and Concord.

This book will present images of daily life in Derry before the recent years of change. Within these pages, the trolley still runs down Broadway; most of our adults are employed in the sprawling shoe factories; boys wear knickers, and girls, long dresses. The Hood cows are seen grazing in their East Broadway pasture, the traffic circle has not been built. Here, Derry has one traffic light, and the Beaver Lake Pavilion is Derry's place to be on a hot summer's day.

It is our hope that through this book the older residents will enjoy reliving their past. We hope that these pictures will help make the newer residents aware of the traditions and events that shaped the modern town. Perhaps, by appreciating what we were, future generations will be more proactive in pursuing a path of conservation and preservation. There is still much in Derry that can and must be protected from the bulldozers of ill-conceived progress and poorly planned change.

—Richard Holmes and William Dugan

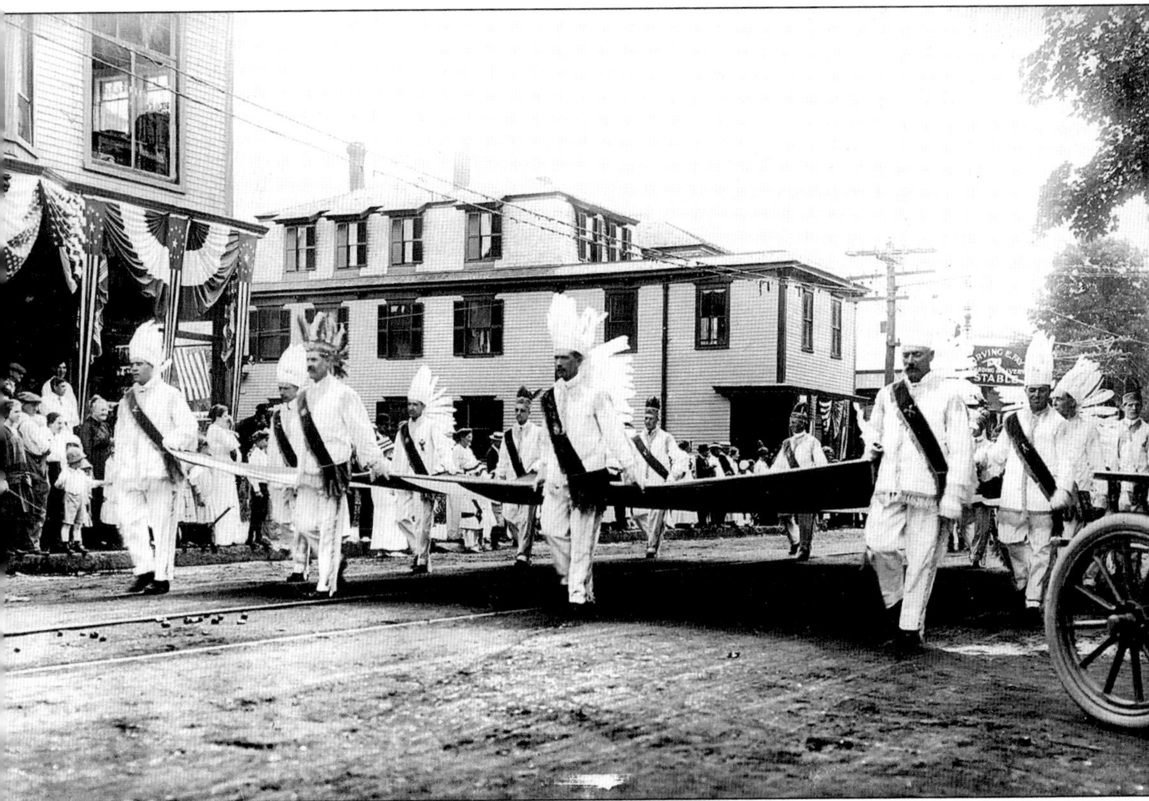

In addition to picnics, baseball games, and church socials, there was always a parade for Old Home Week. Shown here *c.* 1910, Derry's Improved Order of Redmen marches down Broadway in ceremonial regalia. (Allen photograph.)

One

Lakes and Ponds

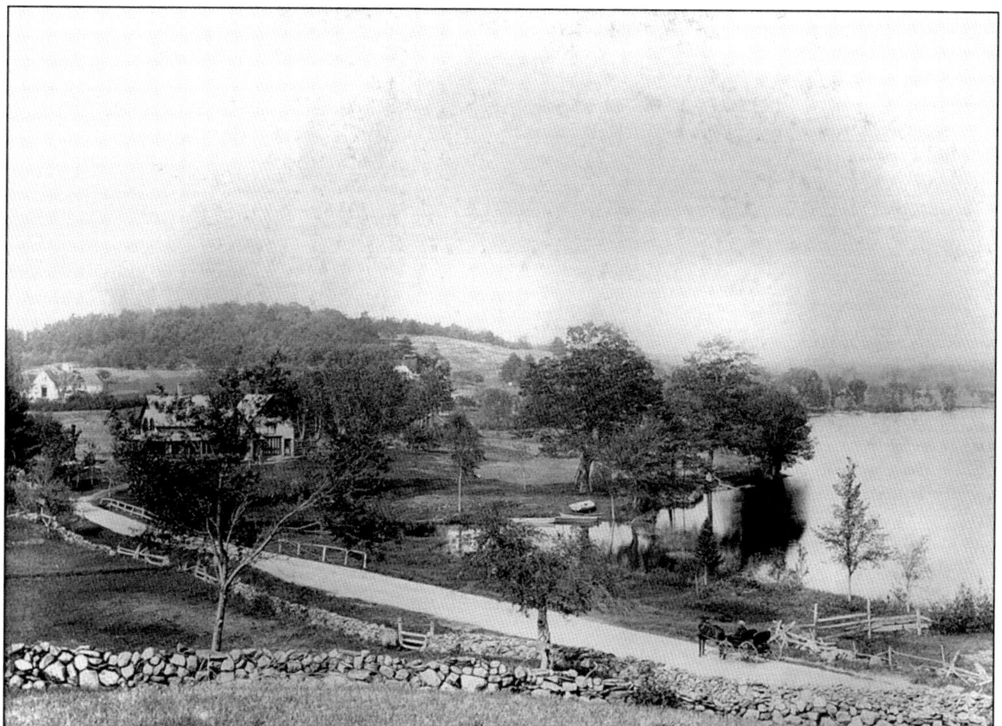

The north end of Beaver Lake was still very rural in 1907. The horse and wagon is likely that of R. N. Richardson, who hired photographer J. W. Bowley to record this scene. Richardson published the picture in *Tsienneto*, a promotional booklet about the area.

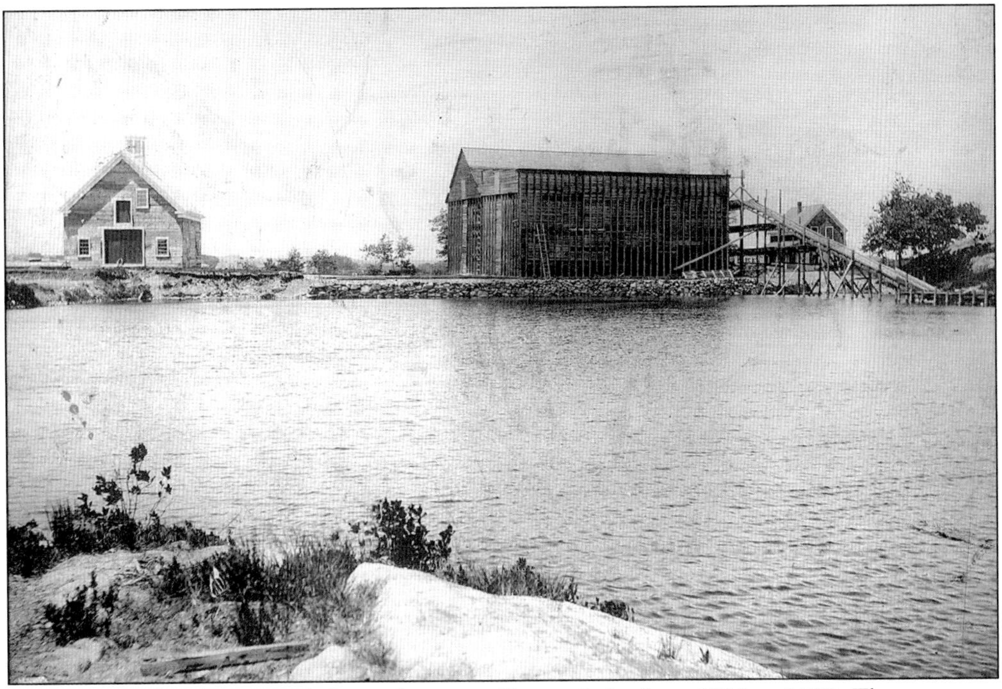

The Madden family operated this icehouse on Beaver Lake from 1910 to 1922. The conveyor belt on the right side of the building was used to move fresh-cut blocks of ice into the building. In 1953, Albert Gallien opened this area of the shorefront as a public beach. It is now a town-owned park.

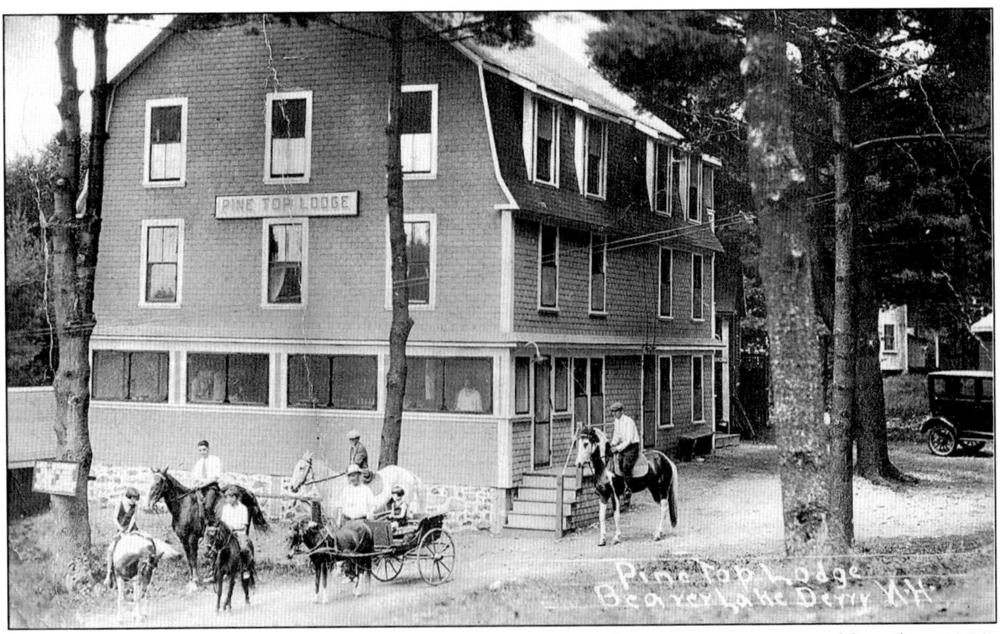

Desire Bellavance built the Pine Top Lodge on Beaver Lake as a restaurant and hotel c. 1919. Guests could rent horses and ponies by the hour. The lodge was destroyed by fire in 1932.

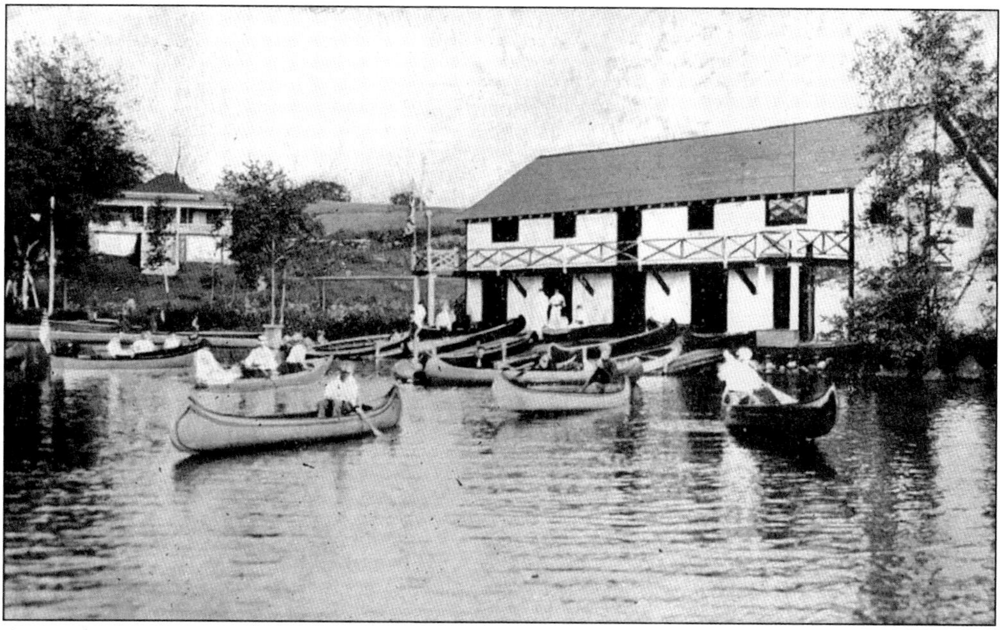

A popular way to spend a summer's day was to rent a canoe at the Beaver Lake Pavilion and paddle on Beaver Lake. This 1920s photograph shows Jim Comeau's armada. In addition to swimming and paddling, visitors to the pavilion could see a movie for a dime and go dancing for a quarter.

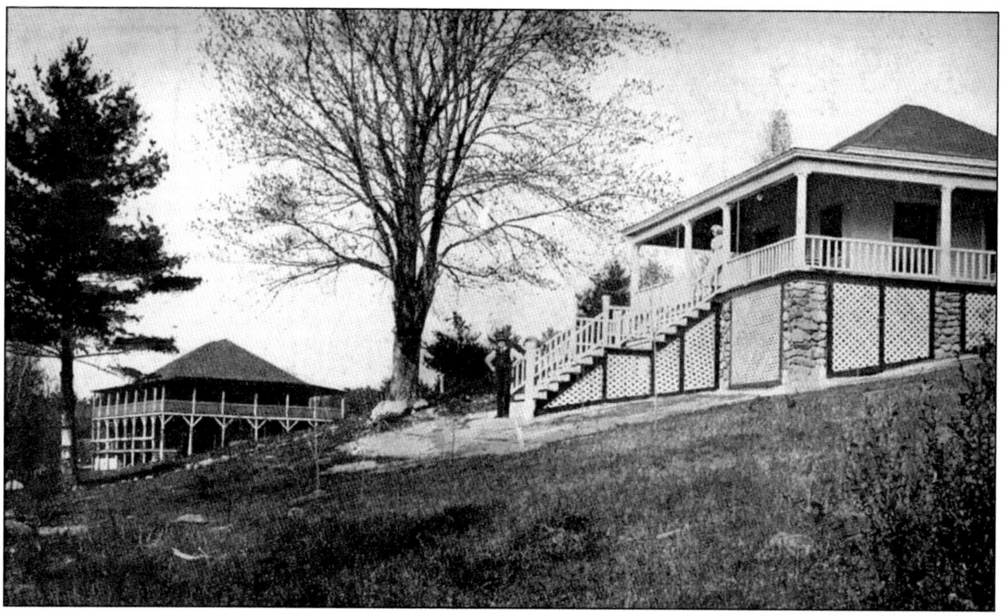

James Comeau, who lived in this Caribbean-style bungalow on the right, managed the Beaver Lake Pavilion. In the years when he did not win the contract to run the pavilion, Comeau operated a swimming area and snack bar from his home. Comeau is seen here standing in front of his home.

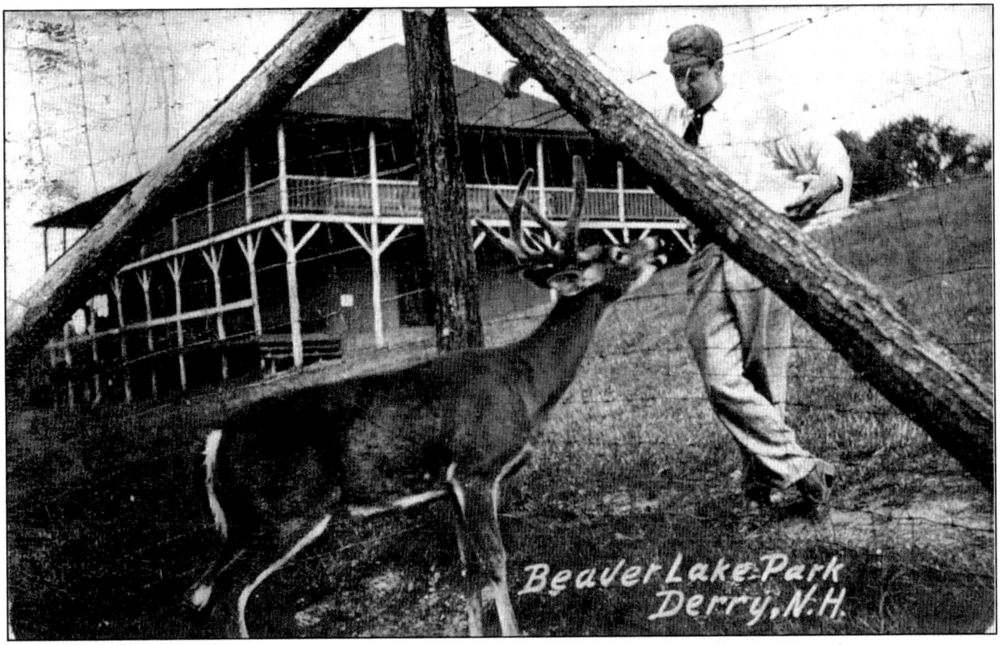

Among the attractions offered at the Beaver Lake Pavilion was a small zoo. Seen here is manager James Comeau with the deer he bought from Corbin Park in 1907. In addition, his menagerie included ducks, turkeys, and a dancing bear cub.

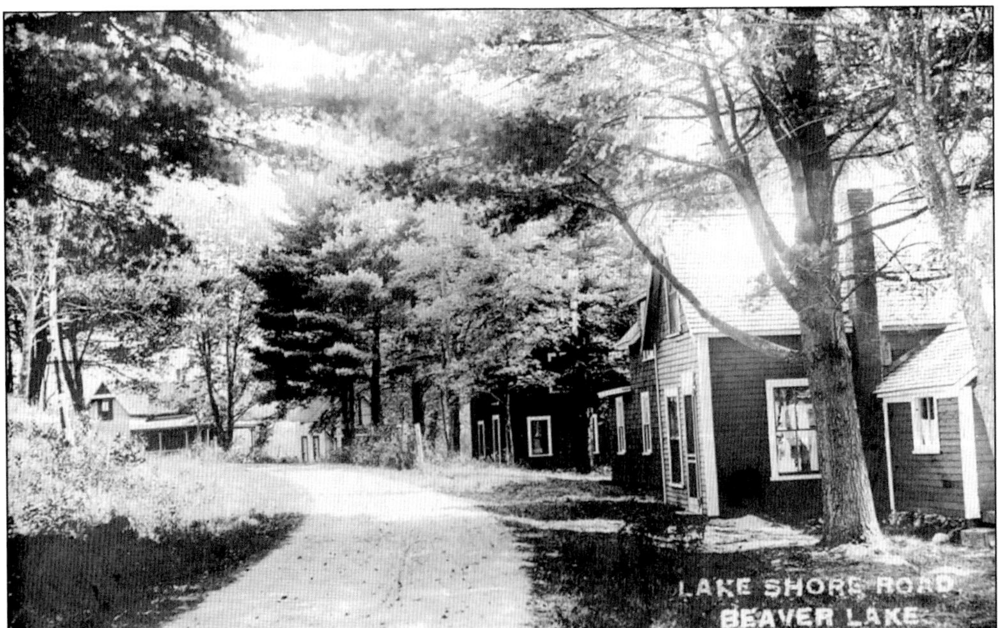

North Shore Road began to be developed during the last few years of the 19th century. Originally the street was called Lake Shore Road. By the 1920s, most of the waterfront was divided into tiny building lots. Soon, cottage colonies surrounded the whole lake.

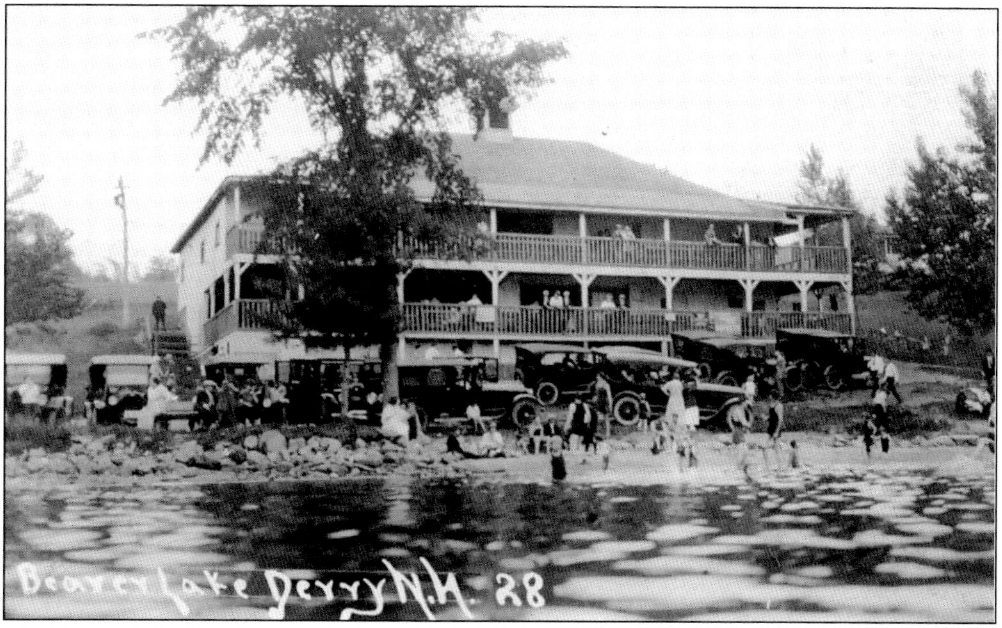

The Beaver Lake Pavilion was built in 1896, as an attraction that was accessible just a few steps from the tracks of the Chester and Derry Streets railroad. After the First World War, few rode the trolley, so the pavilion had to change with the times. The pavilion owners built a 200-car parking lot to attract the Model T Ford crowd.

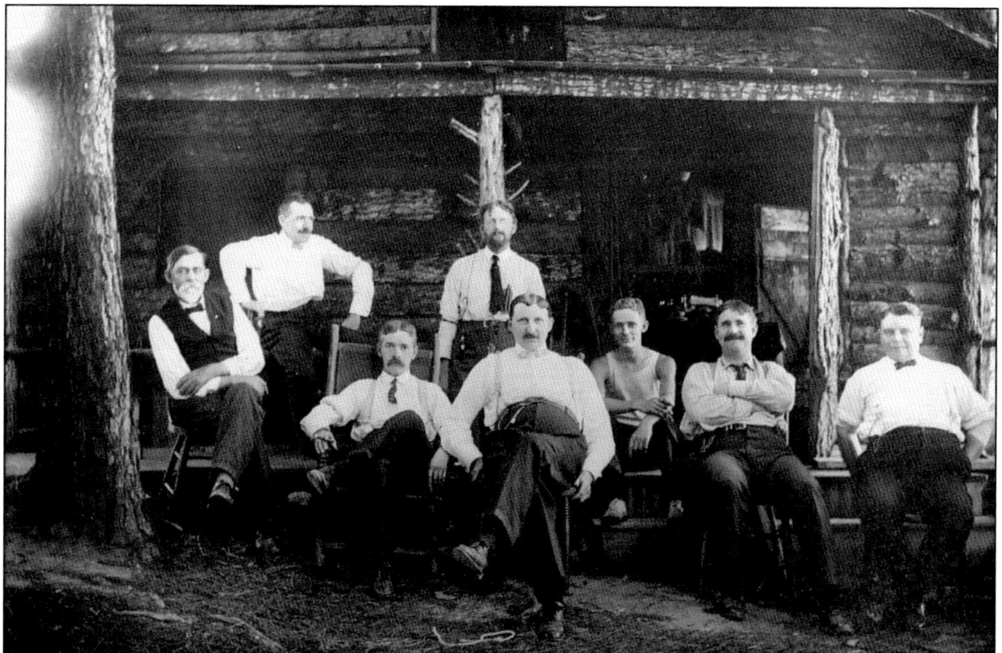

Around 1900, a group of local businessmen formed the Pickerel Club in Nottingham. Originally over the lodge's front door was a sign proclaiming the place to be "Liar's Paradise." The sign was stolen by Nottingham locals and put on "Dud" Leavitt's country store, which for generations has called itself the Liar's Paradise Store.

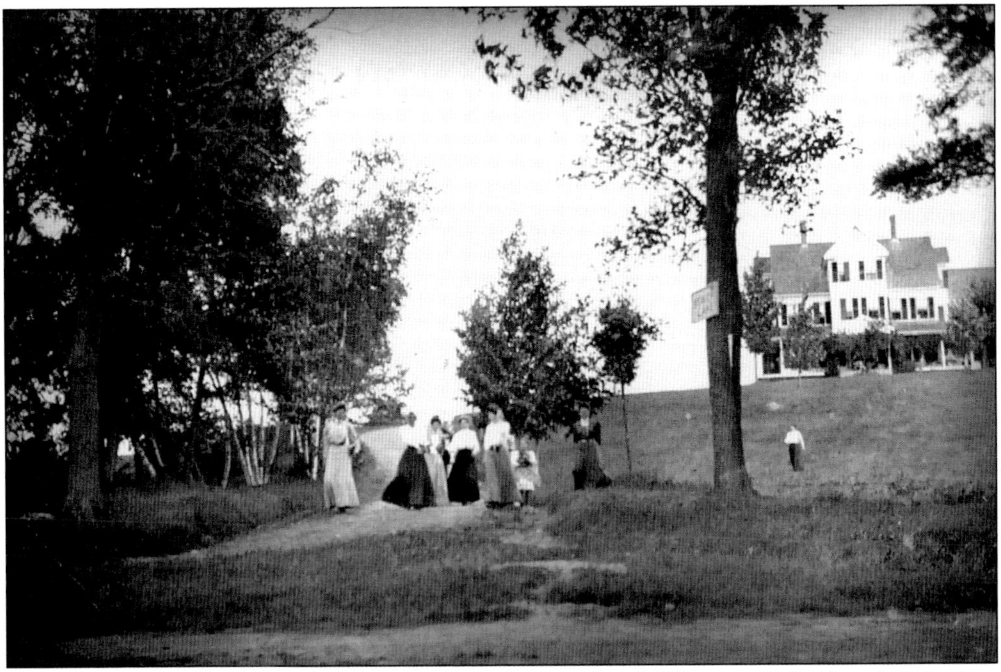

The Beaver Lake House was built in 1892 as a summer hotel. Wives and children left the hot cities and spent all summer in the cool of Derry. Husbands visited on weekends, traveling by railroad coach and trolley. This photograph was taken around 1900.

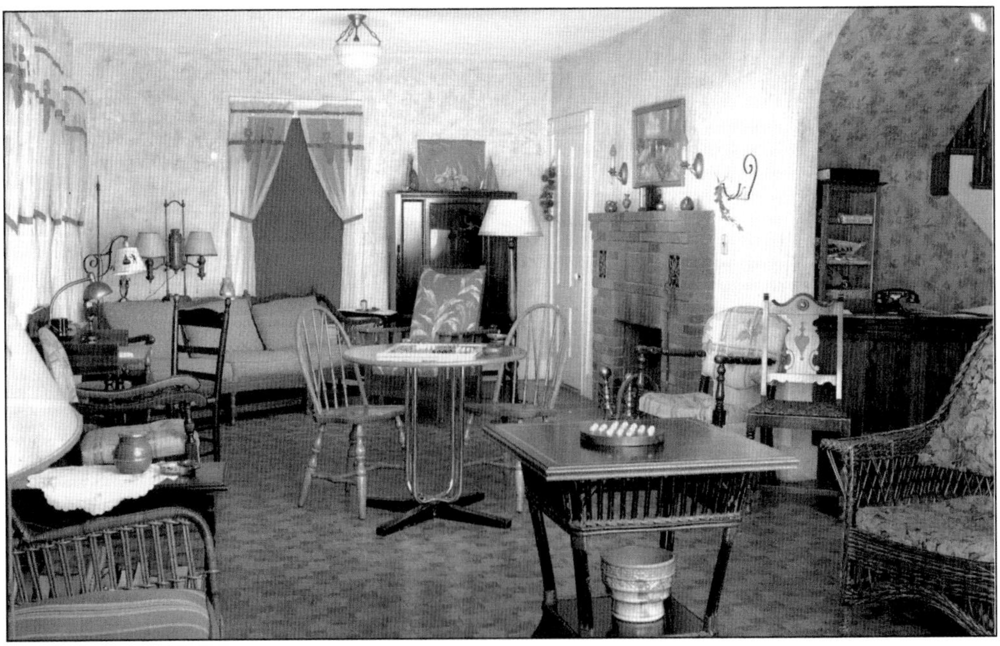

The old-fashioned informality of the public lounge of the Beaver Lake House, c. 1940, was very appealing to generations of city dwellers who sought out the piney woods of Derry. The building on the north shore is now a private health-care center.

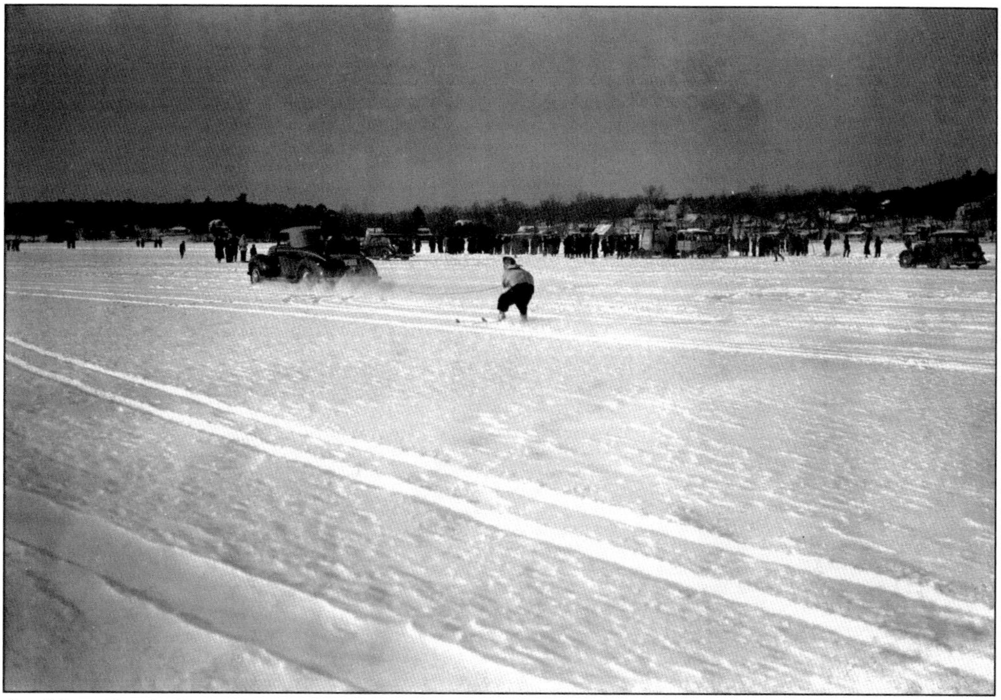

On New Year's Day 1940, a new sport was tried on Beaver Lake. In front of a few hundred spectators, a local sportsman on skis was tethered by a long rope fastened to a sporty car. Along a snow track, the car pulled the skier in a sport called "skijoring." A friend in the car's rumble seat shouted directions to the skier. (Arthur Lear photograph.)

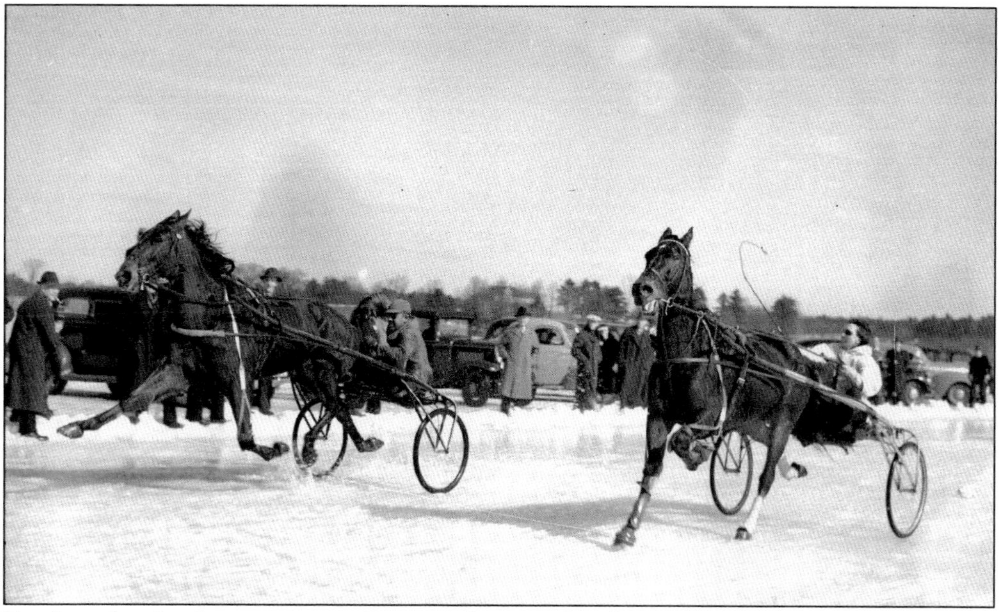

For three decades, horse racing on Beaver Lake was a locally accepted sport. This is the race for the Senator Cole Trophy in March 1943. Here Arthur Sears's *Great Baron* is beating Dillion Vollo's *Dewey*, while also besting the old lake record by three seconds on the quarter-mile track.

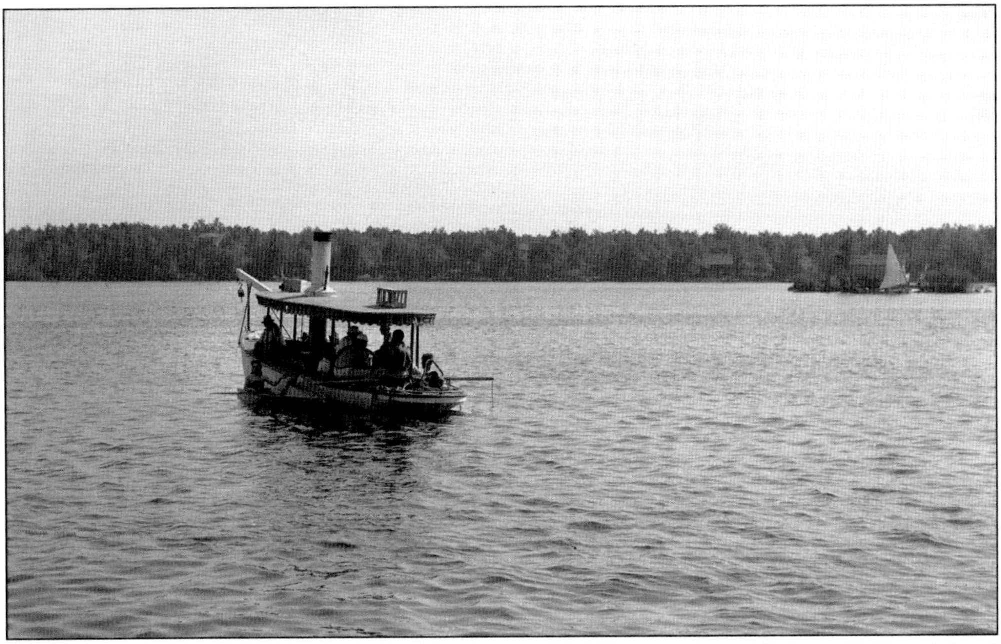

The good steamship *Ida F* was operated by George Eli Whitney from 1900 to 1948 on Island Pond. The 31-foot-long boat, shown here in 1939, could hold up to 25 passengers. (Arthur Lear photograph.)

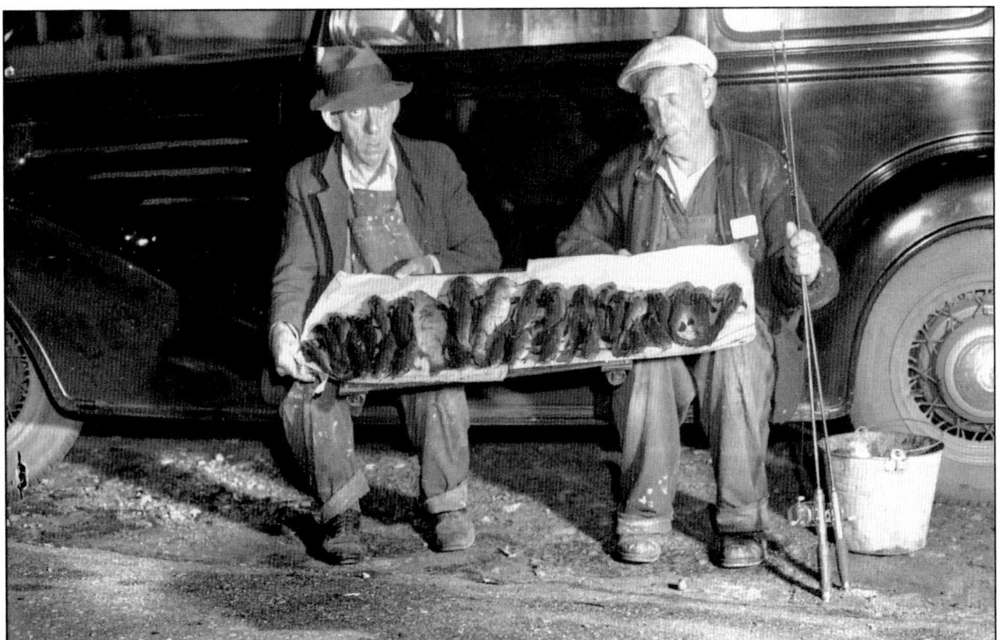

The first day of fishing at Scobie Pond in 1940 was better for some than for others. Pictured are 76-year-old Charles Sawyer (left) and 60-year-old Owen McAdams, showing off their "mess of pouts." Altogether the yield that night was 27 hornpout and 1 bass.

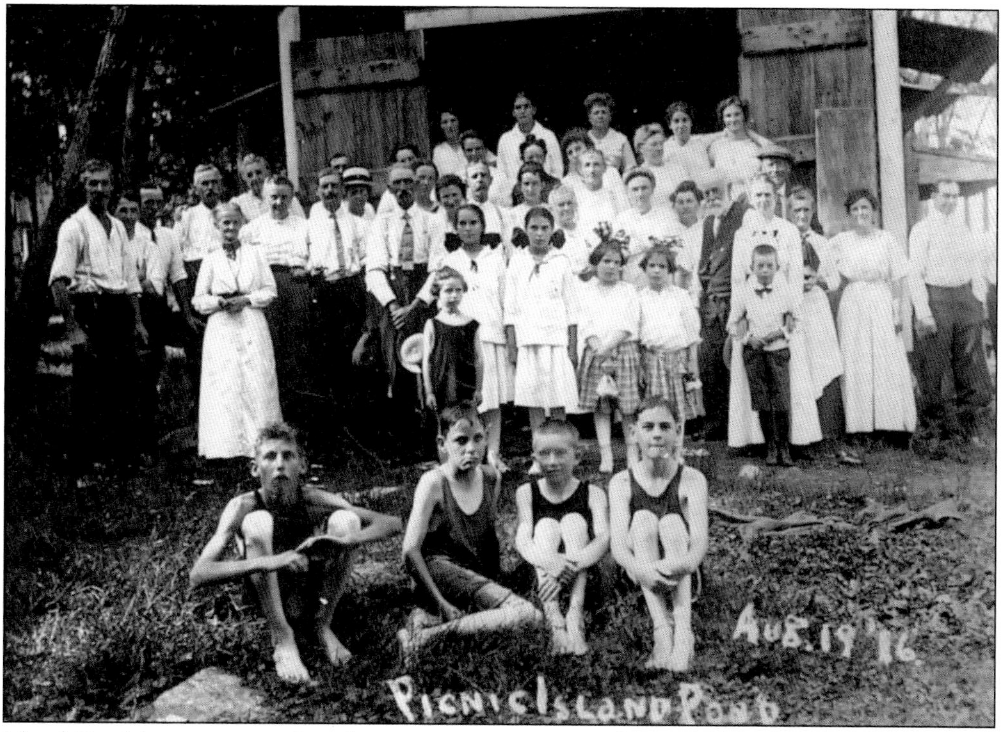

Island Pond has a century-long history as a picnic spot. Here in August 1916, the Nutfield Grange came for a day of fishing, baseball, swimming, eating, and dancing. The Goldsmith twins, standing at the center of the front row, celebrated their 12th birthday.

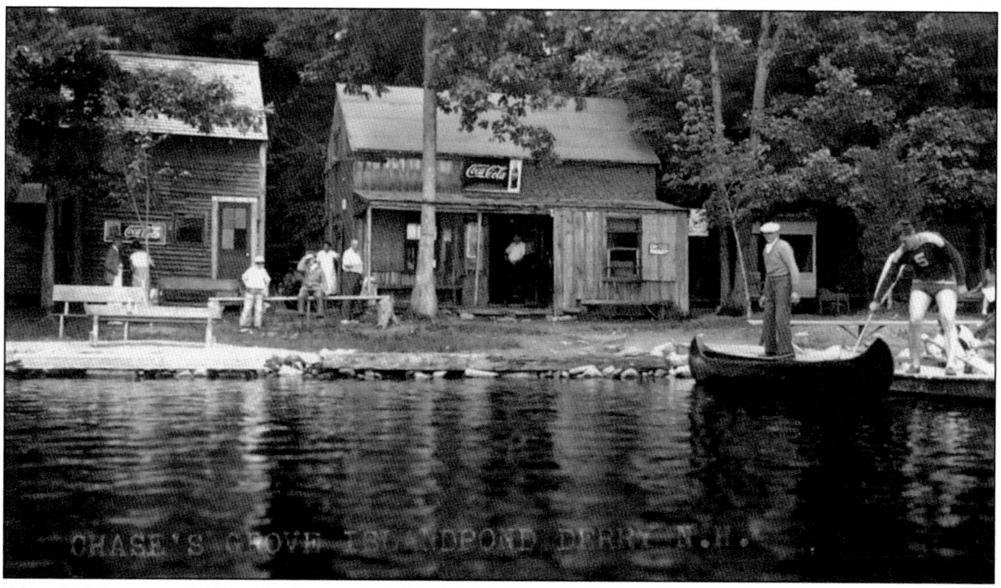

This 1934 view of Chase's Grove at Island Pond shows the refreshment stand that was popular with the summer cottage colonists. During the 19th century, the Chase family operated a picnic ground for day-trippers. Over the years, the area developed into a full-service summer vacation destination.

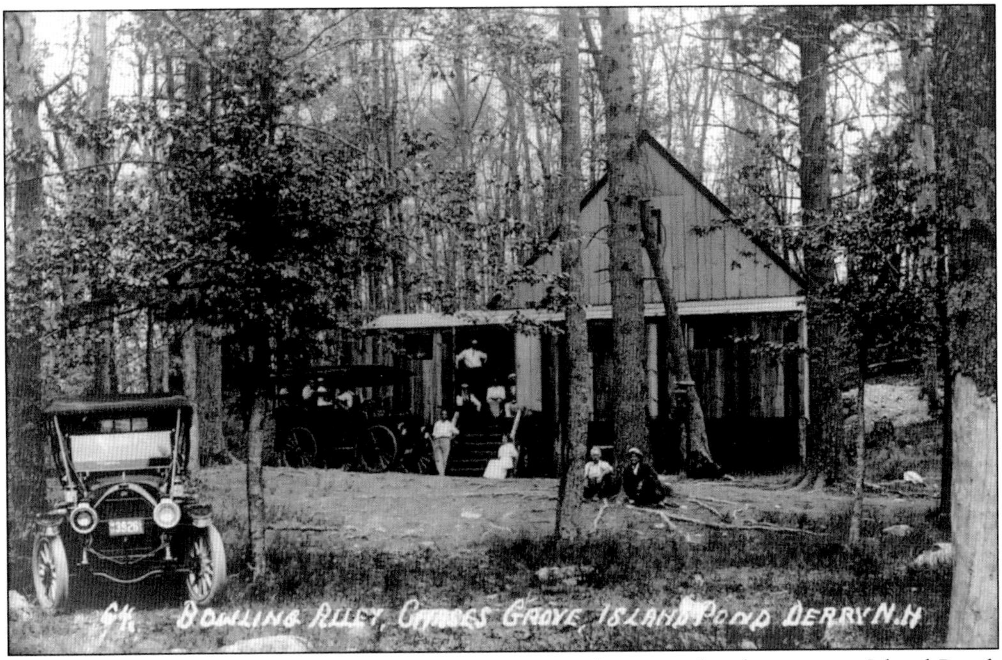

In 1910, the bowling alley at Chase's Grove was a popular rainy-day diversion at Island Pond. At night the dancehall became the center of activity. Chase's Grove was a safe, tame area when compared to the riotous activity at the nearby Rockingham Hotel, which was suspected of being both a brothel and speakeasy. The infamous hotel burned down in 1915.

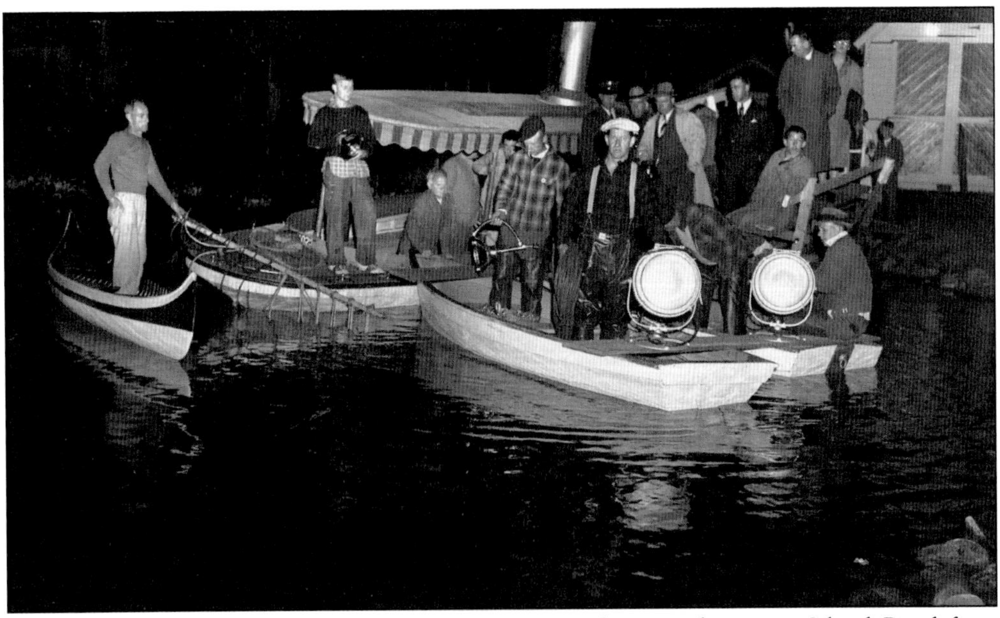

On July 7, 1938, Alfred Grassini of Lawrence, Massachusetts, dove into Island Pond from his rowboat while trying to retrieve a lost oar. The 16-year-old never resurfaced. Divers with grapples and huge underwater lights were brought in to search for the victim in the 30-foot-deep pond. In the background is George Eli Whitney's steamboat *Ida F.* The body was recovered two weeks later.

Two

FARMS

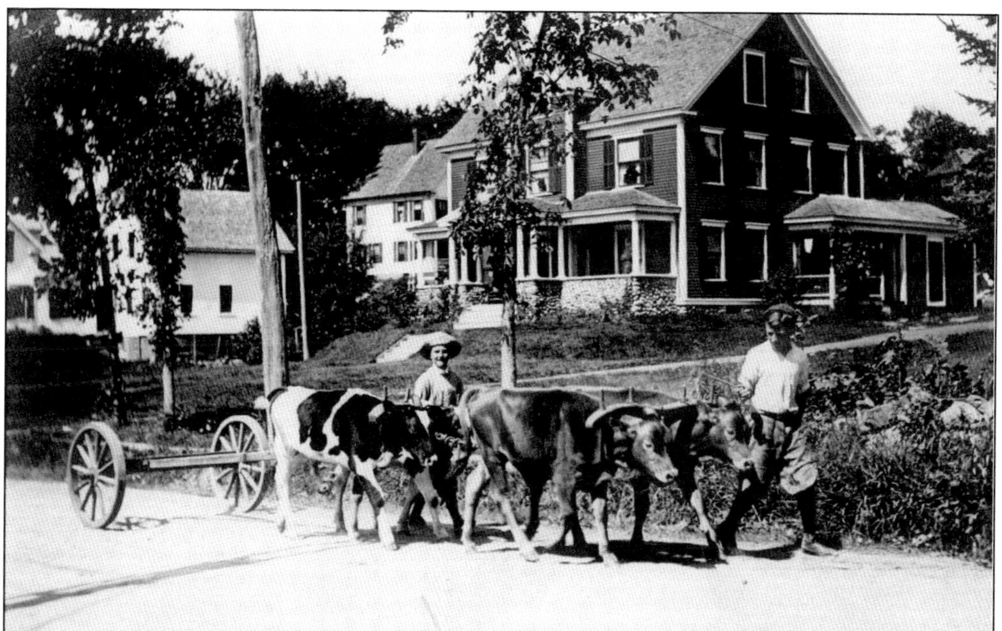

Photographed in 1908, Ralph Miltimore (1895–1971), on the left, and Gilbert Hood Jr. (1899–1985) are training their four young steers to become draught animals. In the background is the residence at 132 East Broadway, near the Danforth traffic circle.

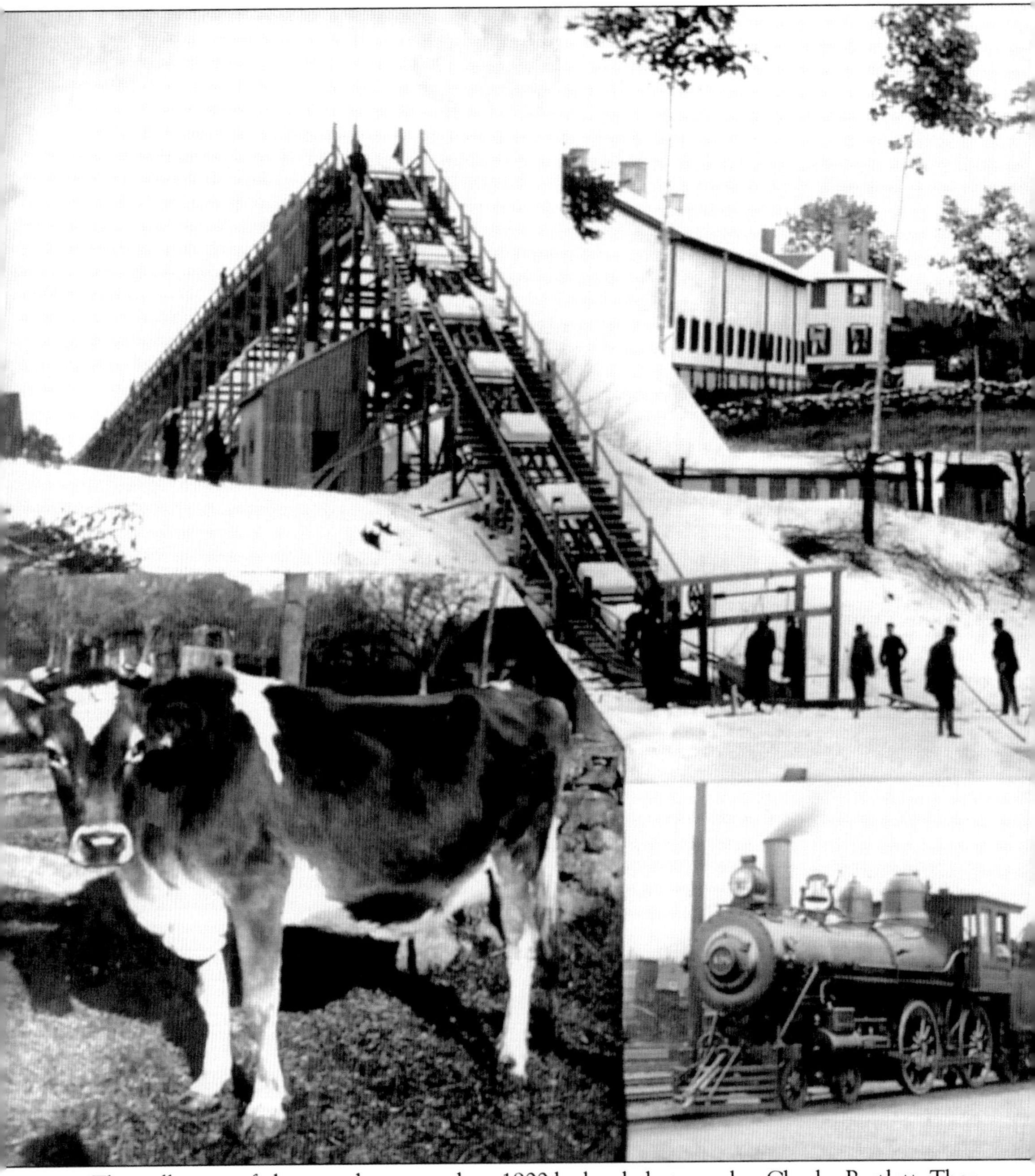

This collection of photographs was made c. 1900 by local photographer Charles Bartlett. They chronicle the Derry aspect of the great H. P. Hood & Sons milk company. Viewed clockwise from the top left is the conveyor belt that brought ice from Horne's Pond to the Hood icehouse; the Hood Homestead on East Broadway; the creamery where Hood's blue-ribbon butter was

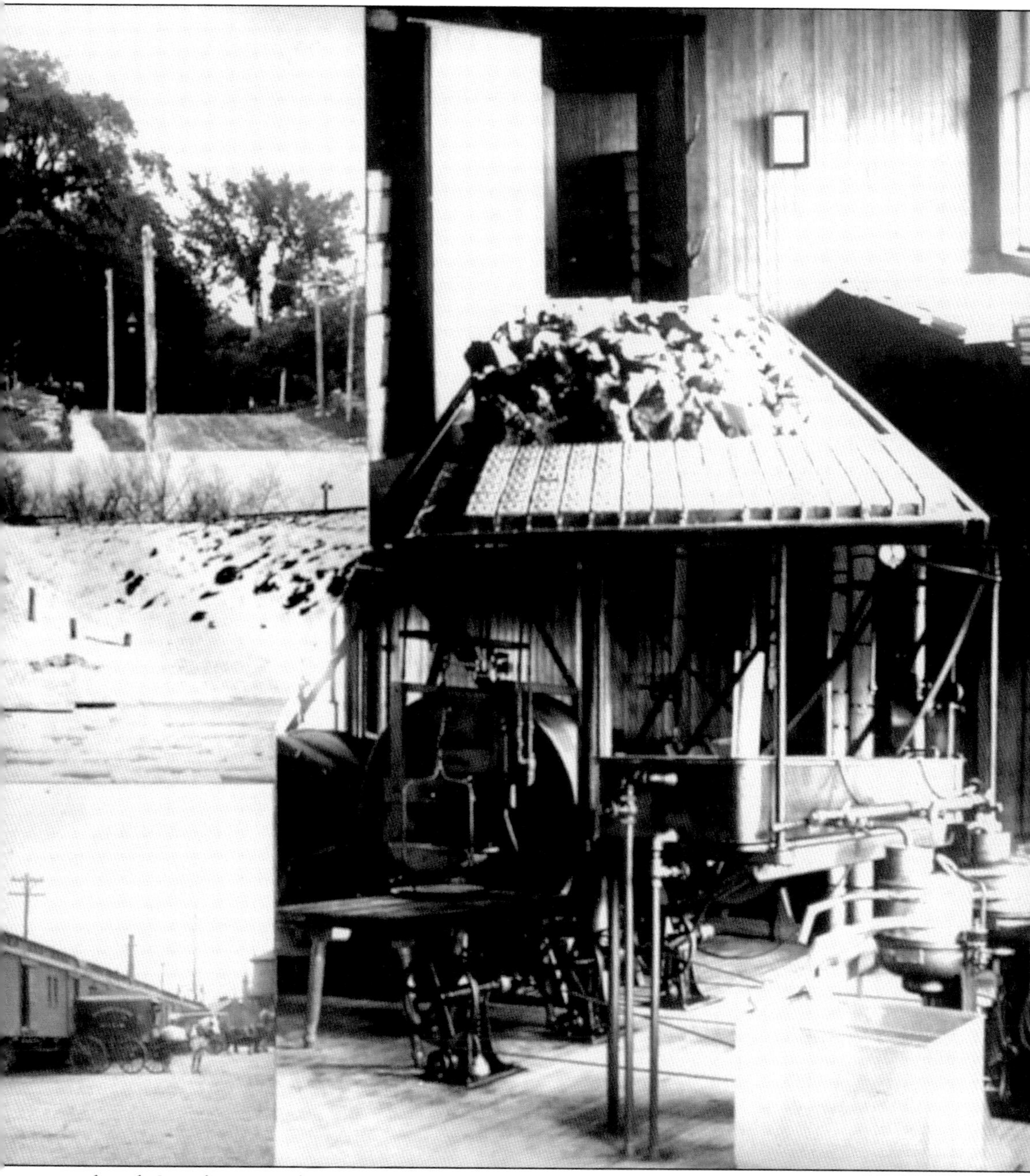

produced; Hood's state-of-the-art sanitary bottling equipment; the Hood refrigerated railroad car that carried Hood's products to distant markets; and Brown Bessie, Hood's champion Jersey cow from Derry, whose face became the company's symbol in all its advertisements.

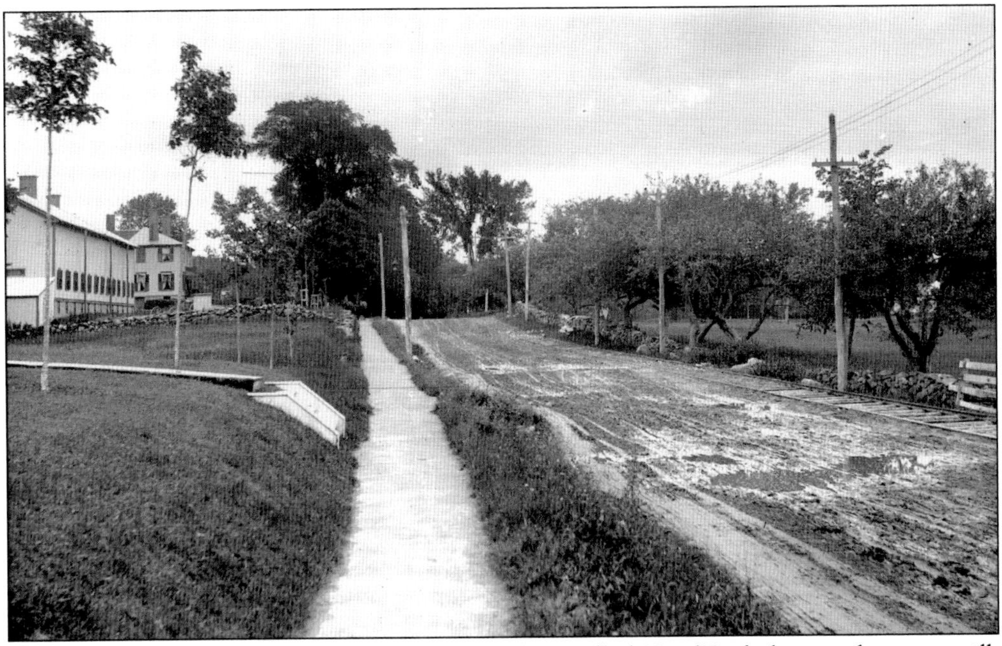

This 1900 photograph shows the East Broadway farm called HoodKroft that was home to milk king Harvey P. Hood from 1858 until his death in 1900. The massive, 140-foot-long barn was destroyed in a 1962 fire. Its former site has been occupied by a Chinese restaurant since 1982. The pasture on the right is now the Hoodkroft Country Club. Notice the Chester and Derry trolley tracks on the edge of the dirt road.

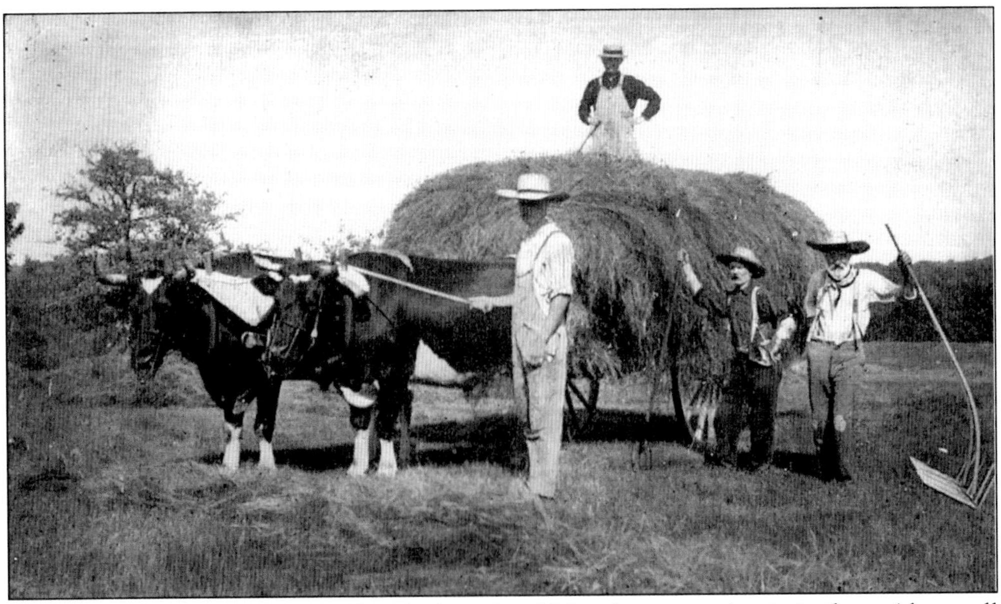

The Hood company in Derry employed a large local labor force to maintain its farm. Almost all of the fodder for the company's cows was raised here. The Derry air was a lot different during the Hood years: In 1961, Hood spread 200 tons of cow manure on its fields, which produced a yield of 550 tons of hay and 640 tons of silage.

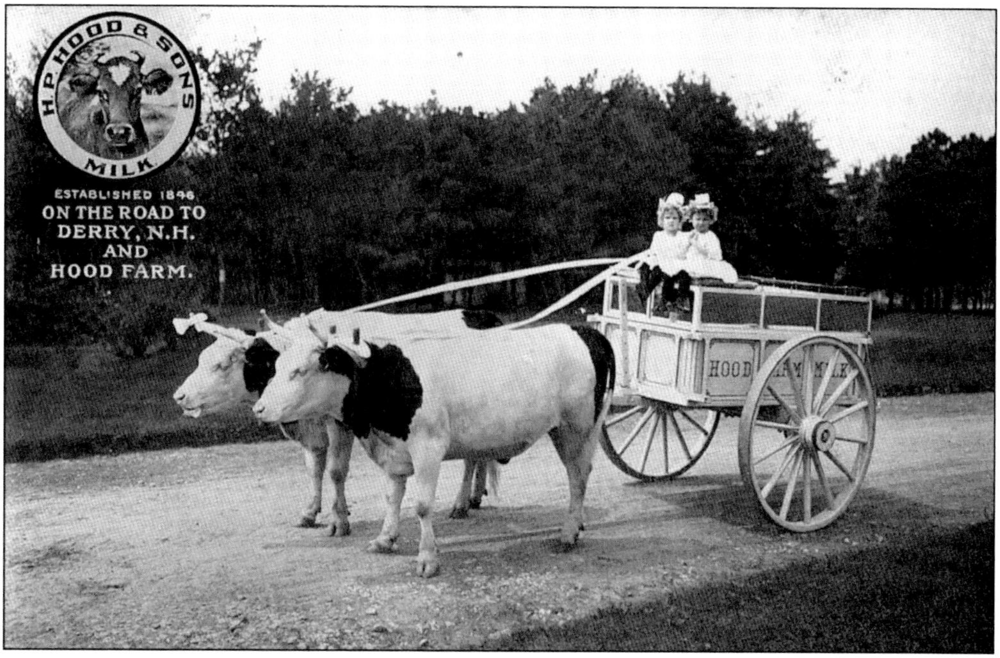

In 1919, H. P. Hood & Sons produced a series of postcards about its milk business. A number of these cards showed scenes from Derry. This card features two girls in an oxcart "on the road to Derry." (Courtesy of H. P. Hood Inc.)

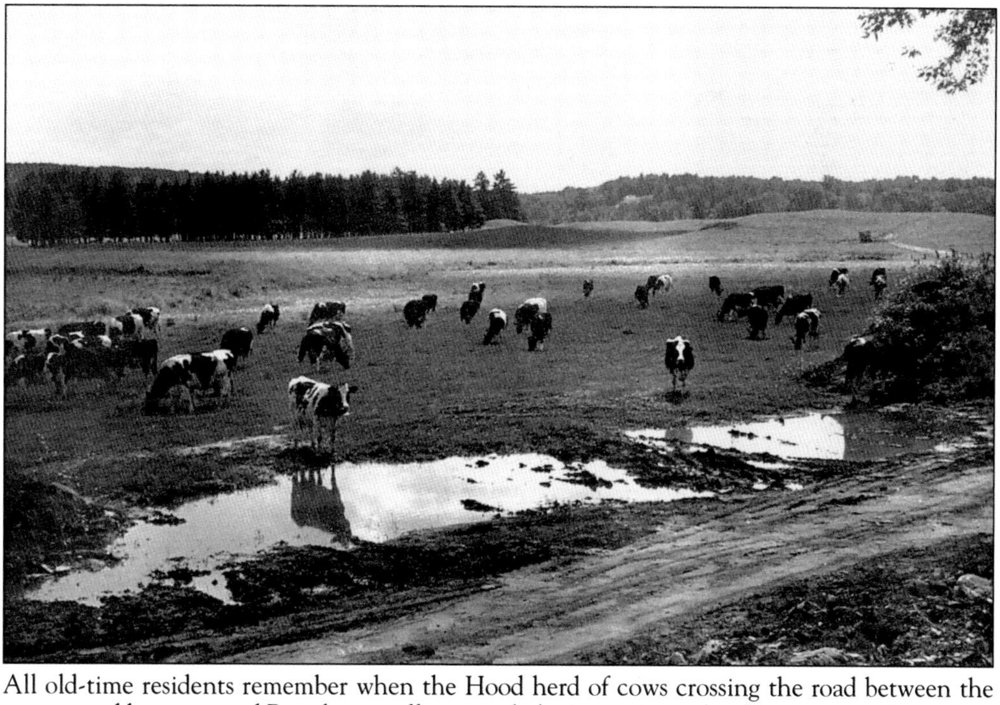

All old-time residents remember when the Hood herd of cows crossing the road between the pasture and barn stopped Broadway traffic twice daily. In 1969, on the day after this photograph was taken, the herd of 200 cows was sold at auction. The pasture was converted to the golf links of the Hoodkroft Country Club. (*Derry News* photograph.)

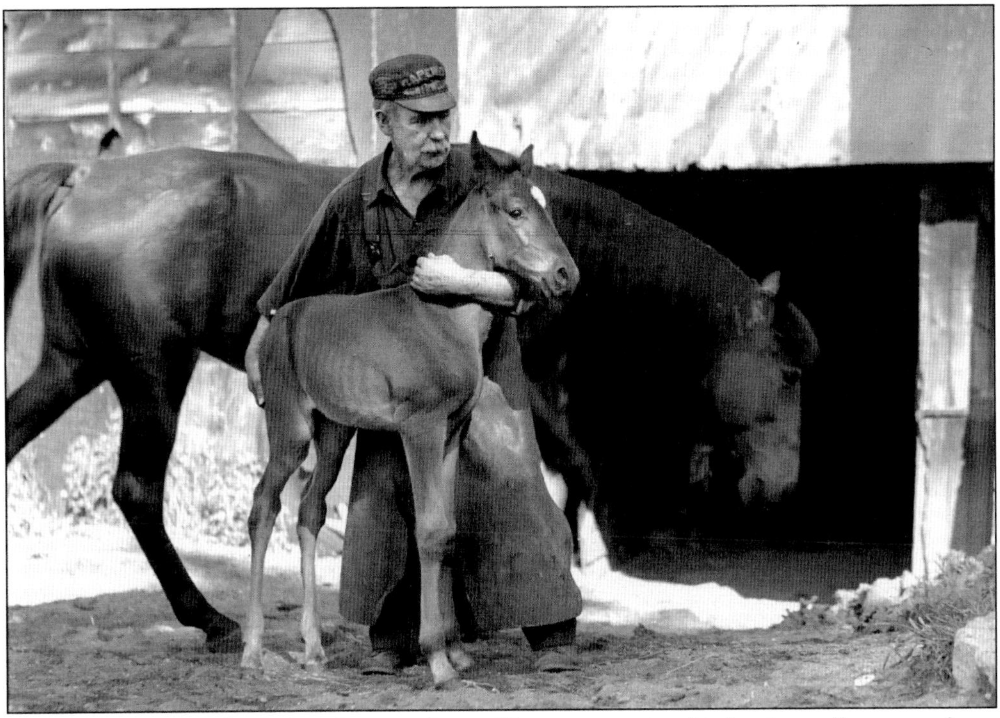

When it was time for Judge George Grinnell's mare to give birth, the call was made to blacksmith Charlie Doherty (1872–1966). Charlie was a local legend because of his speedy racehorses. The gentleness of his face in this 1940 photograph speaks to the old man's earnest love of horses.

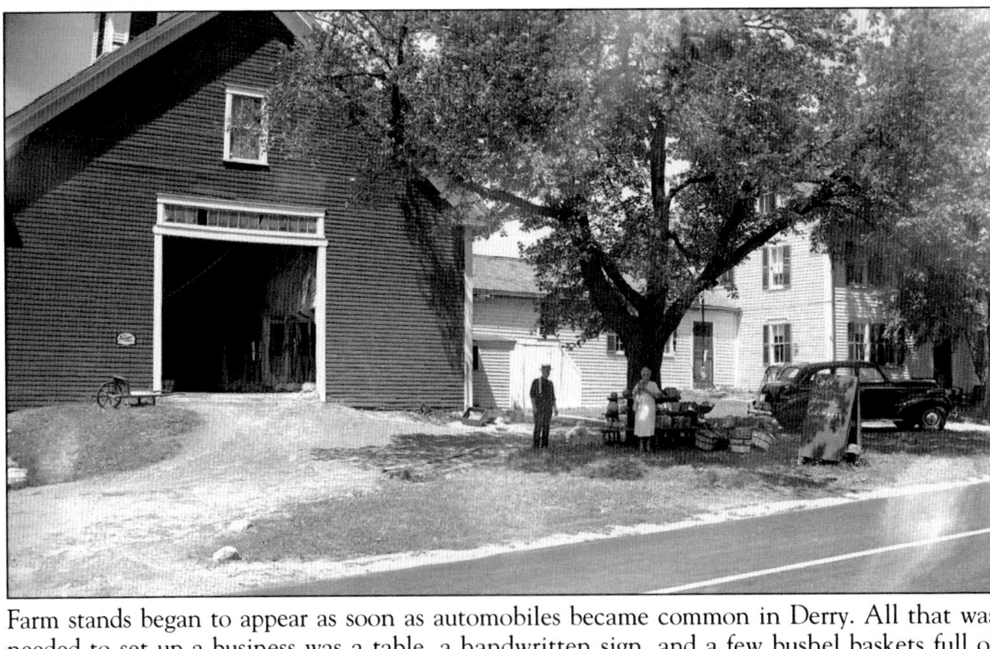

Farm stands began to appear as soon as automobiles became common in Derry. All that was needed to set up a business was a table, a handwritten sign, and a few bushel baskets full of vegetables. Here in 1941 is the Emerson Farm at 108 Chester Road. It is now the location of G. R. Trading Post. (Arthur Lear photograph.)

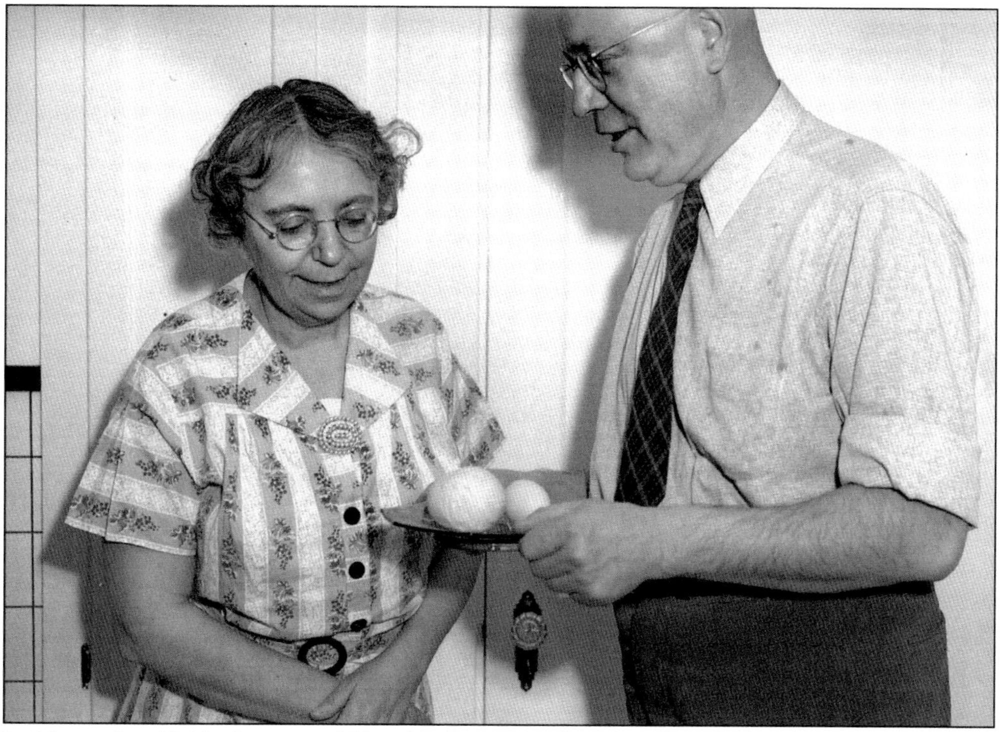

In November 1940, Annie and Tim Vaillancourt discovered in their chicken coop a huge white egg. This pride of the henhouse measured about six inches in length and weighed more than five ounces. There is obvious pride on the faces of these two local farmers for their hen's accomplishment.

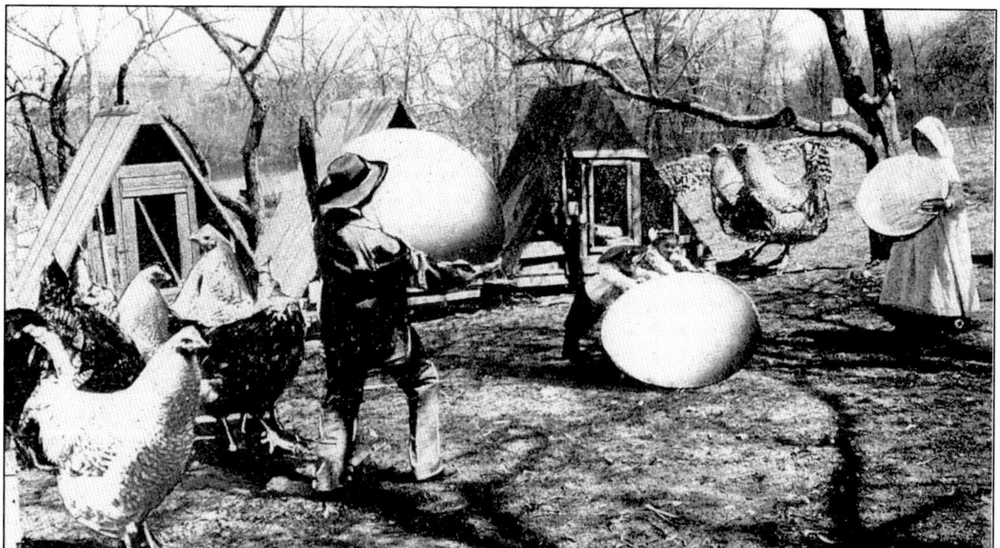

In this view published by druggist William Benson in 1911, the poultry farmers in Derry are beyond compare. At this time there were more hens in Derry than ever before. Each year the Derry poultry farmers put on a chicken show that attracted huge crowds. Derry's most famous chicken rancher was poet Robert Frost.

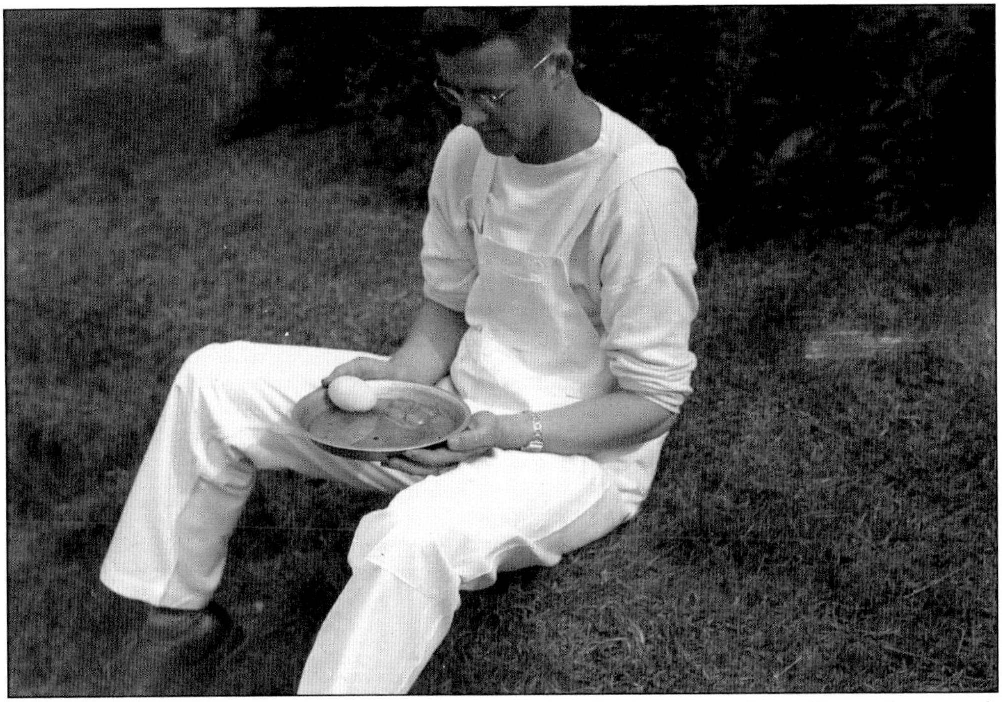

The Derry Egg Auction, on Crystal Avenue, was a distribution center for millions of eggs each month. In 1939, Roger Beliveau (pictured) was candling eggs to find cracks in their shells. He was very surprised that day to find an egg that had four yokes. Such an occurrence had never happened in the billion-egg history of the auction.

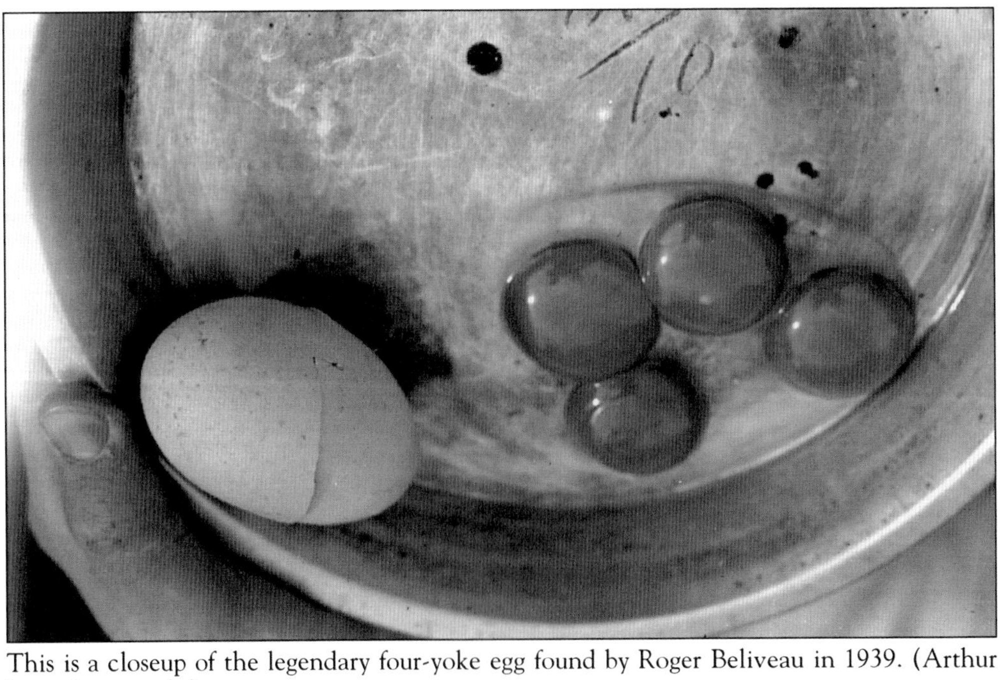

This is a closeup of the legendary four-yoke egg found by Roger Beliveau in 1939. (Arthur Lear photograph.)

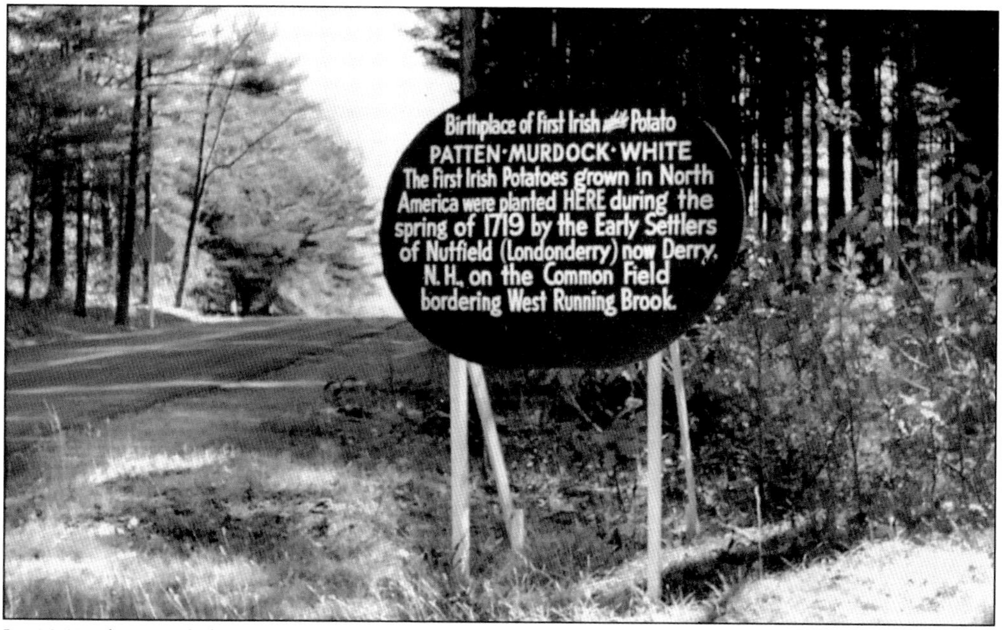

In 1960, the Nutfield Grange spearheaded the drive to memorialize Derry's role in the history of the potato. This sign was erected on the side of the Route 28 bypass near the site of the Common Field of 1719. The sign stood for several decades before disappearing in the 1990s.

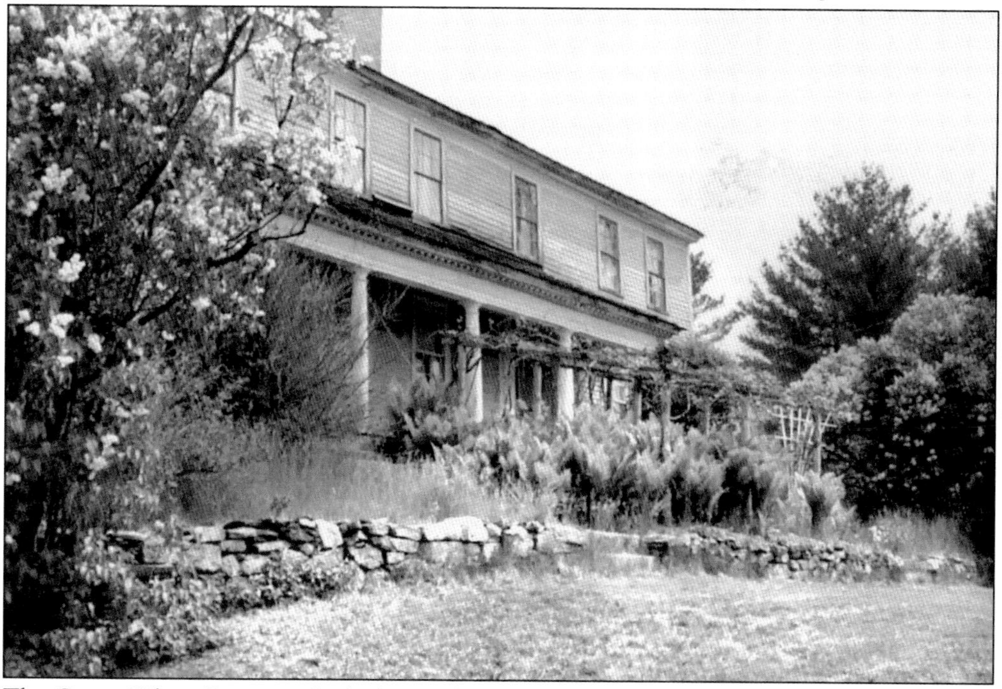

The Carrie White Farm was built during the Revolutionary War on the site of the Common Field. Here America's first potato crop was planted in 1719. During the 1970s, three town meetings voted to have the town buy the historic farm. The selectmen did not carry out that assignment. The farm was instead sold to a developer who bulldozed the house and built 850 apartment units.

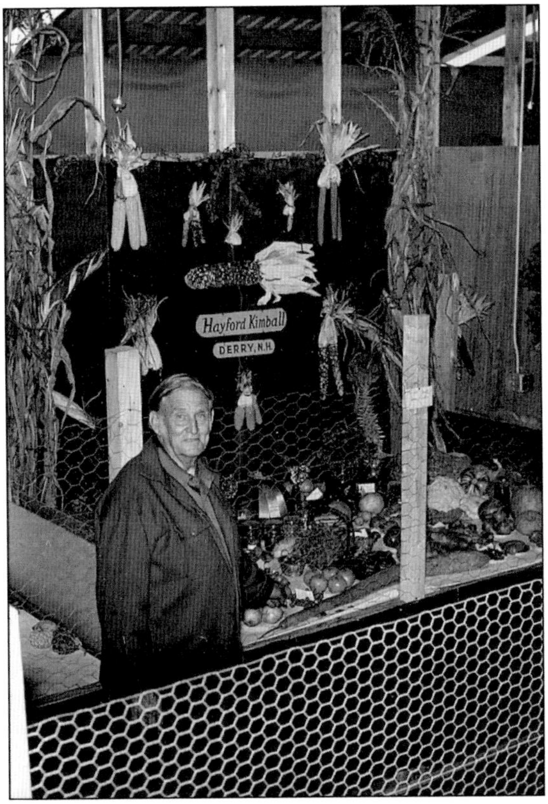

Hayford Kimball (1893–1989) was a respected commercial and social leader in Derry. He owned Kimball's Lumber Company, was a state legislator, and was a master of the Nutfield Grange. He is shown with his 1963 vegetable display that won blue ribbons at the Hopkinton, Rochester, and Deerfield State Fairs. (*Derry News* photograph.)

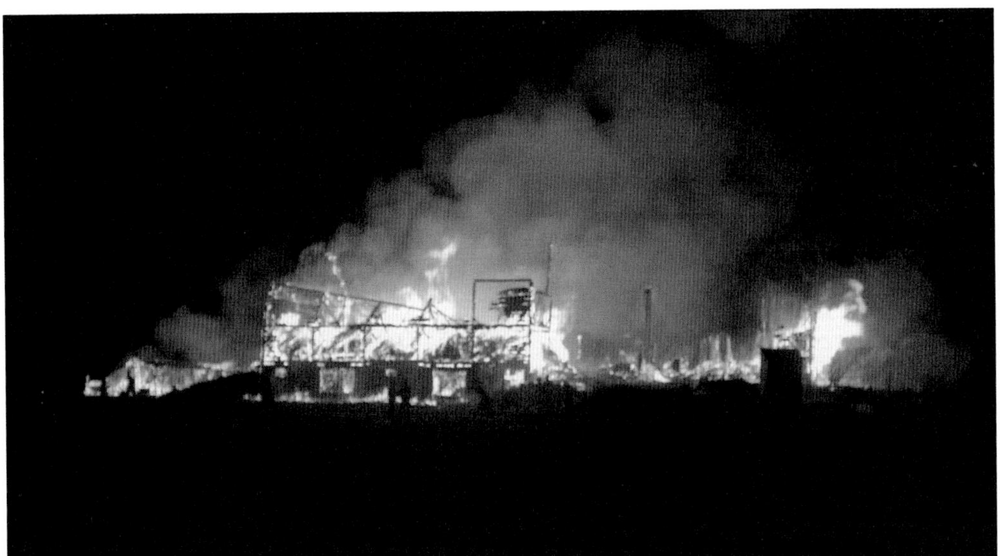

Late on the night of November 17, 1939, the sounds of panicking cows awoke farmer John Yeronis of Scobie Pond Road. Seeing the flames coming out of the barn window, he ran to his car and drove two miles in his underwear to get help. The house was saved, but Yeronis lost most of his herd, hay, and equipment. Such fires were an all-too-common occurrence in agricultural Derry.

Three

PEOPLE

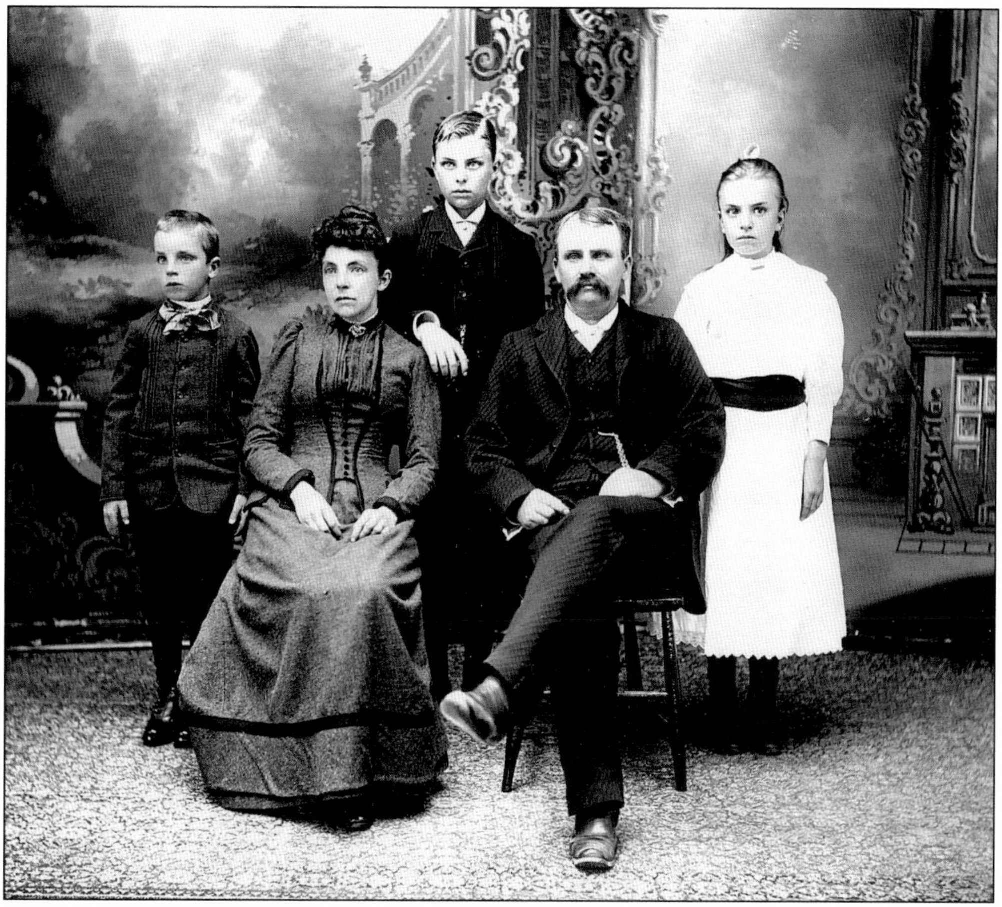

Carmi Norton (seated right) is pictured with his family *c.* 1890. He was a local insurance agent who, in 1895, divided his family farm on Birch Street into house lots. He offered loans at 5 percent interest to those who wished to build homes on his development. By 1898, there were 10 homes in the section now known as Nortonville.

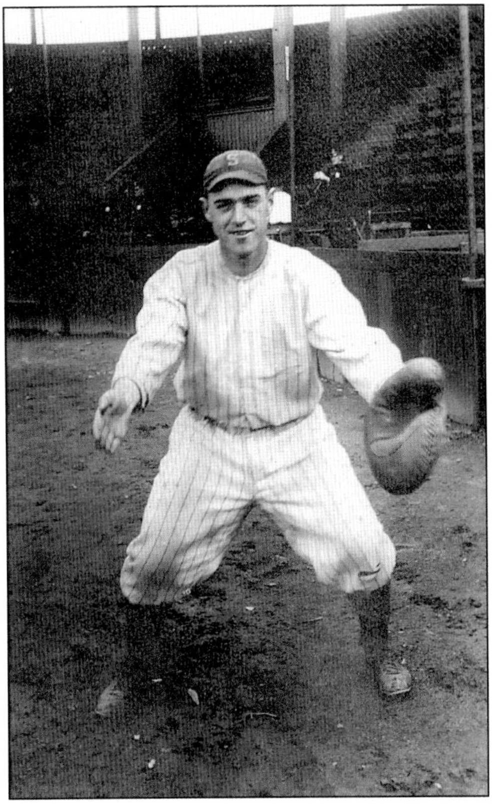

Fred "Casey" Tyler (1892–1945), brother of major-league pitcher George "Lefty" Tyler, was a star catcher with the Derry Athletic Association. In 1914, Casey joined his brother on the Boston Braves. Casey played in 18 games that year and had a respectable .333 batting average. He was later sent to play in the minor leagues, and retired in 1926.

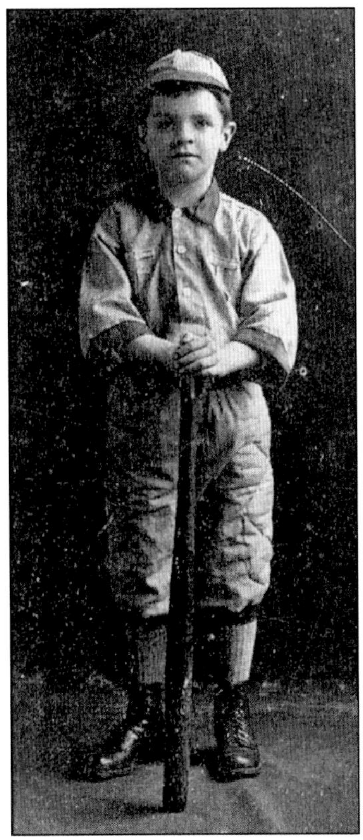

Young Alexander "Shine" Bogle (1902–1984) wanted a pony in 1910. The Dunlop Pony Company was giving away Shetland ponies and carts to whomever got the most friends and neighbors to mail in preprinted postcards with the contestant's picture on them. Seen here is one of Shine's postcards. He did not win, however. In time Shine became a truck driver for Beacon Freight Company and a popular local sportsman.

George "Lefty" Tyler (1889–1953) played ball for the Derry Athletic Association before going on to the Boston Braves and the Chicago Cubs. He pitched in the World Series of 1914 and 1918. The 6-foot, 175-pound hurler is best remembered as being one of the stars of the miracle Braves of 1914, who went from being in last place at midseason to winning the World Series.

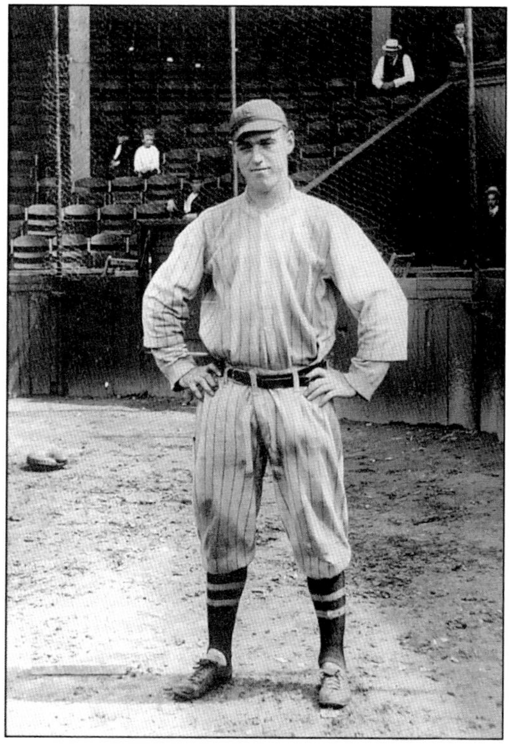

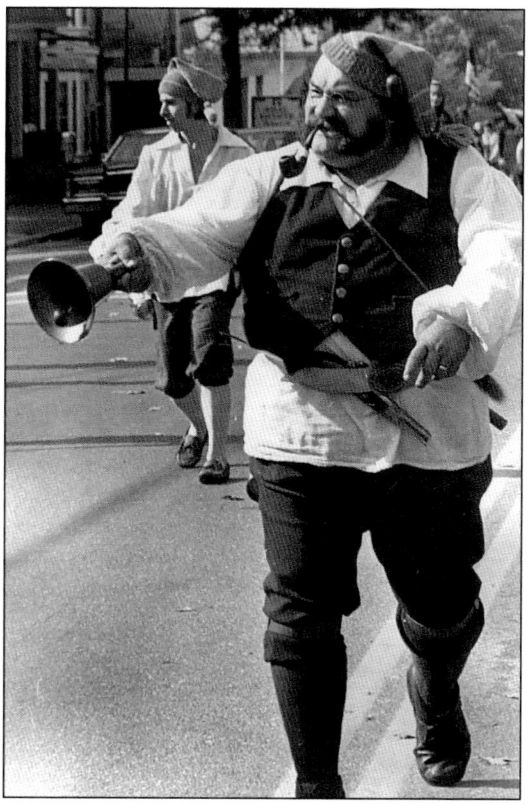

Gerry Cox served as Derry's first recreation director for 28 years. He is pictured here as leader of Derry's militia during the bicentennial celebration in 1976. On one Memorial Day in the 1980s, Cox could not get a band to march in the parade so he bought hundreds of plastic kazoos and invited everyone to join his improvised marching band. (*Derry News* photograph.)

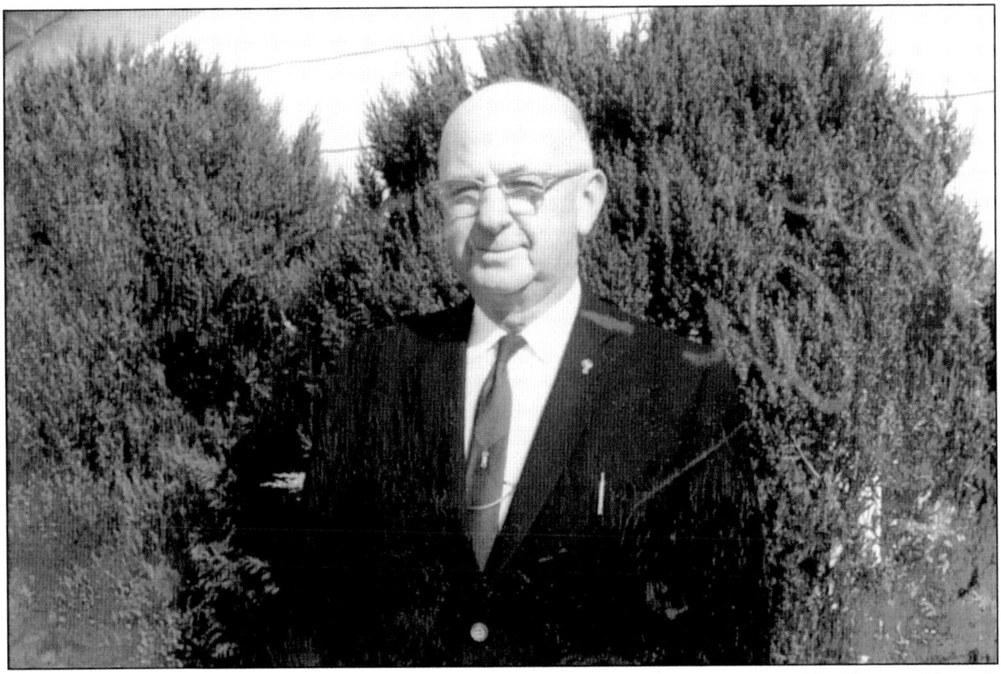

Bertrand Peabody (1906–1994) founded the Peabody Funeral Home in 1933. He was Derry's citizen of the year in 1982. Peabody was trustee of Forest Hills Cemetery for more than 30 years, and was the founder of the Derry Co-op Bank. He belonged to the Kiwanis, Masons, Odd Fellows, and Knights of Pythias. Grandsons Eric and Craig Peabody now operate the Birch Street funeral home.

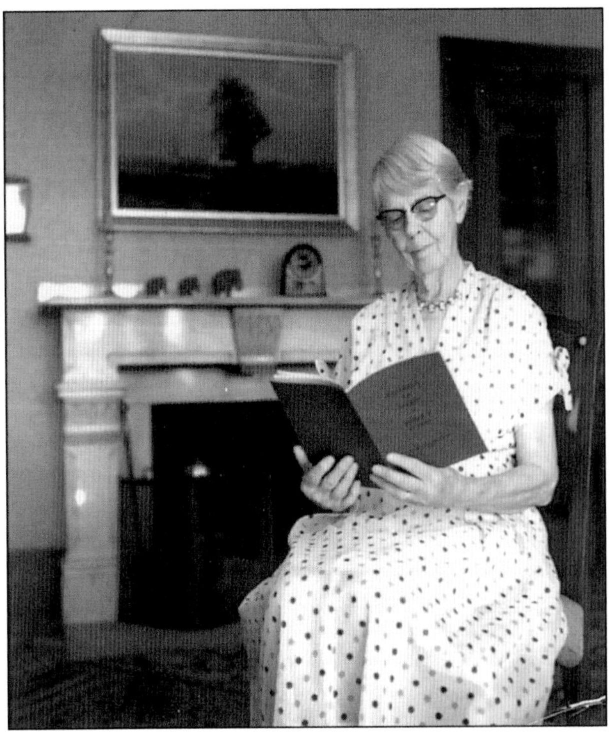

Harriett Chase Newell (1881–1976) was Derry's most prolific historian. She wrote eight books on local history, including her *Houses of Derry* series. In 1966, she was selected as Derry's citizen of the year. Newell was very active in the local chapter of the Daughters of the American Revolution (DAR) and the Central Congregational Church.

Judge Leonard H. Pillsbury (1835–1933) stands in the front row, surrounded by family members. He served with honor in the Civil War and operated a Broadway furniture store. Pillsbury was a district judge, a peace activist, an ardent foe of alcohol, and a zealous supporter of Prohibition. Family legend has him arresting his nephew Rosecrans Pillsbury when he found the young man having a drink at a party celebrating the 1914 announcement of Judge Pillsbury's candidacy for governor of New Hampshire.

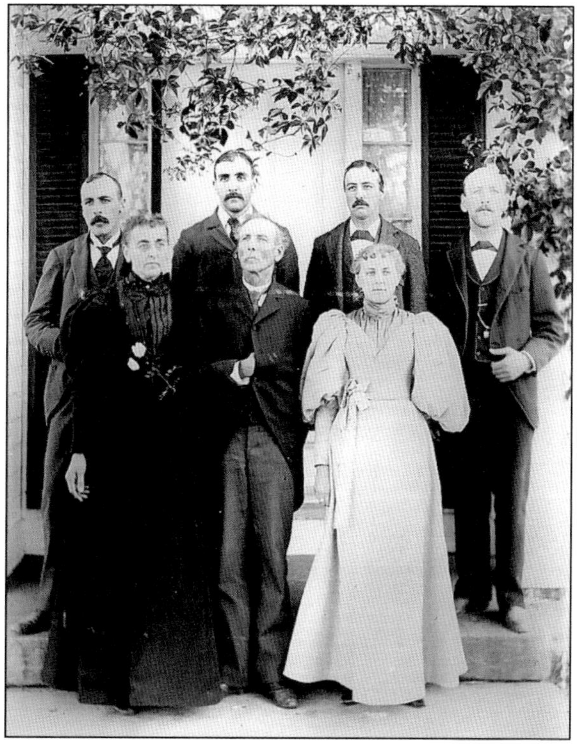

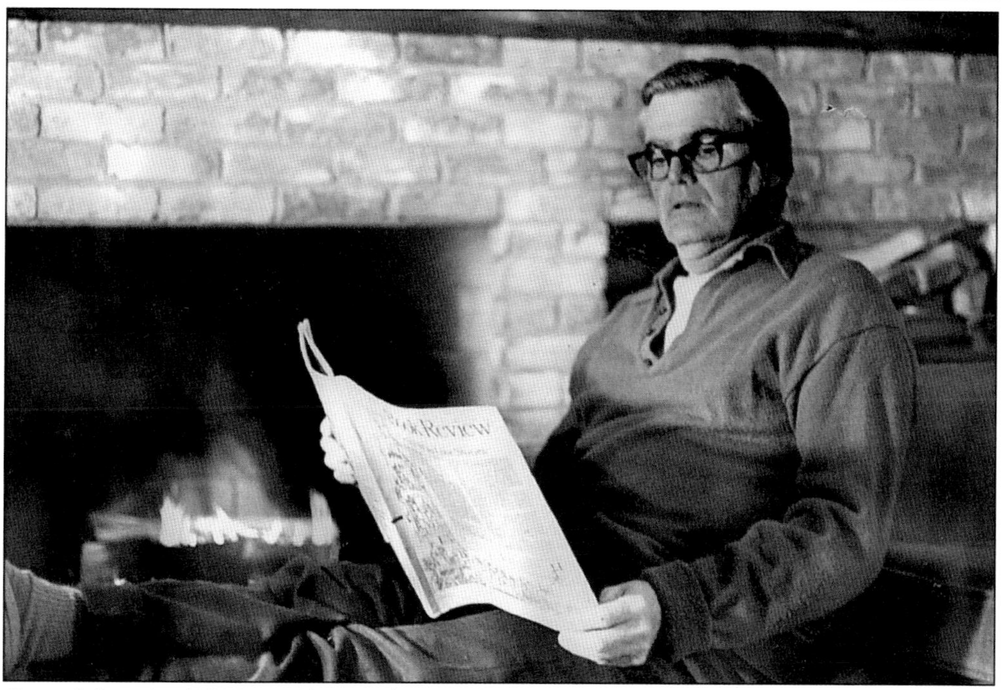

Conrad Quimby (1925–1997) was editor and publisher of the *Derry News* from 1963 to 1987. A popular Derry personality, he was a member of the state legislature and served on many local committees. Quimby is remembered for bringing an urban sense of style to the small-town newspaper. (*Derry News* photograph.)

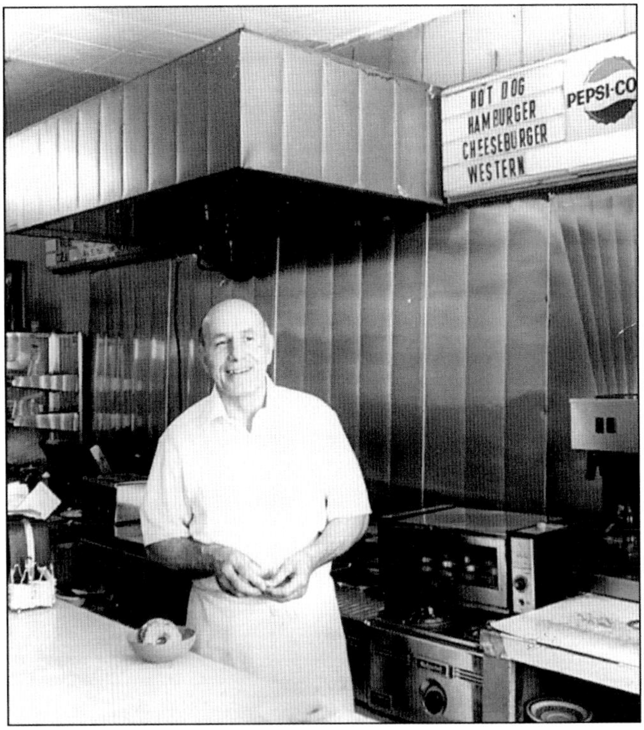

George Katsakiores was born in Derry in 1924 and attended local schools. He owned White's Restaurant from 1948 to 1988. Since 1982 he has served in the state legislature, where his wife, Phyllis, is a fellow legislator. She is also a member of the town council and the Heritage Commission.

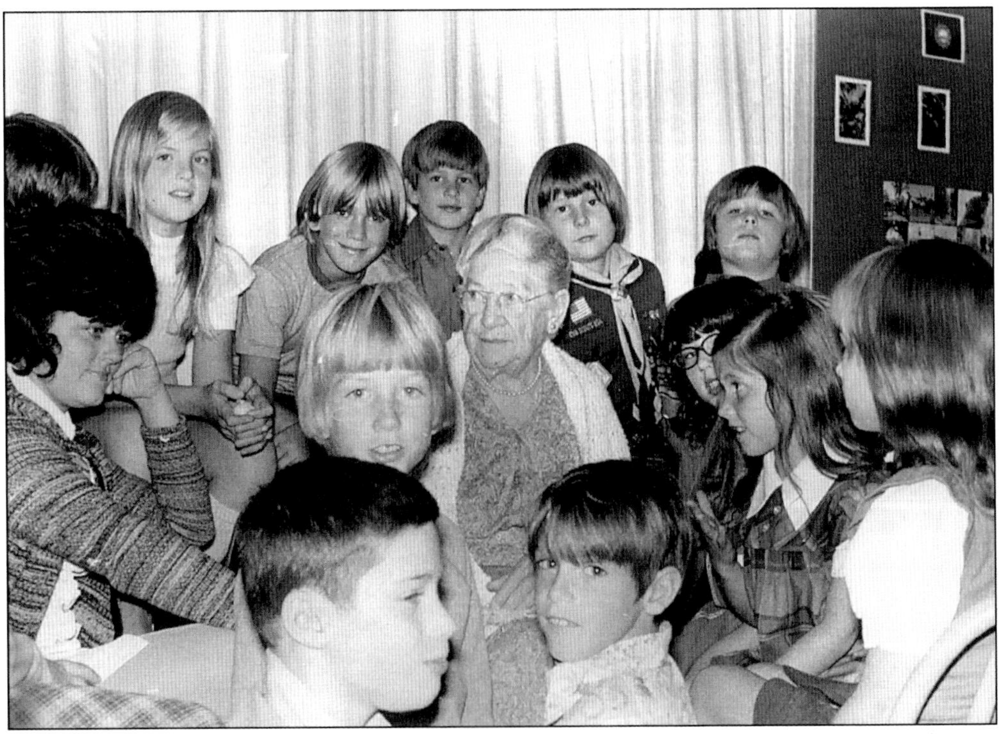

Lula Reynolds (1879–1981) is seen surrounded by young admirers on her 96th birthday. She was the holder of the "Boston Post Cane" as the oldest person in Derry. Her motto was, "Nothing bothers me, I don't have time."

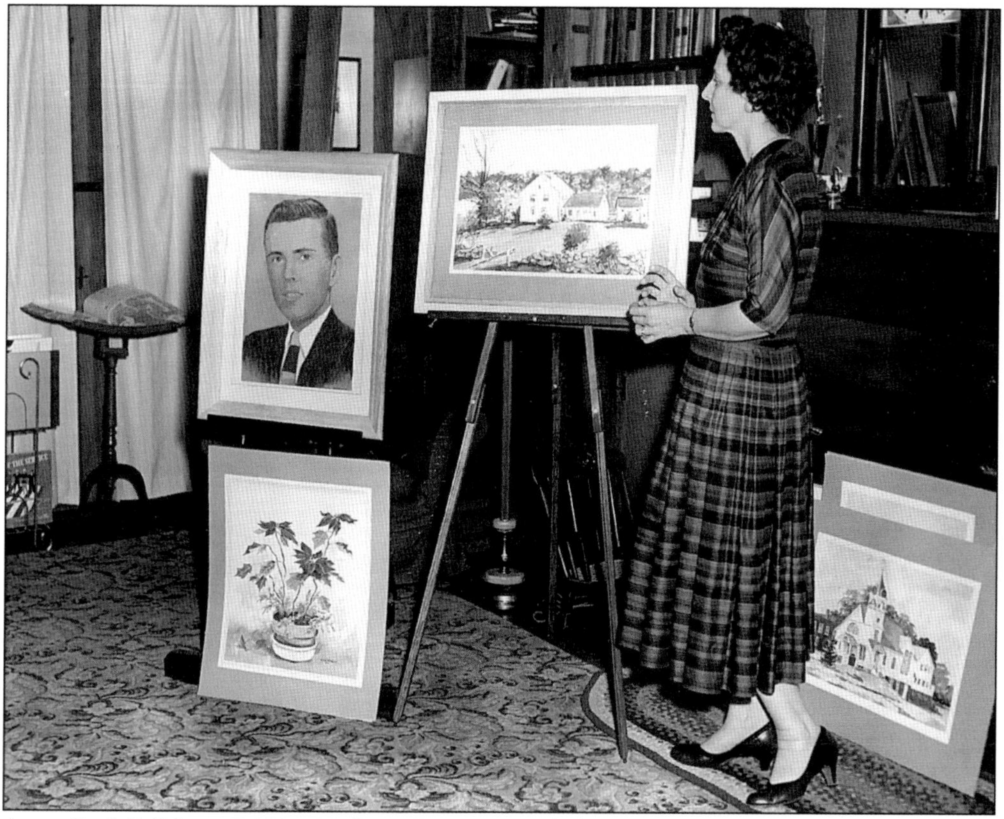

Artist Ruth Pillsbury (1908–1991) was Derry's most beloved artist and the wife of Judge Walter Pillsbury. Over her career, she painted the cover artwork for 25 town reports. She is seen here in 1963 surrounded by her works. Her rendering of the Baptist church at the lower right was used on a town report in 1980.

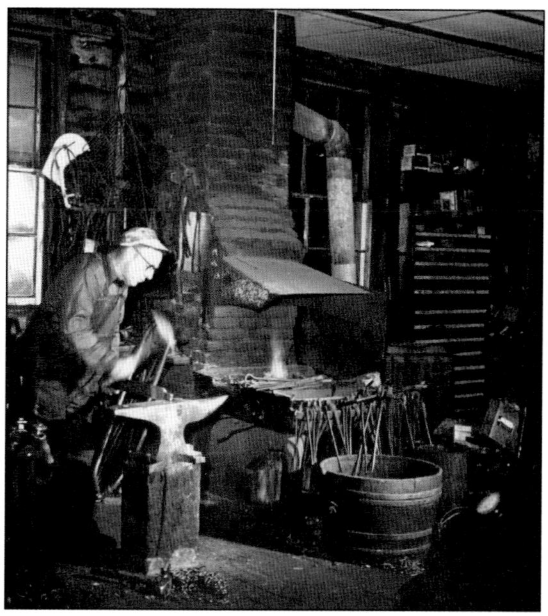

For decades blacksmith William E. R. Smith (1891–1954) worked his magic with iron at Chase's Garage on Central Street. His hammer could turn the white-hot metal into any shape he desired, to fix wagon wheels or automobile shocks. (Photograph courtesy of Bertha MacDougall.)

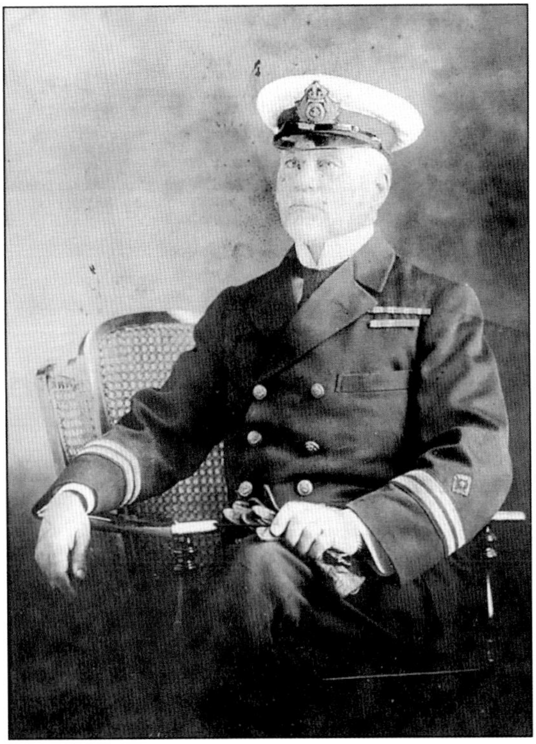

Dr. Charles B. Charest (1868–1944) may be unique in the world's military annals. He was a combat officer for four different countries in three different wars: the Canadian Army in the Rebellion of 1885; the British Army in the Boer War; and in World War I with the French Navy (1914–1917) and the U.S. Navy (1917–1918). He was a Derry physician from 1906 to 1940 who was "too busy to marry."

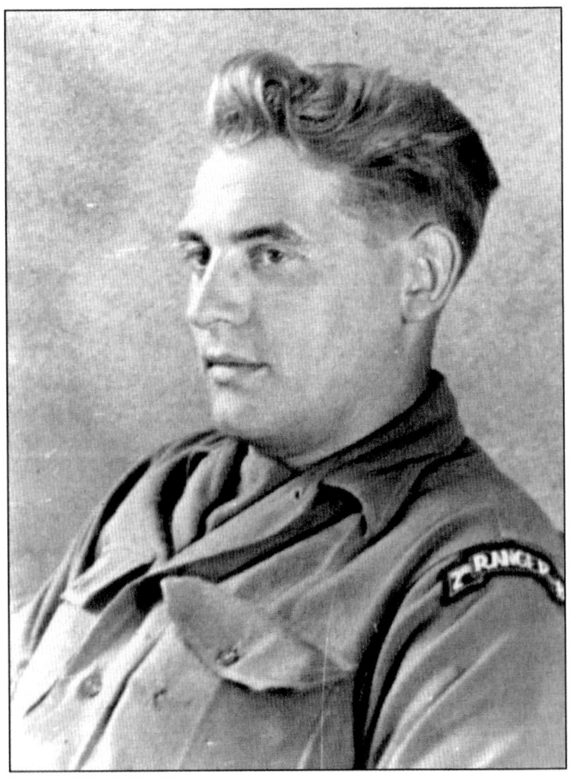

Walter Borowski was born in 1920 and is a lifelong Derry resident. During World War II, while under fire, Sergeant Borowski led his Army Rangers up the cliff during the invasion of Normandy on D-Day. He earned the Silver Star, Bronze Star, and Purple Heart. Borowski always denies any credit for himself, and says the real war heroes are those like his brother Eugene who did not come back home to Derry.

Harry Smart (1891–1979) is seen laying a wreath during the 1971 Memorial Day ceremony. Smart was then the oldest member of the local Veterans of Foreign Wars (VFW) post. He served with the 103rd Machine Gun Battalion between 1917 and 1919. On this day in 1971, Smart said he was "too old to march but too young to forget those buddies I left over there." (*Derry News* photograph.)

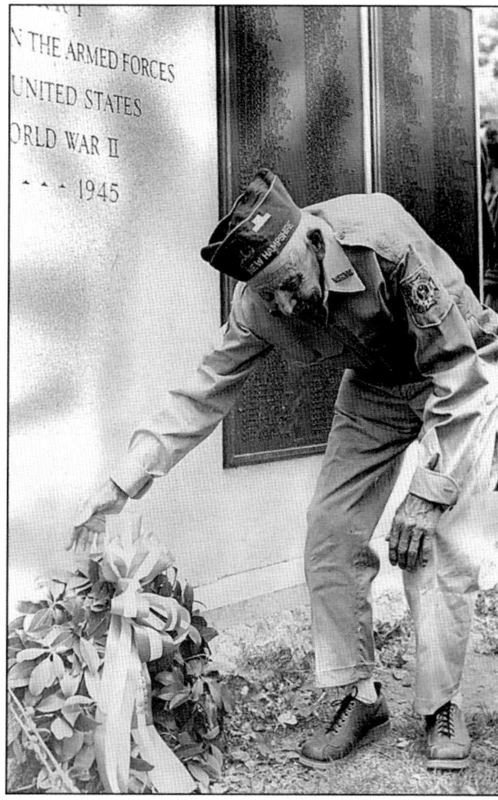

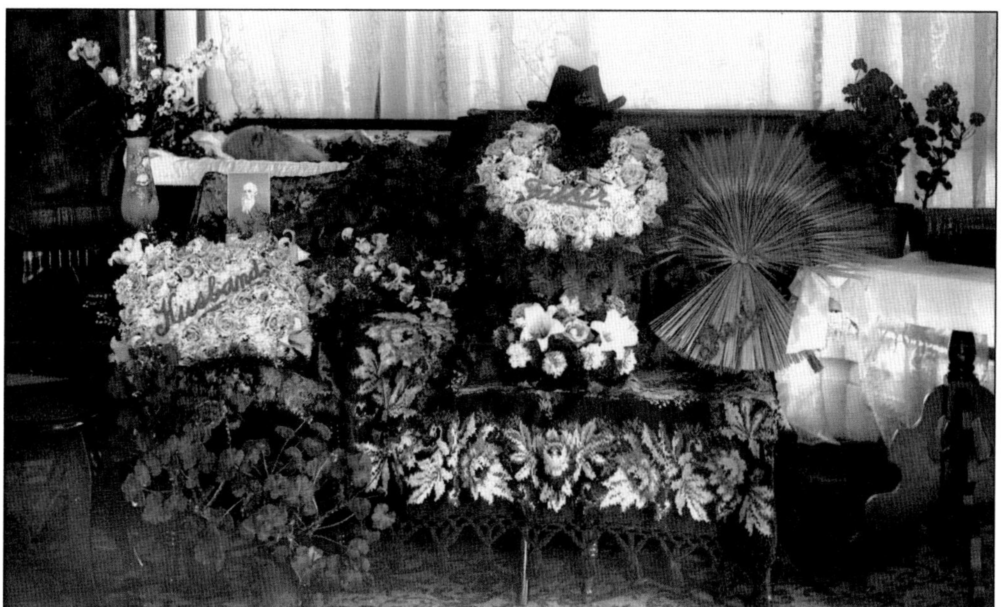

This funeral for an unidentified soldier took place in the 1890s. On the top of the casket is the Grand Army of the Republic hat of a Civil War veteran. A sheaf of wheat from the Grange is on the right. Photographer Charles Bartlett recorded this final tribute for the benefit of the soldier's distant family members who could not attend the funeral.

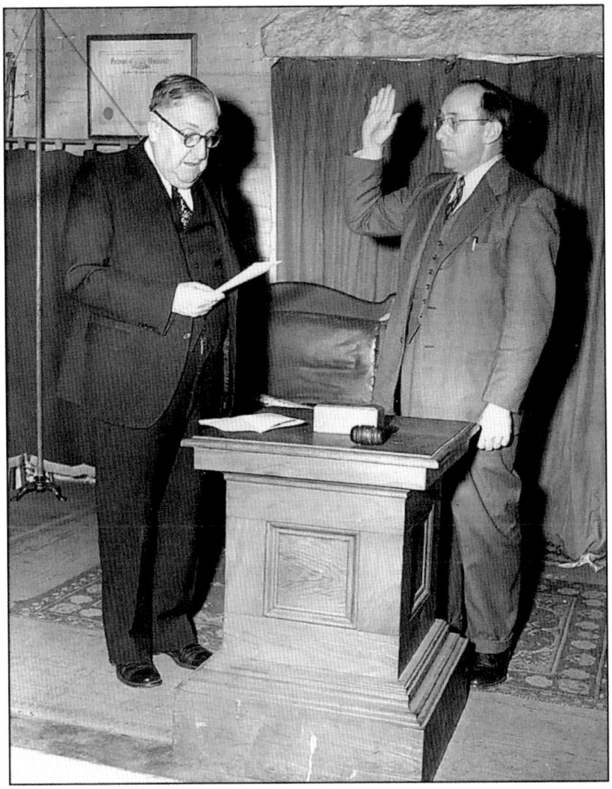

In 1951 Judge Herbert Grinnell (1881–1956), left, is shown swearing in his son George (1910–2000) as the new judge of the Derry District Court. Herbert had been the local judge since 1915, but had been forced to retire at age 70. George, a legendary aviator, retired in 1980 when he reached his 70th year. (F. J. Sullivan photograph.)

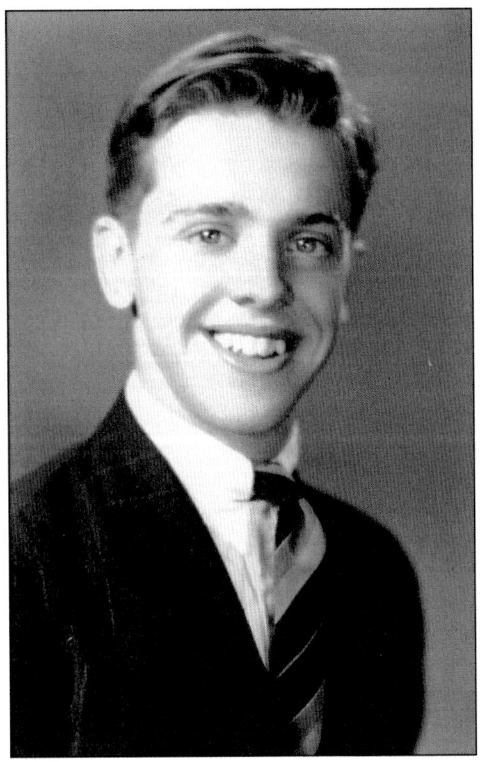

Astronaut Alan B. Shepard Jr. was born in Derry on November 18, 1923. He is seen here in his Pinkerton Academy graduation photograph from 1940. On May 5, 1961, Shepard became America's first man in space, and in 1971 he walked on the moon. He spent a total of 216 hours and 57 minutes in space. Shepard died on July 21, 1998. His memorial stone is at Forest Hill Cemetery in East Derry.

Four

INSTITUTIONS

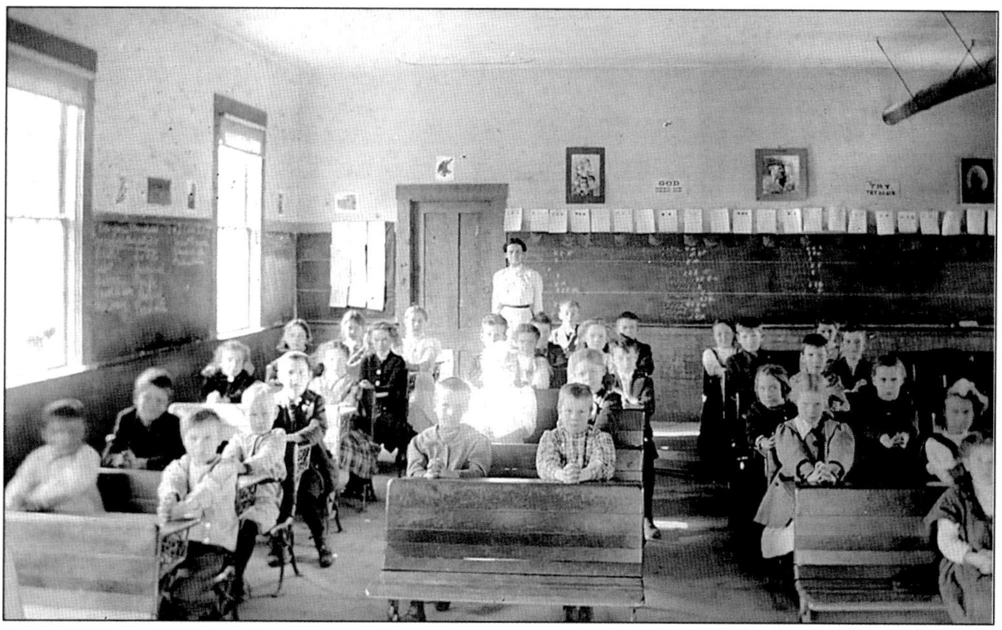

From 1824 to 1887 the Adams Female Academy was a nationally respected girls' school. Among the school's trustees were Ralph Waldo Emerson and Franklin Pierce. By the time of this c. 1905 photograph, the academy had become a Derry public school. The chalkboard shown here is merely wooden boards painted black. The teacher's 30 students are kept on the right path by signs on the wall that say, "Try, try again," and "God sees me."

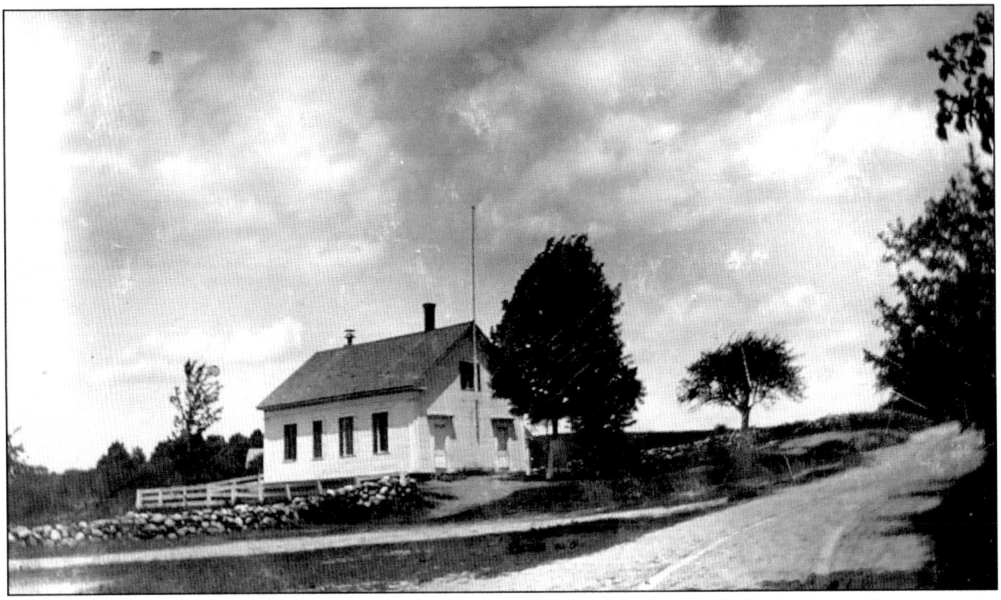

In the 19th century, Derry had a dozen-one room schools scattered throughout the town. In 1914, No. 8 School was on the Chester Road (Route 102) near English Range Road. That year, the school required all students to bring their own drinking cup to school to replace the common dipper that had been shared by all the students as well as the teacher. The school was open from 1856 to 1932, and is now a private residence.

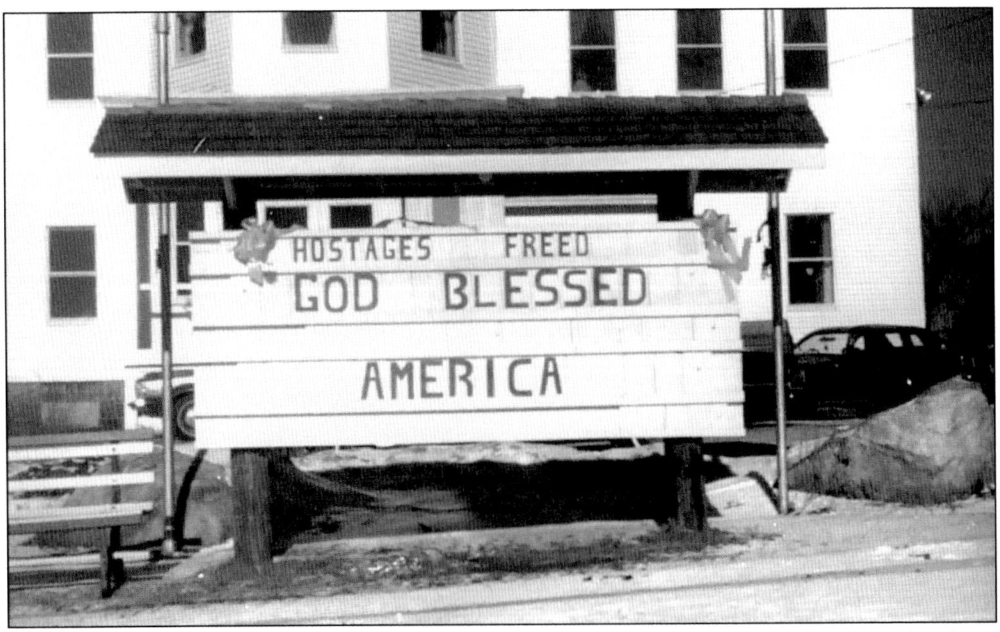

For a decade, the signboard at the West Side Community Center told Broadway passersby about school plays, championships won by local teams, theatrical productions, and town fairs. On January 20, 1981, the sign announced that the American hostages in Iran had been freed after their 444 days of captivity at the hands of extremists. The former West Side School was made into a community center in 1972.

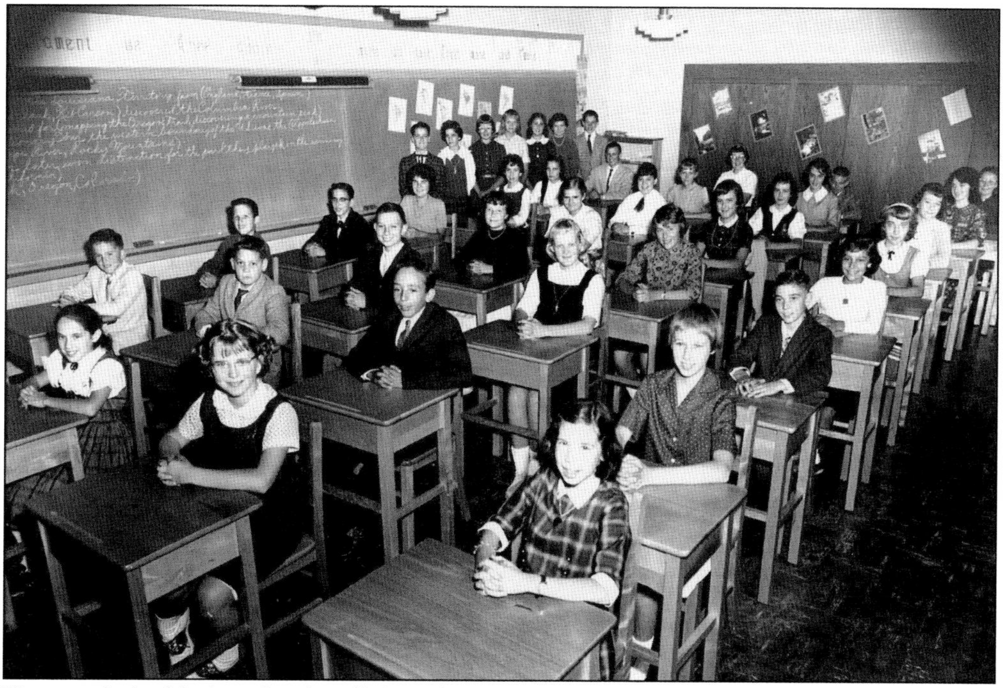

Here are the highly disciplined, well-dressed students of Derry's St. Thomas Aquinas School during the 1950s. Certainly this class appears to represent every teacher's dream. The school was founded in 1952, and currently has an enrollment of 275 students. In 2004 the school and church's facilities were greatly increased in size with the opening of the multipurpose Aquinas Center.

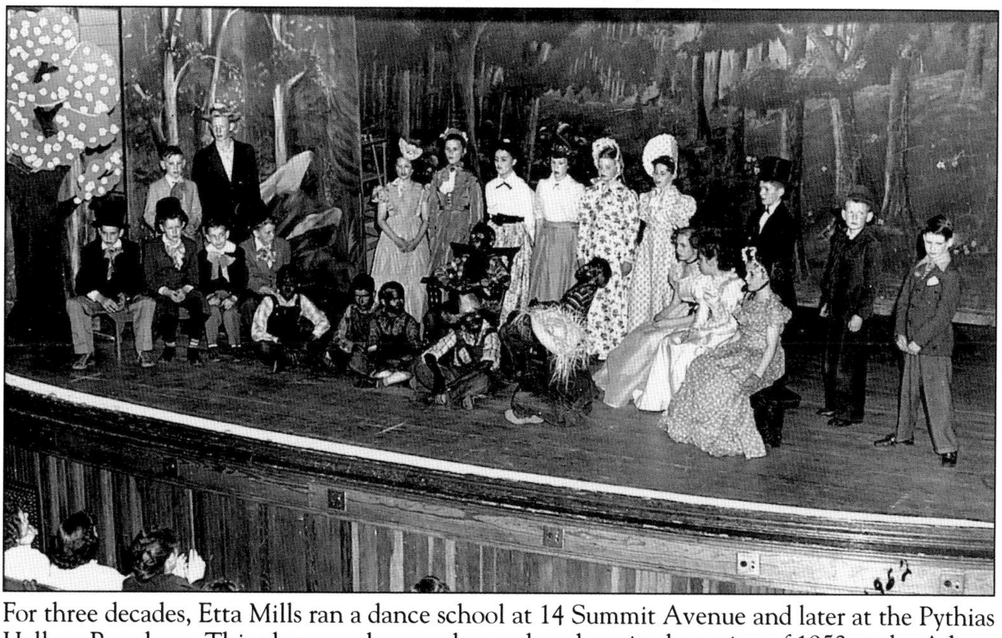

For three decades, Etta Mills ran a dance school at 14 Summit Avenue and later at the Pythias Hall on Broadway. This photograph was taken at her show in the spring of 1952 at the Adams Memorial Building. The production kept her audience enthralled for more than two hours. This is a scene on the "Gay Nineties." The singers in blackface are performing a salute to composer Stephen Foster. (F. J. Sullivan photograph.)

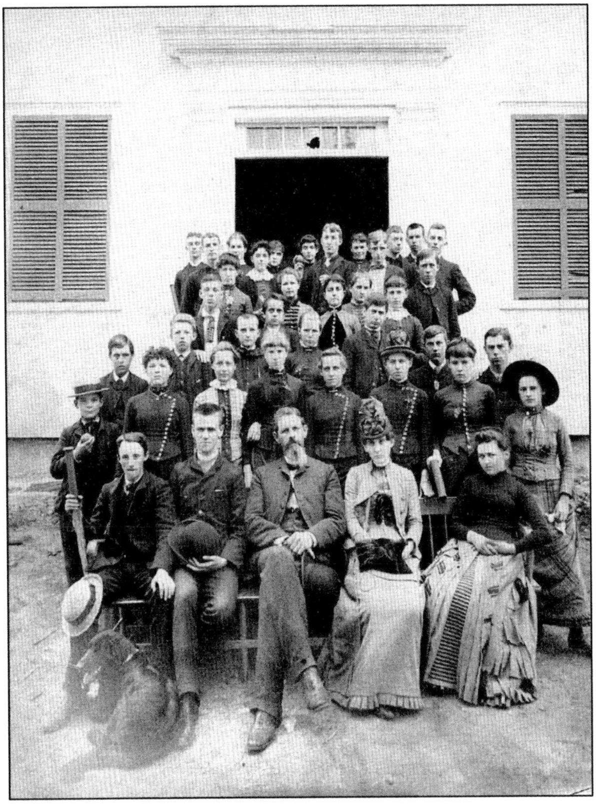

Pinkerton Academy was a much smaller institution in 1887, when this photograph was taken in front of the original academy building. Four of the boys here have baseball equipment in their hands. The three adults in the center of the front row are, from left to right, teacher Robert Lincoln O'Brien (1865–1955), who later became chairman of the U.S. Trade Commission; principal George Bingham; and teacher Mary Pearson.

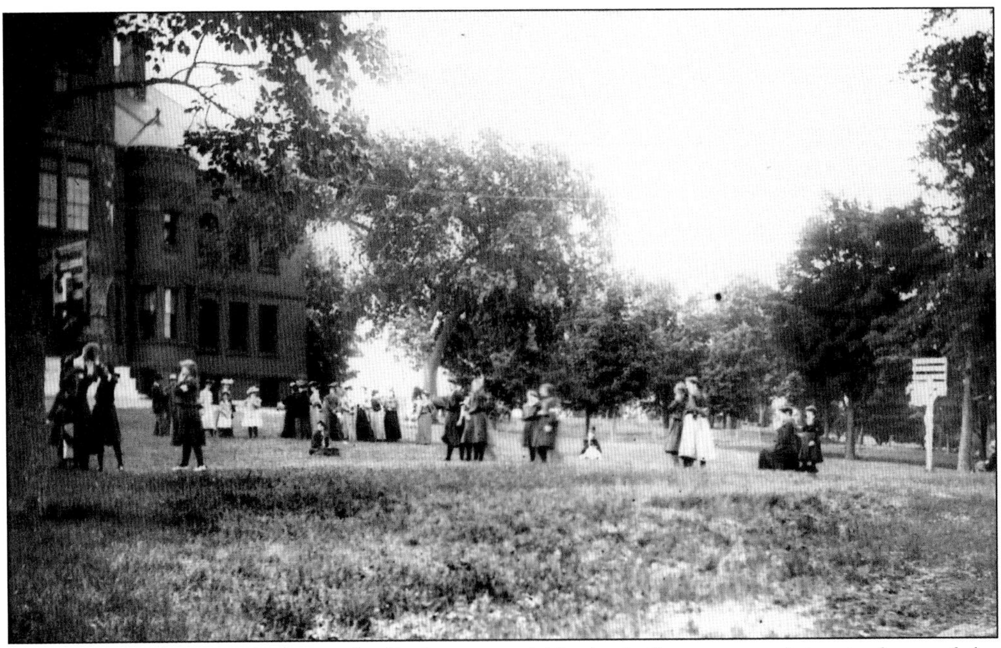

This c. 1898 photograph shows the Pinkerton girls' basketball team practicing in front of the Pinkerton Building. Each of the players is modestly outfitted in long black bloomers. The school did not officially recognize girls as athletes until 1904. (Bertha MacDougall photograph.)

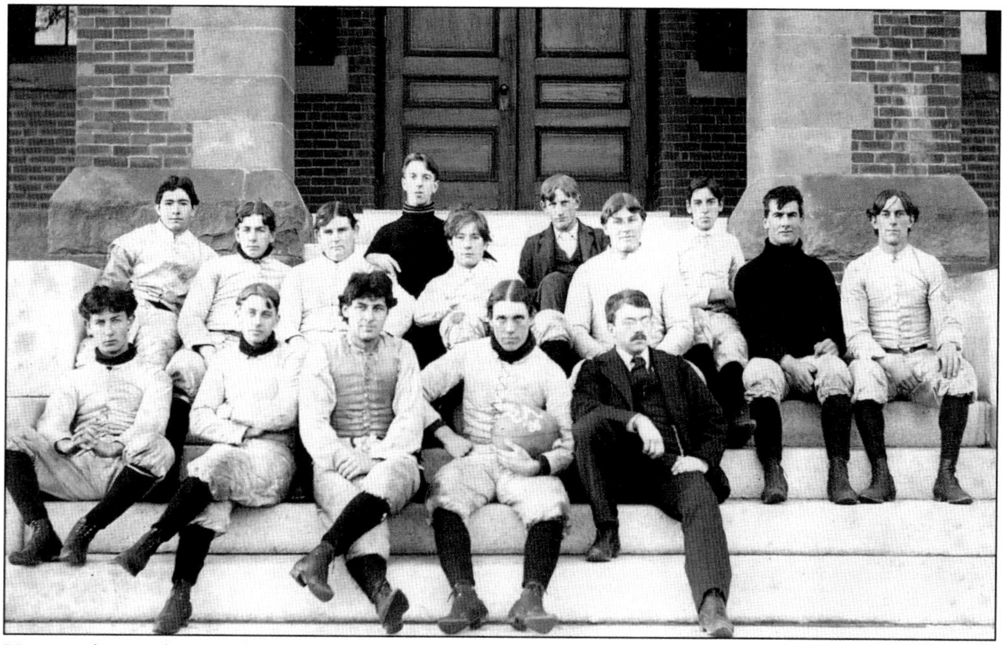

Here is the mighty Pinkerton Academy 11 in 1896 with coach Harry Newell and his assistants. In its only recorded game that year, the squad lost to Drummer Academy 14-0. The football team did not receive official recognition and support from the academy until 1904.

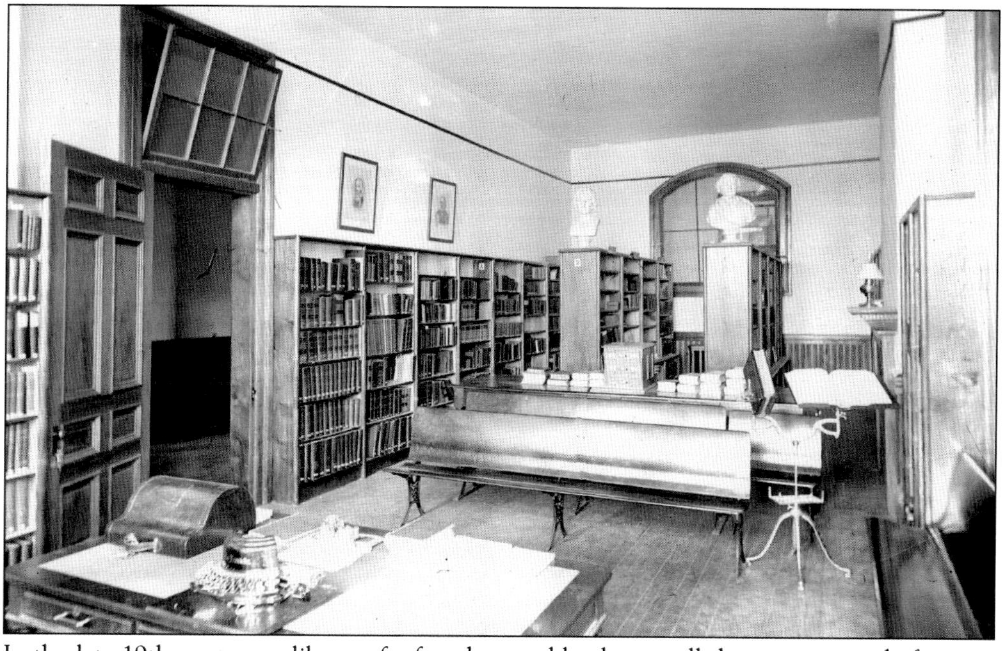

In the late 19th century, a library of a few thousand books was all that was required of even a progressive school like Pinkerton Academy. On the librarian's desk, at lower left, a very primitive typewriter can be seen. A kerosene lamp sits on the fireplace mantel on the right. In 1895, the library collection consisted of 3,447 titles. In 1959, the Saltmarsh Library was built by a donation from Rev. Frank N. Saltmarsh and his wife, Mamie. (Edmund Angell photograph.)

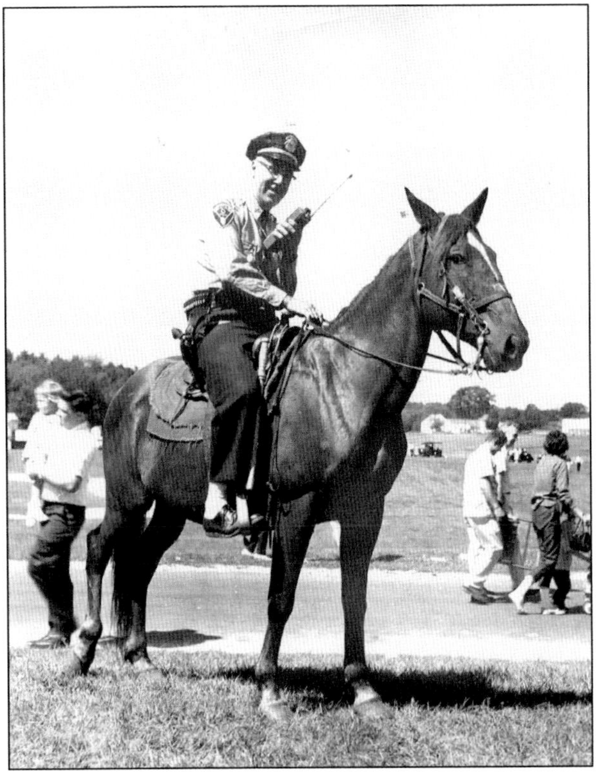

Police officer Ernest Gaines is seen here on a rented horse at the 1965 LaborFest. He rode the steed in the day's parade and then used it for public-relations duty at the Hood-Grinnell school grounds. Each year thousands came to Derry on Labor Day to take part in activities in honor of the American worker.

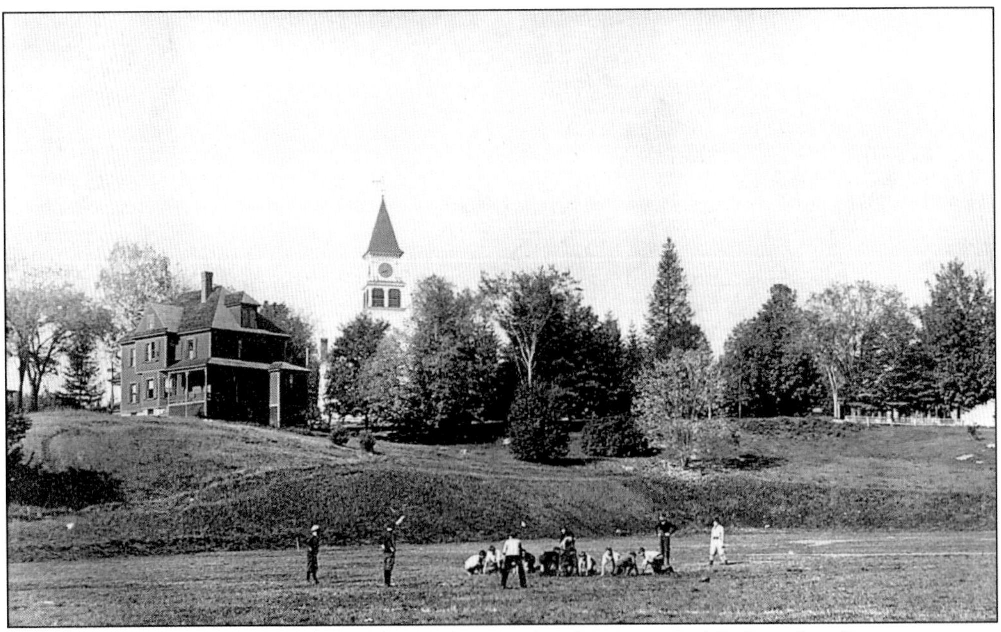

This photograph from 1909 shows the Pinkerton Academy oval. All the school's sports teams used this athletic field for more than 70 years. The Pinkerton Astros now play on a large modern field near the school's former agricultural training farm. On the ridge above the oval is the steeple of the Central Congregational Church.

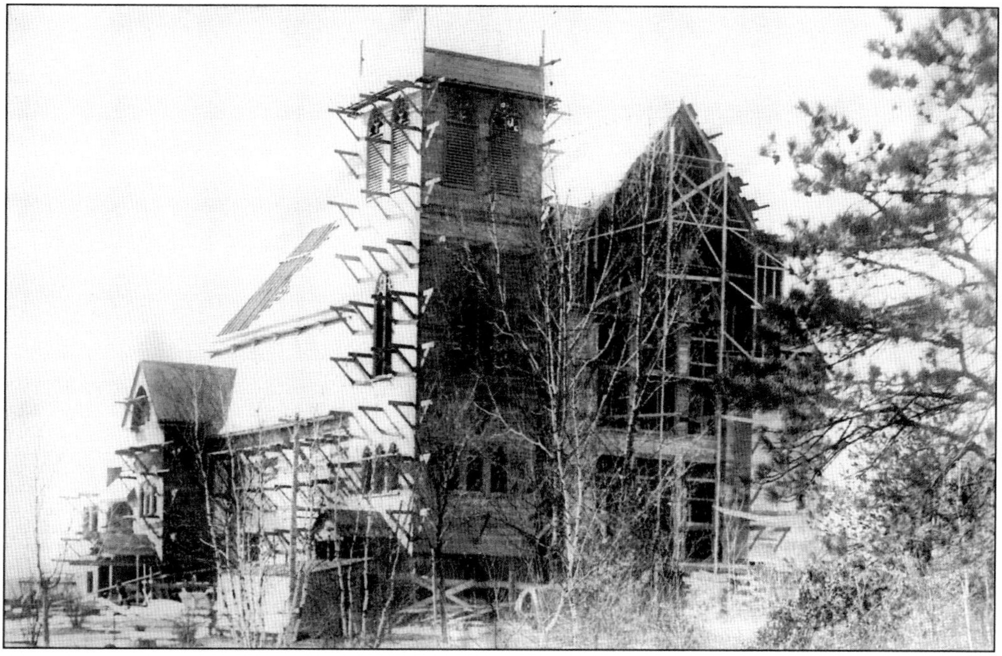

The new St. Thomas Aquinas Church was dedicated in November 1917, more than three years after a fire had razed the original building. The congregation, which consisted mainly of low-paid shoe factory workers, had spent much of that time in raising funds for the reconstruction. The new church shown here being built is much larger and ornate than the former chapel. (Allen photograph.)

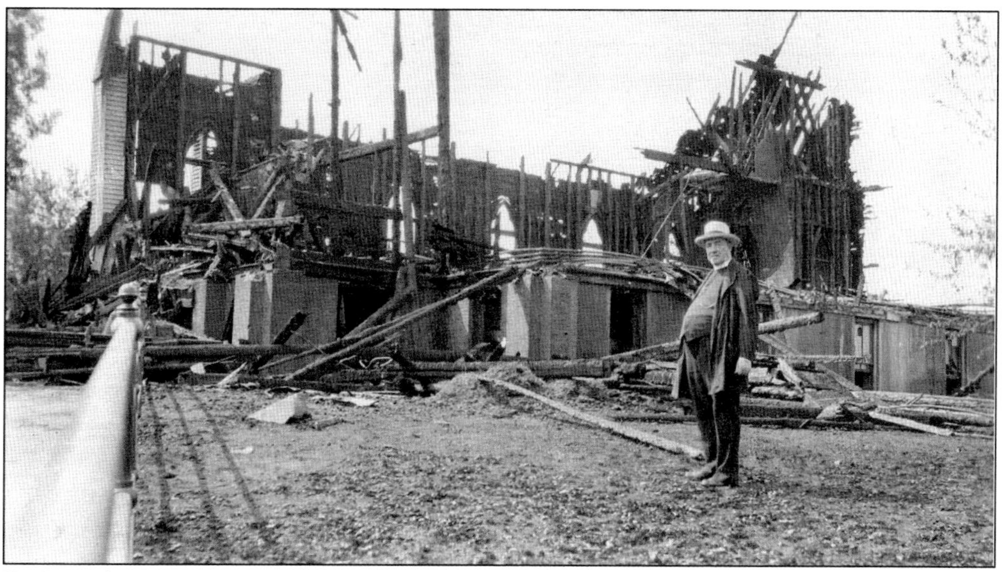

Fr. Daniel Dunn was out of town when the August 1914 fire destroyed the 25-year-old St. Thomas Aquinas Catholic Church. The portly priest returned to Derry the next day and is seen here surveying the damage. Following the fire, the parish held Mass at the Scenic Theater on Railroad Avenue for nearly three years, until a new church could be built.

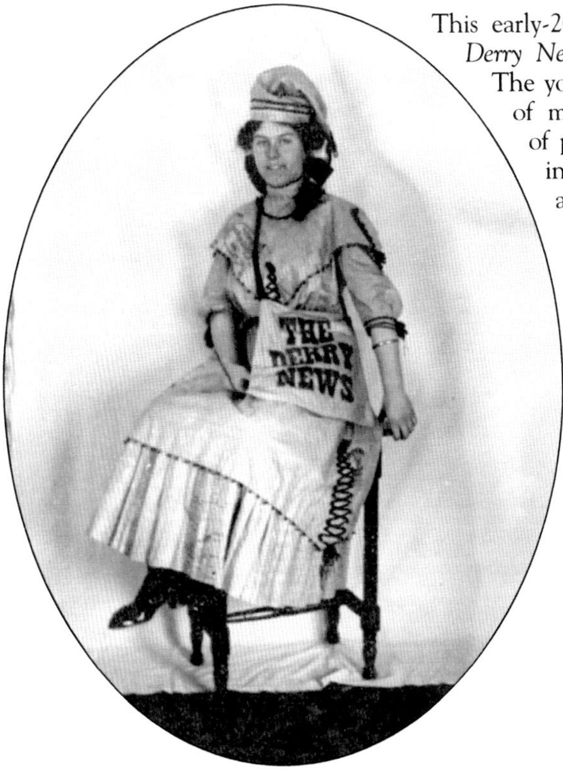

This early-20th-century photograph shows that the *Derry News* was an equal-opportunity employer. The young woman's dress and hat are all made of muslin-type cloth with a printed design of pages from the *Derry News*. This design includes ads for stoves, baking powder, and a Broadway paint store. The *Derry News* ceased using door-to-door paperboys and papergirls in 2003.

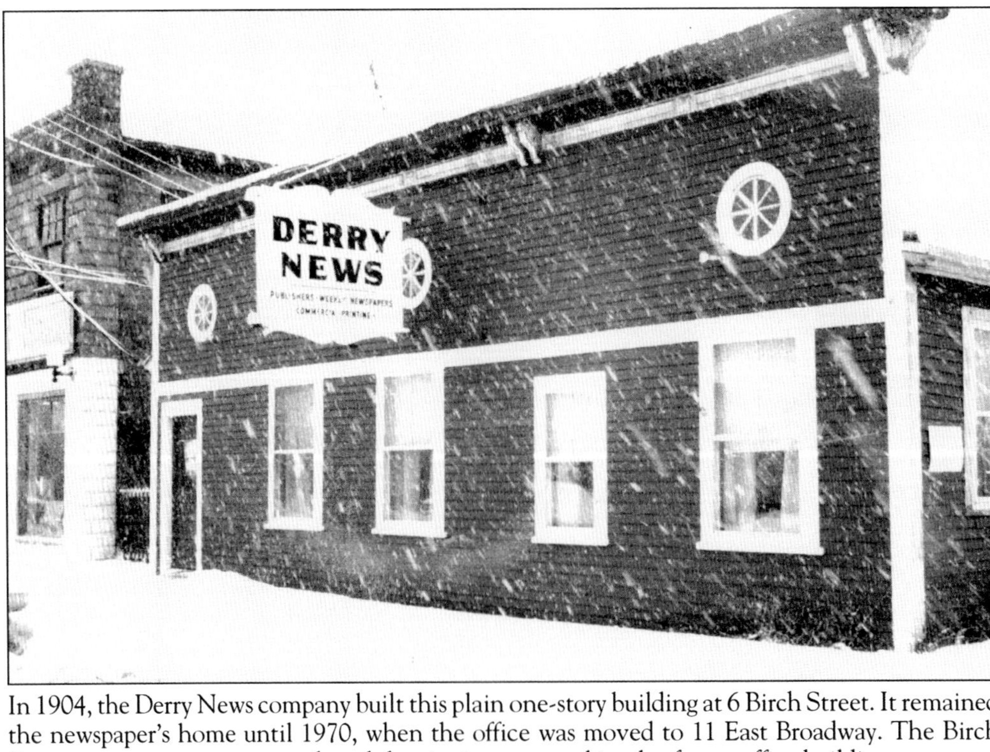

In 1904, the Derry News company built this plain one-story building at 6 Birch Street. It remained the newspaper's home until 1970, when the office was moved to 11 East Broadway. The Birch Street structure was soon razed, and the site is now a parking lot for an office building.

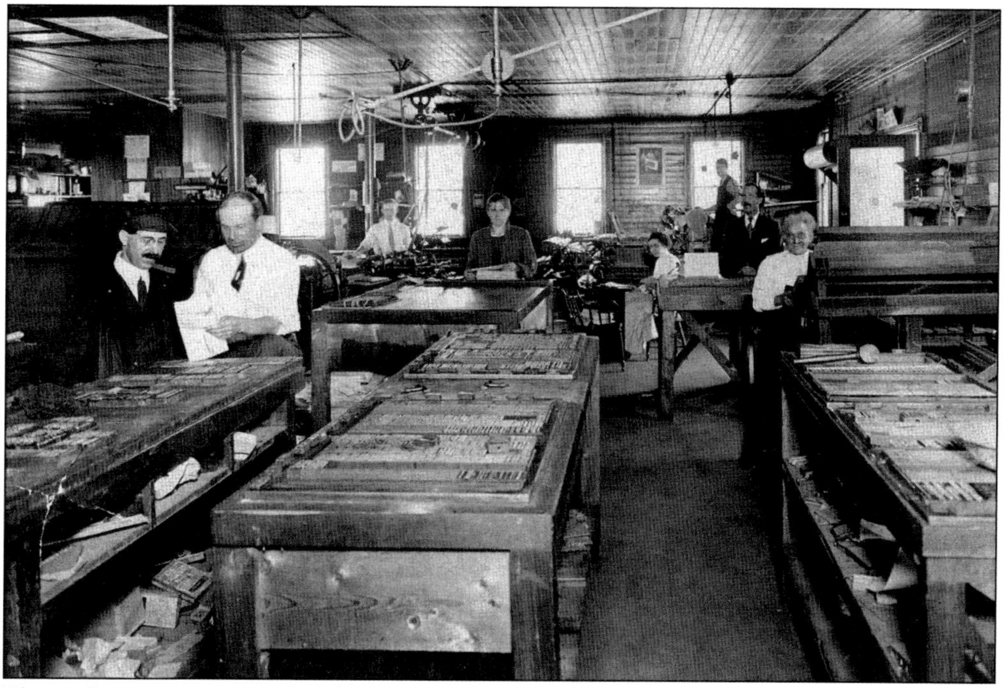

This is the composing room of the *Derry News* in 1911. The publisher, Edmund P. Trowbridge, is seen on the left talking to an employee who is wearing the printer's traditional leather eyeshade. In the background are the noisy printing presses that would shake the whole building when they ran.

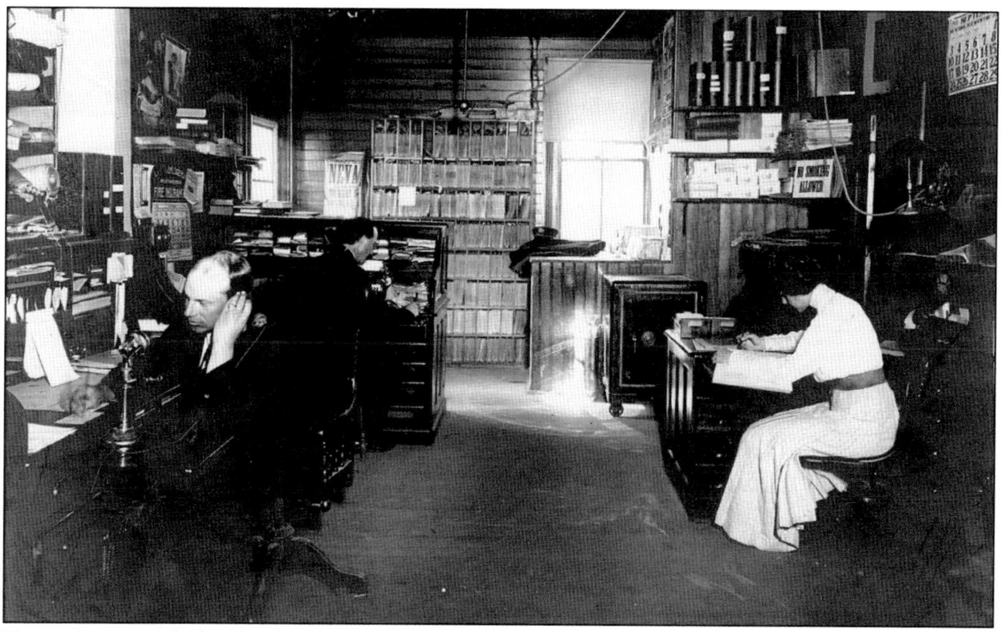

From this crowded office, Edmund P. Trowbridge published the *Derry News*. He owned the paper from 1903 to 1944. He is seen on the left talking on the telephone. On the counter by the window at the back is a fireman's uniform; it is carefully laid out in anticipation of the next conflagration. Gaslights light the room.

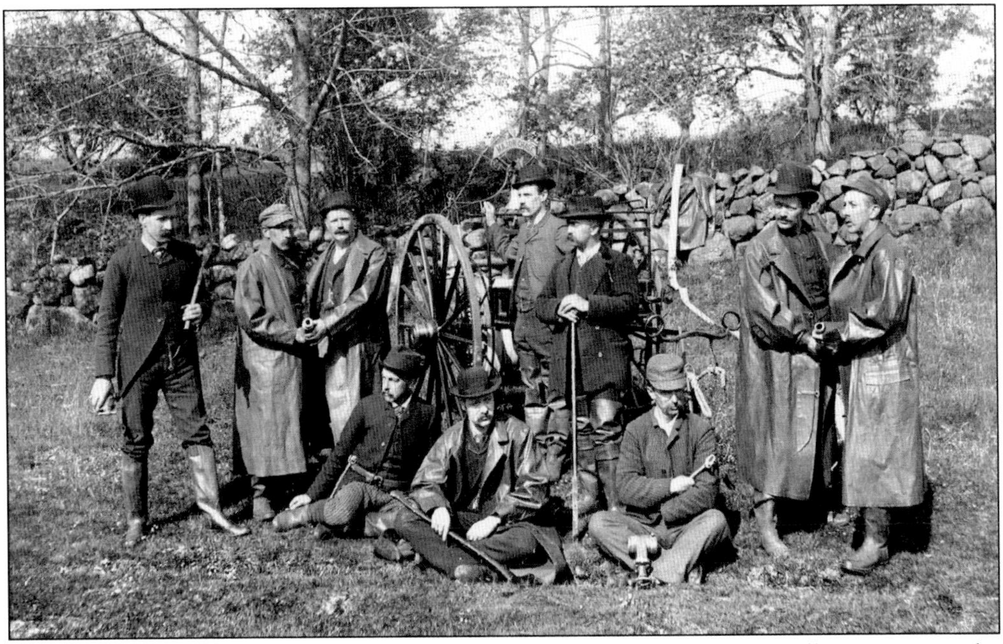

In the 1880s, there were separate fire departments in each of the three villages. Here is the pride of the Lower Village. This secondhand, two-wheeled fire apparatus was pulled from the Crescent Street fire station to the fire by a team of men. Many of these men are attired in protective leather coats and high boots, and have elected to wear the more-stylish derby or baseball cap in place of the traditional fireman's helmet.

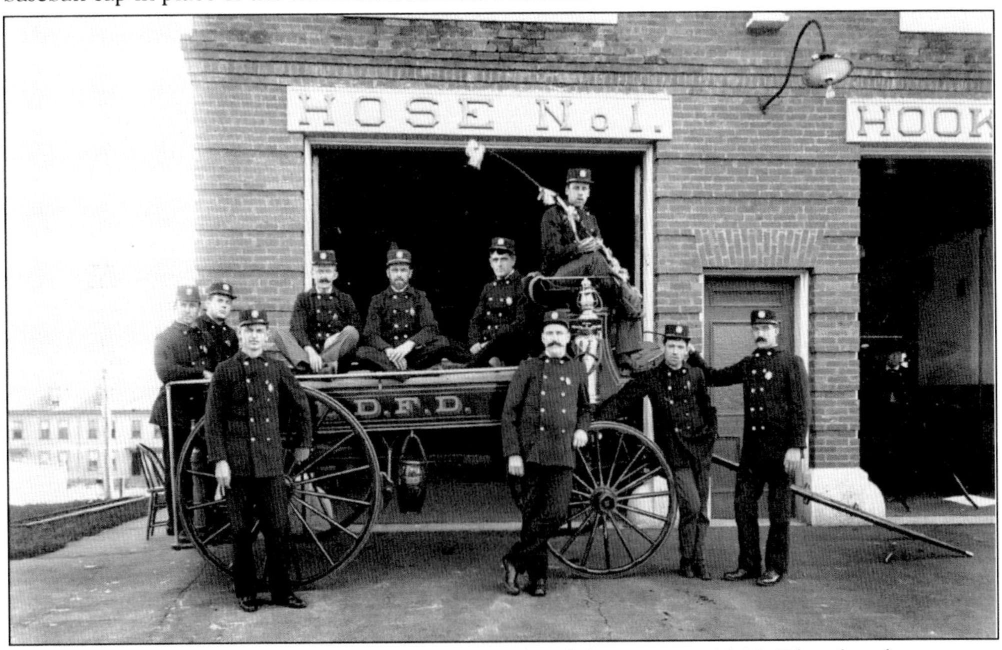

This piece of firefighting equipment was the pride of the town *c.* 1900. This fire department was organized in 1885 after a Broadway fire wiped out most of the area's buildings. The brick fire station was completed in 1899 and was enlarged in 1961. The horses that pulled the department's two-wagon force were stabled down the street.

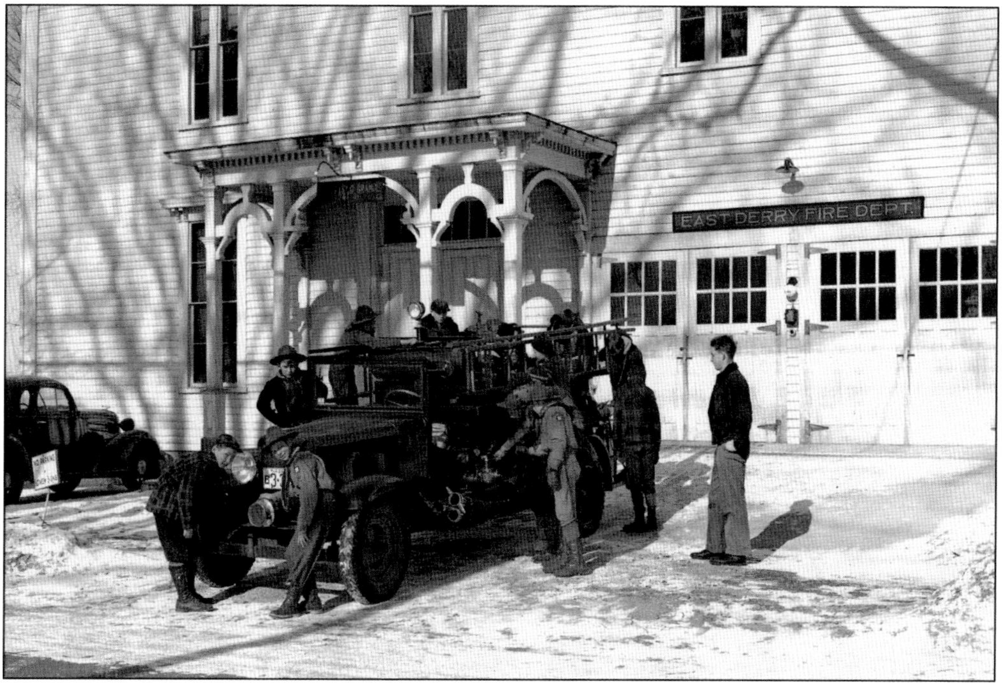

In January 1940, Scoutmaster Duncan Cameron (right) brought Troop 98 to examine the fire engine of the East Derry fire station. Notice that most of the boys are wearing knickerbockers. The vehicle is a 1929 Chevrolet truck that had been retrofitted into a fire engine. The East Derry Fire Department called the Upper Village Hall its home from 1934 to 1970.

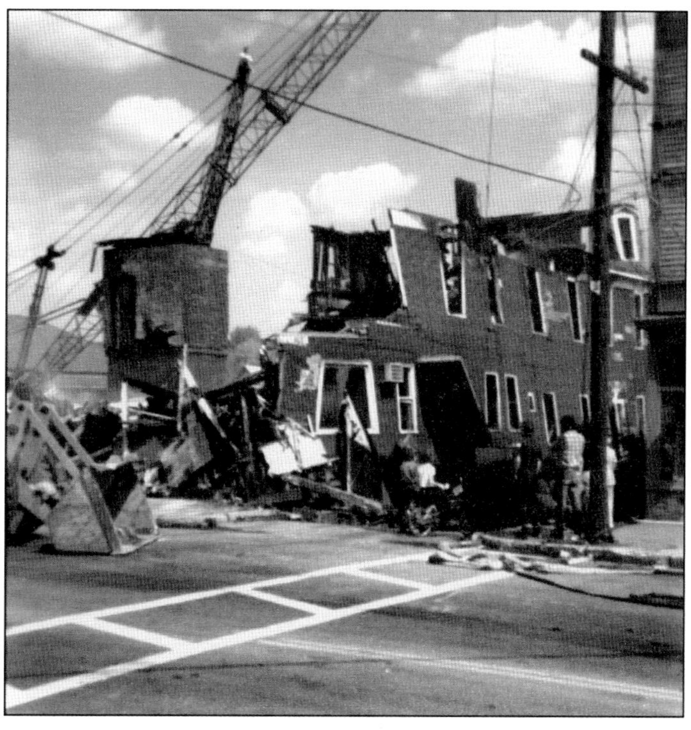

For more than a century, shoe factories lined Broadway. In 1915, the owners converted their factories into apartments and stores. A fire on January 1, 1979, destroyed most of the buildings between the railroad depot and the West Derry fire station. Left homeless were 30 apartment dwellers. What parts of the buildings had been spared from the flames were declared unsafe and were soon demolished.

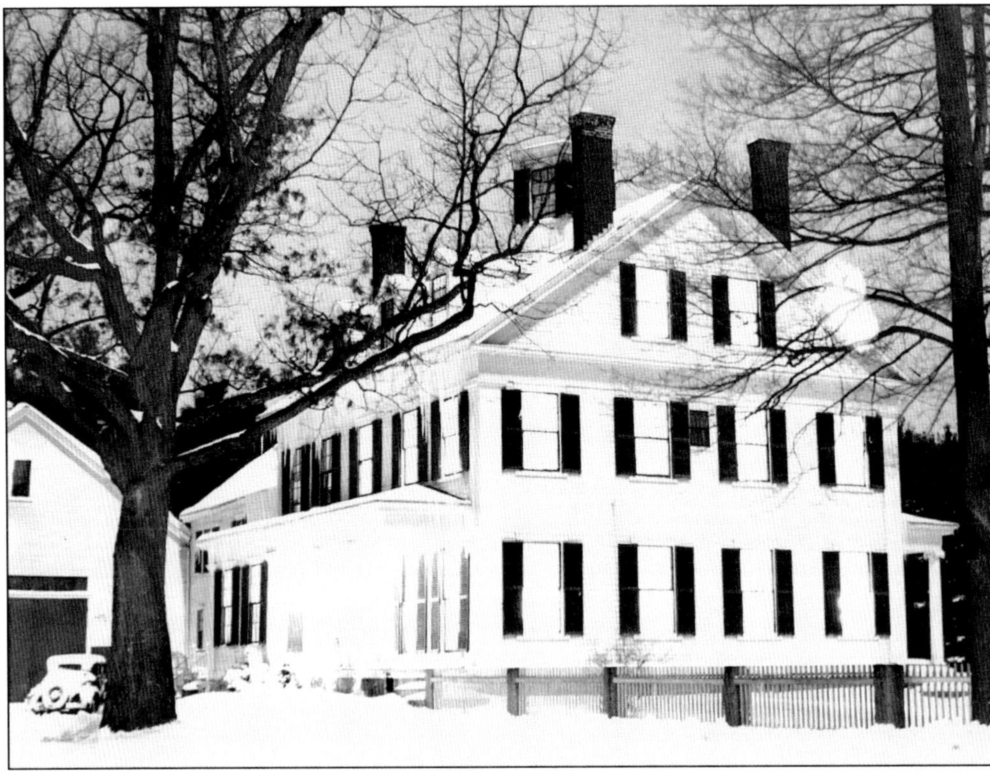

Benjamin Eastman built this stately Old Chester Road house in 1849. In 1933, his granddaughter Katherine Hood gave the house to the town to be used as the Alexander-Eastman Hospital. It was co-named for Dr. Harrison Alexander, who had bequeathed money for a hospital. After the hospital moved in 1964, the building was converted into apartments.

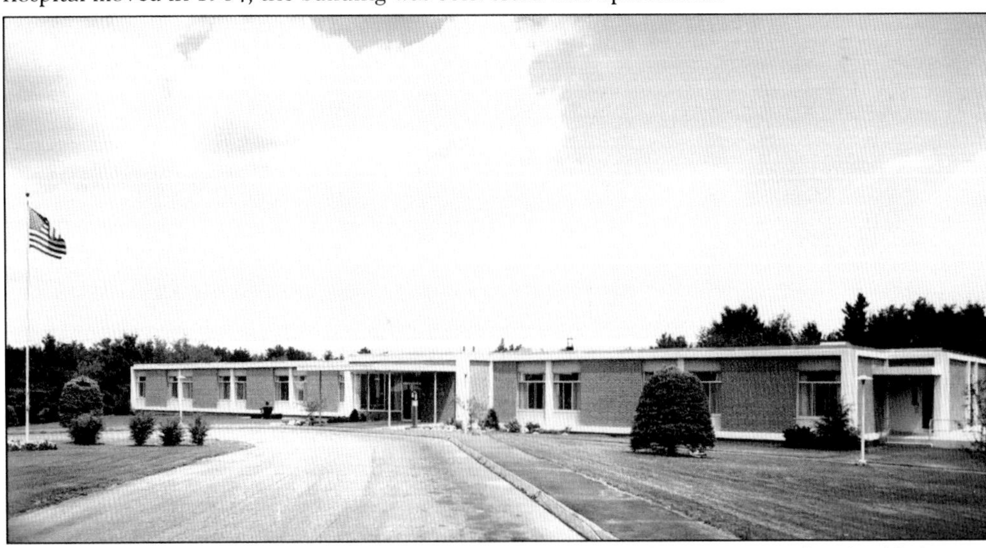

A successful fund-raising campaign in 1961 raised much of the money used to build the new Alexander-Eastman Hospital. It was built in 1964 on Birch Street land given to the town by Dr. Harrison Alexander for recreation and public use. It was closed in 1983 and replaced by Parkland Hospital. (F. J. Sullivan photograph.)

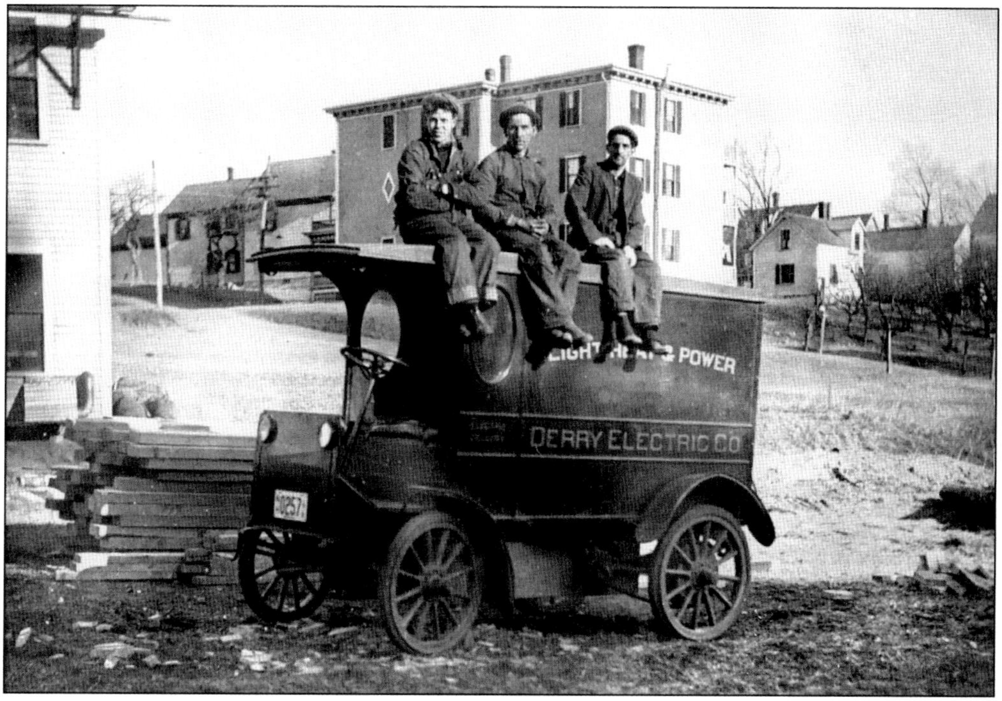

The Derry Electric Company was founded in 1891 and operated from 42 East Broadway. It was not until 1910 that transmission of electricity was allowed after midnight. This electric company service truck is shown near the Maple Street generating plant.

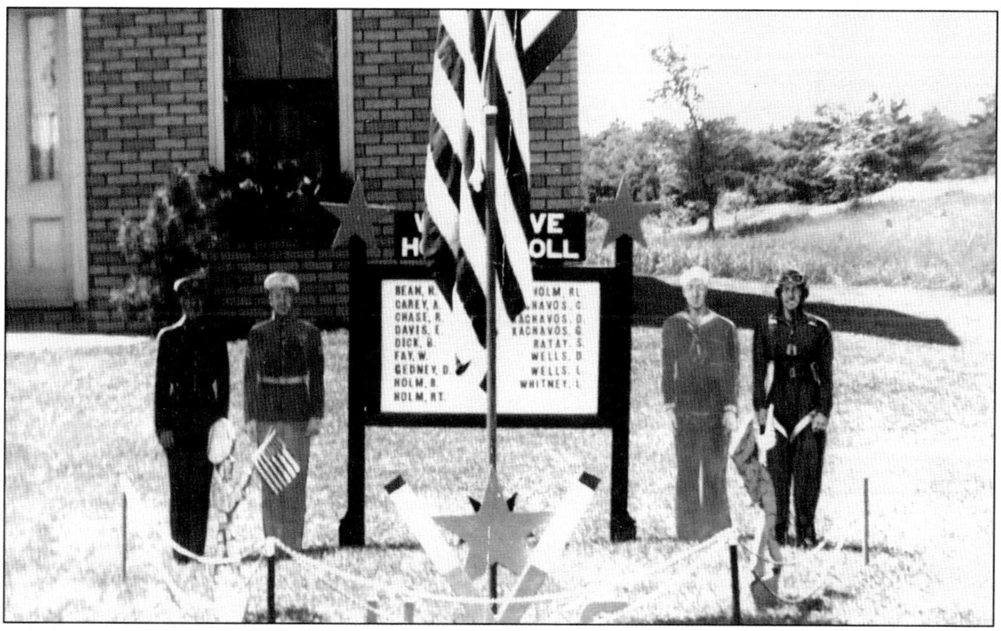

During World War II, the Bunker family of Fordway erected this display at their home. On the sign were the names of the 13 men from their neighborhood who were in the military. That section of Derry is called Peppermint Corners, Ward Five, or Chaseville.

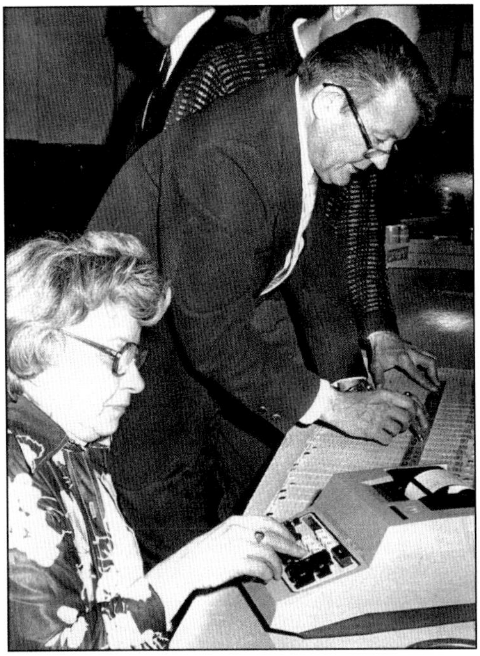

Since 1722 the town's residents have voted at the annual town meeting to elect their civic leaders and decide on how much to tax themselves. Here moderator Joseph Stancik and town clerk Cecile Hoisington are counting the votes that elected Benjamin Newell selectman over Harold DiPietro by a vote of 1,133 to 1,080. After 1985 the town eliminated town meetings and went to a mayor and council form of government.

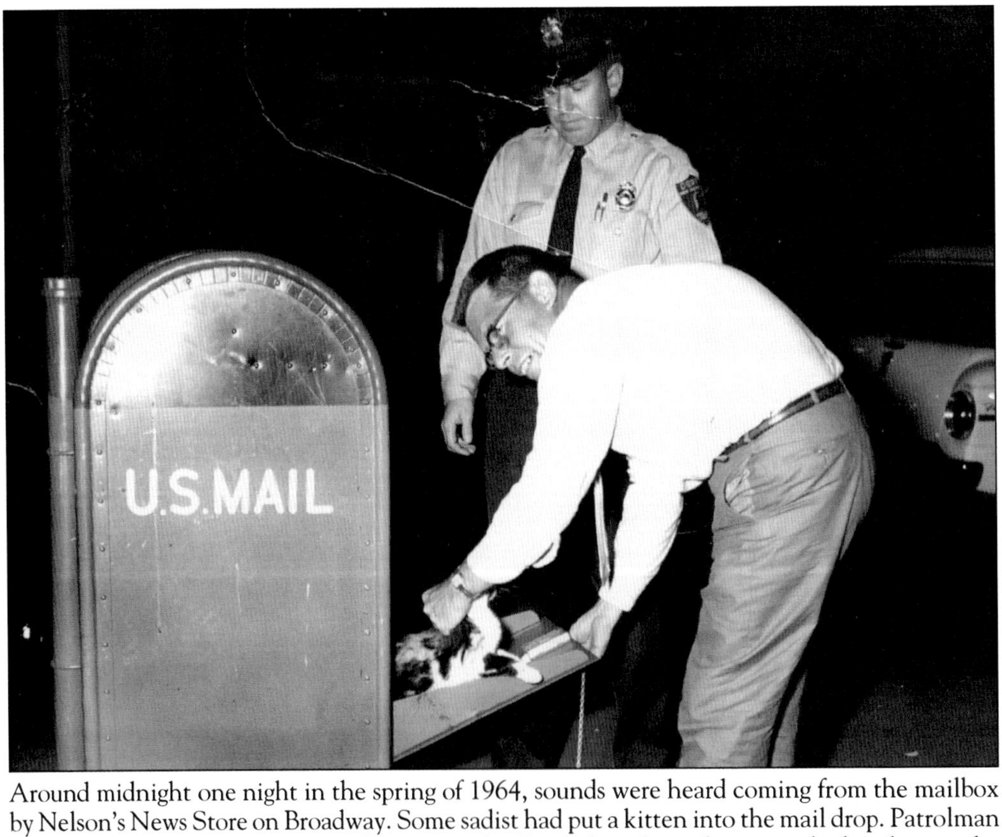

Around midnight one night in the spring of 1964, sounds were heard coming from the mailbox by Nelson's News Store on Broadway. Some sadist had put a kitten into the mail drop. Patrolman Herb Webster called off-duty mailman Leander Burdick to leave his warm bed and open the mailbox. The calico cat was fine thanks to the two men. (F. J. Sullivan photograph.)

Five

TRANSPORTATION

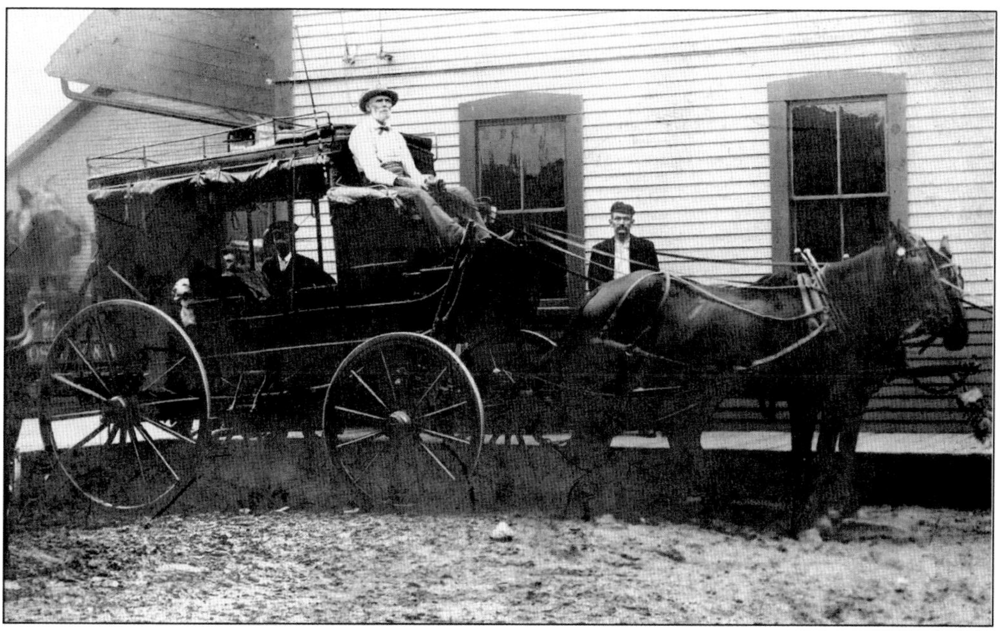

Stagecoach service between Chester and Derry began in 1793. The coach took a couple hours to make the trip. The road was so rough that passengers frequently had to be strapped in to prevent them from being thrown from the coach. The Concord Coach is shown here at Chester center. The construction of the Chester and Derry trolley line ended the need for the stagecoaches.

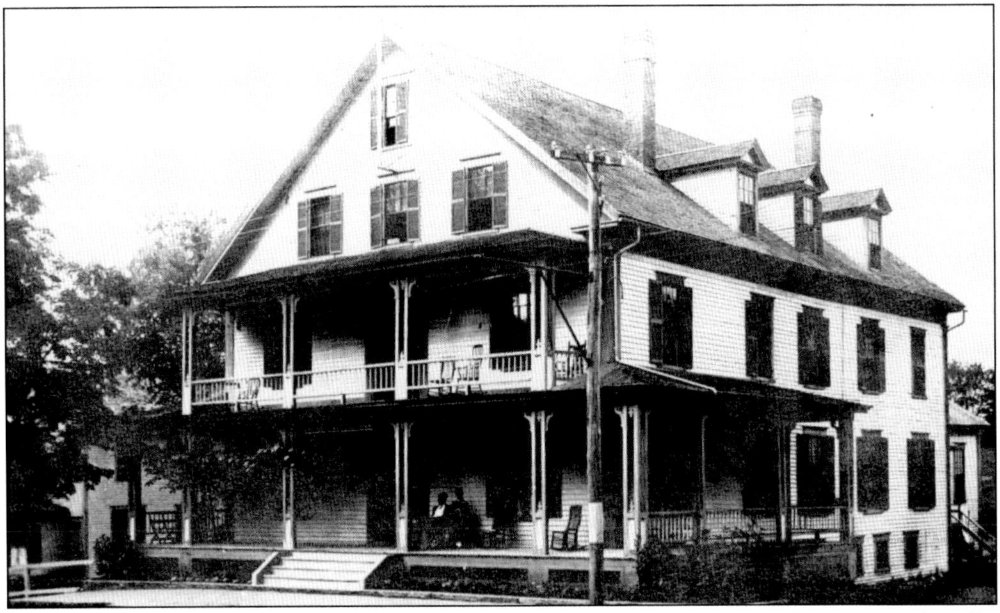

Hildreth Hall was built in 1812 as a stagecoach inn to handle the increased commercial traffic on the new Londonderry Turnpike. The inn burned in 1863 but was quickly rebuilt in the original design. It was purchased by Pinkerton Academy in 1884, and was demolished in 1952 to make way for an athletic field house.

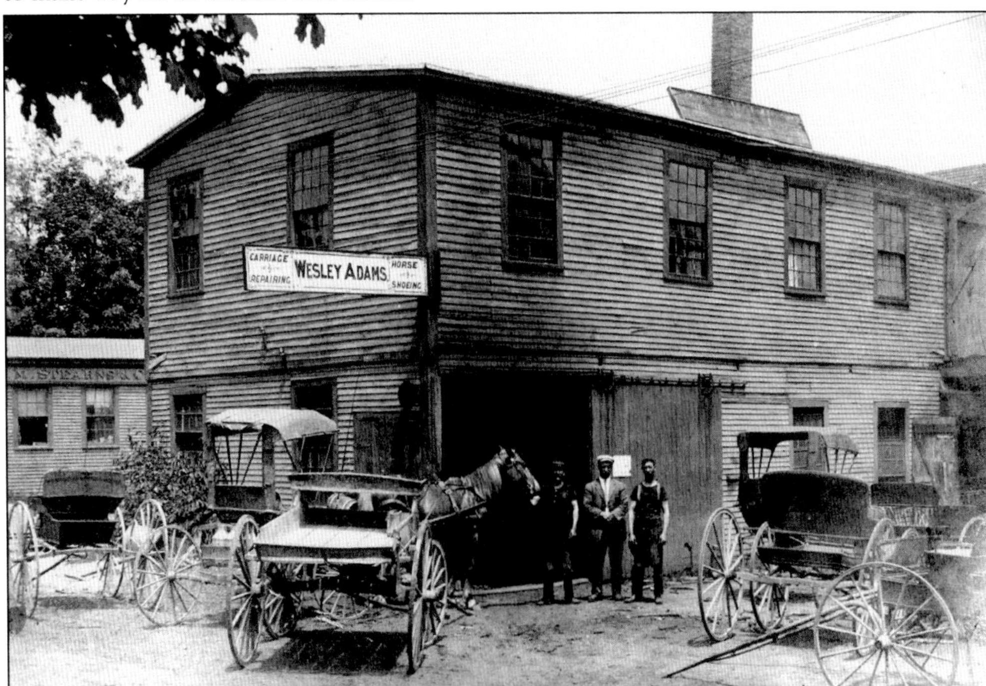

Wesley Adams's carriage shop was located on Franklin Street and advertised itself in 1908 as offering "horse shoeing, [and] carriage repairs," with "special attention given to interfering and stumbling horses." Adams (1872–1943) served as head of the state Grange, president of the New Hampshire senate, and deputy sheriff of Rockingham County.

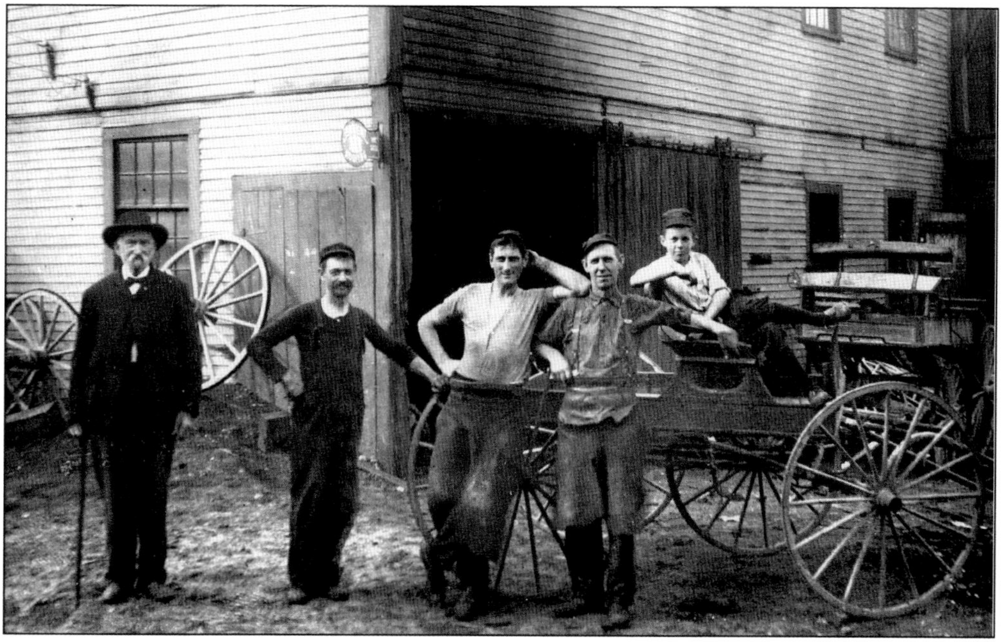

The Abbot, Davis Company of Central Street manufactured "farm wagons, carts, and rigs" in West Derry. The company owned nine buildings, including a four-story wheelwright shop. Altogether the business occupied 85,000 square feet in the Broadway area.

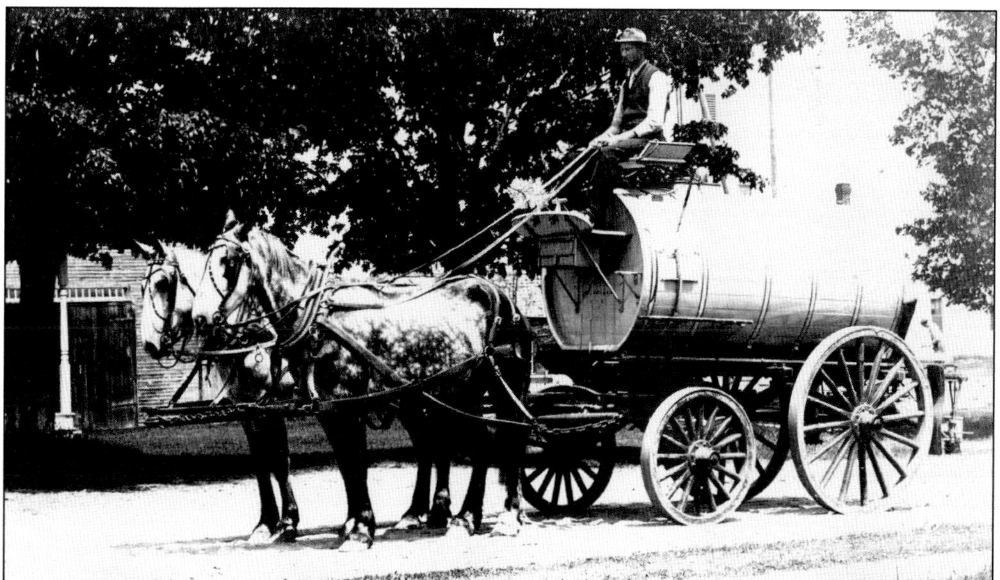

In 1909, there was not a single paved road in Derry. During the long, dry New Hampshire summers, the dust rose with every passing wagon. In the summer of 1916, the town spread 120 gallons of oil directly on the dirt roads off the Broadway area. This was in a time before there was much public concern about pollution.

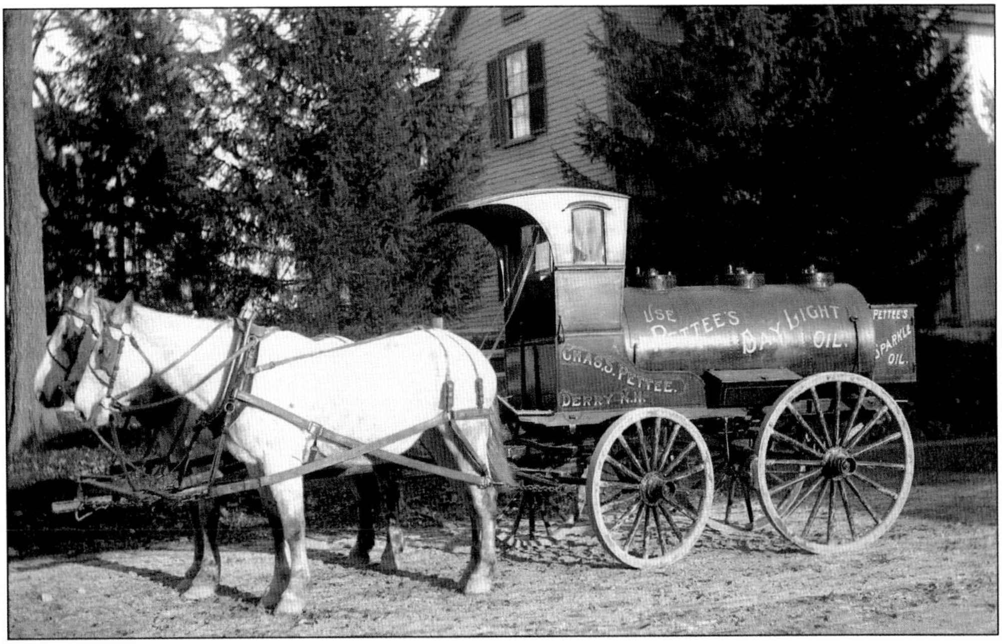

Around 1890, Charles Seneca Pettee's kerosene delivery wagon was a common sight in Derry. He would bring his "sparkle oil" to homes throughout the town. The oil was used in lamps, cooking stoves, and space heaters. Pettee ran the Derry Village Store and operated an ice wagon that offered door-to-door delivery.

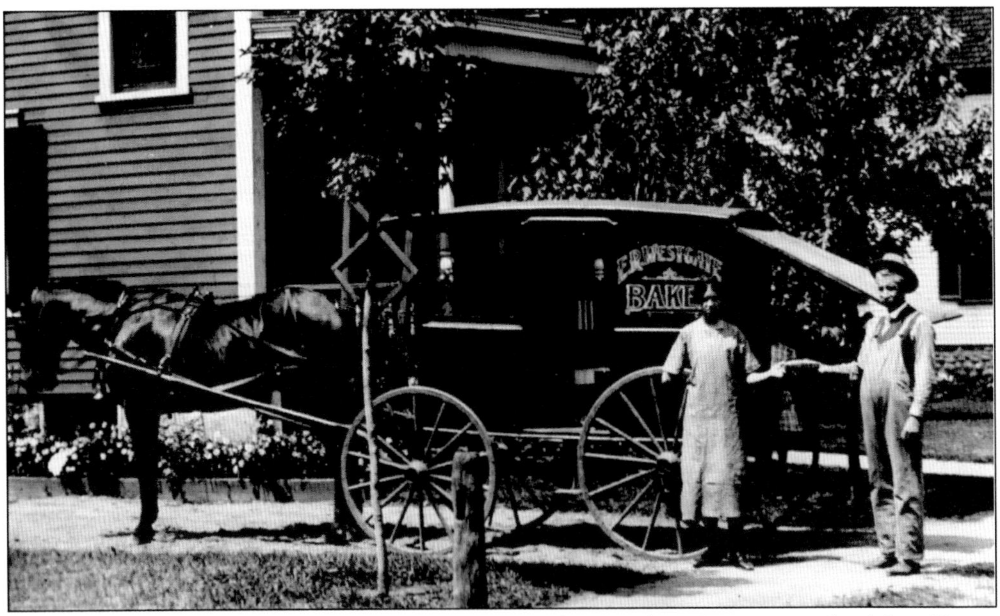

At the start of the 20th century, there were many door-to-door "stores on wheels" in Derry. There was the iceman, the fish man, the tin cart, the milkman, and others who made weekly stops all over town. Here, the baker is seen delivering a pie to a West Derry housewife. A bell around the horse's neck alerted potential customers of the bakery cart's approach.

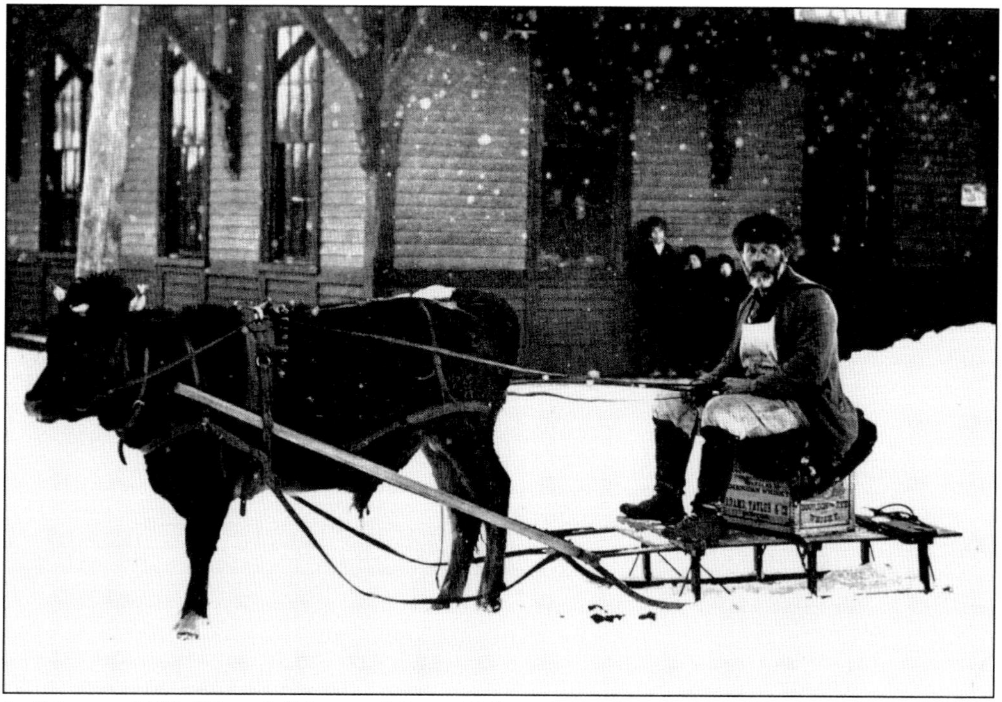

In February 1907, Edward Gilman of Derry Village drove his new rig down Broadway. He had built a sled of old lumber and fashioned the harness from scrap leather. Gilman's seat was an empty whiskey box. He had spent months training his two-year-old bull to be a draught animal. Farmer Gilman claimed the bull-powered cart could do light hauling. (L. H. Rand photograph.)

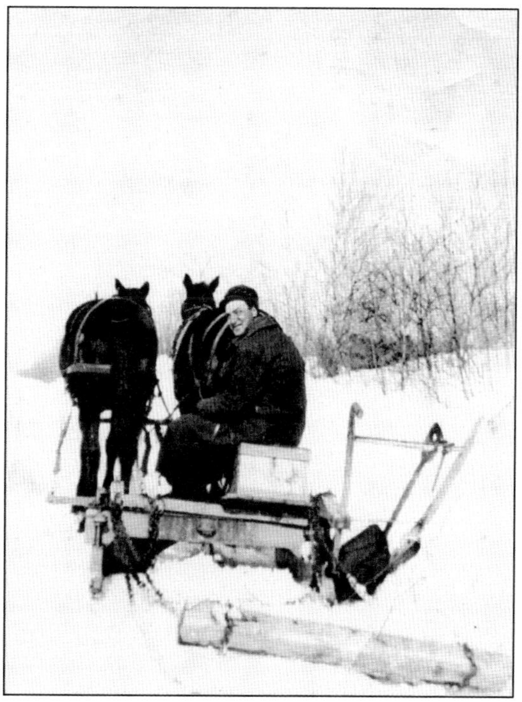

It was well after the First World War before motor trucks with plows began to clear the snow-covered roads of Derry. During the town's first two centuries, winter travel was usually accomplished in horse-drawn sleighs. In this c. 1910 Derry photograph, a team of horses is dragging a log to break a path through a snowdrift.

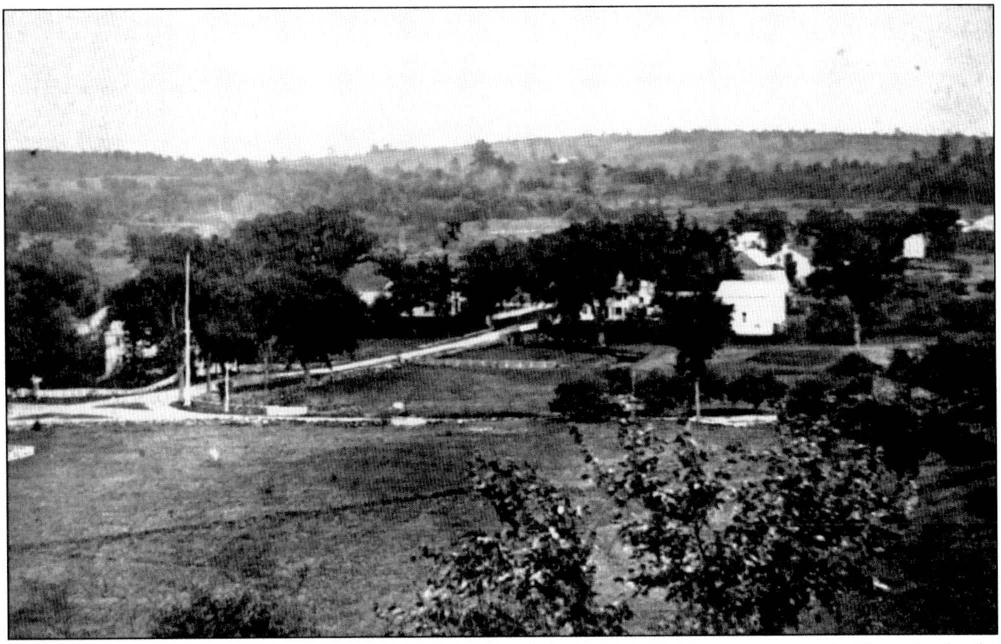

This 1880 photograph, taken from the steeple of the Central Congregational Church, looks south toward the site of the present traffic circle. During the spring mud time, this intersection was often an impassible quagmire for horse-drawn wagons. The flagpole in the center left was erected during the Civil War as the town's liberty pole. The Danforth traffic circle was built in the late 1930s.

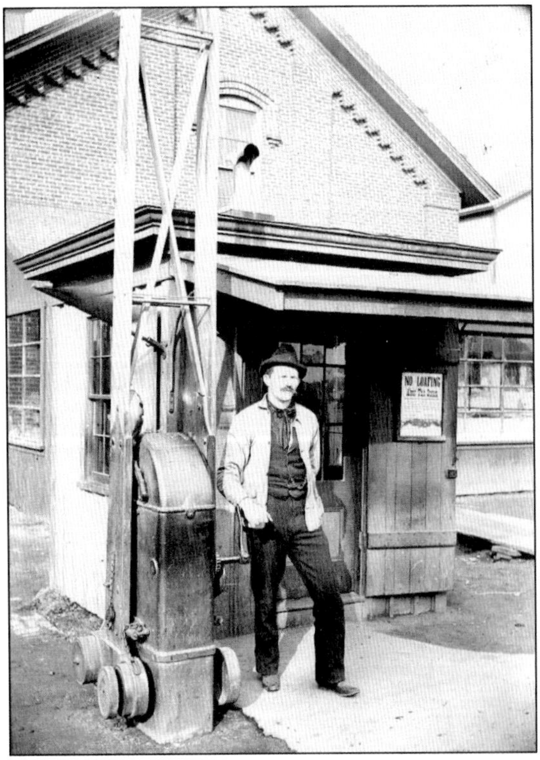

For 131 years, speeding railroad engines crossed Broadway on their way to and from Manchester or Boston. A pair of 30-foot-long safety gates were lowered to halt horses, automobiles, or pedestrian traffic. This c. 1905 photograph shows Thomas Henry Ford, the Broadway gate-tender. The sign on his hut warns, "No loafing about this building."

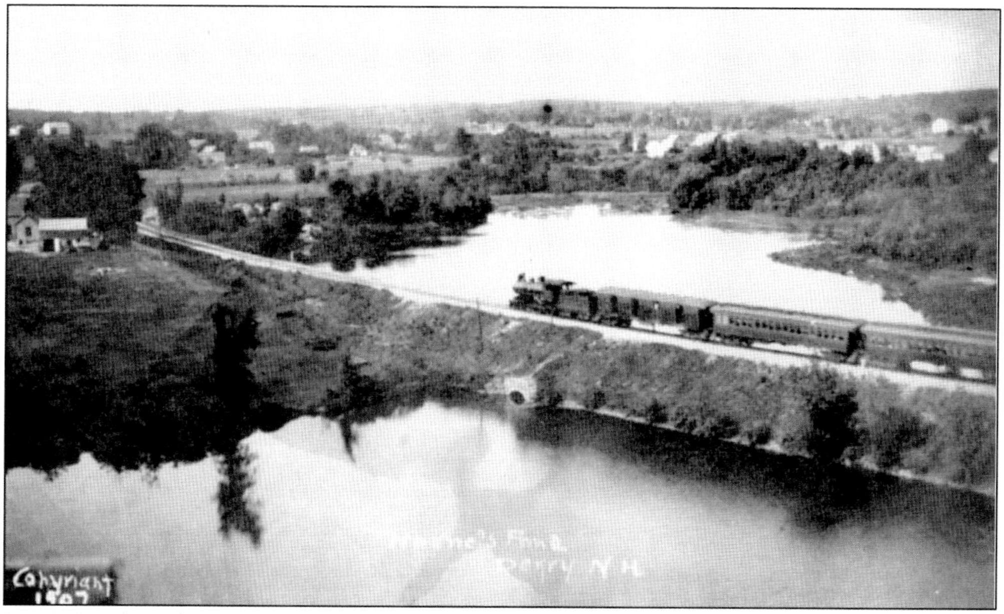

In 1848, when the Manchester and Lawrence Railroad line was built, there were many hills to be made level and waterways to bridge. The millpond at Horne's sawmill was right in the railroad's path. Rather than go around the small pond, the rail company decided to build an earthen causeway, which split the pond in half. Today one side is called Hood Pond and the other called Horne's Pond. (L. W. Rand photograph.)

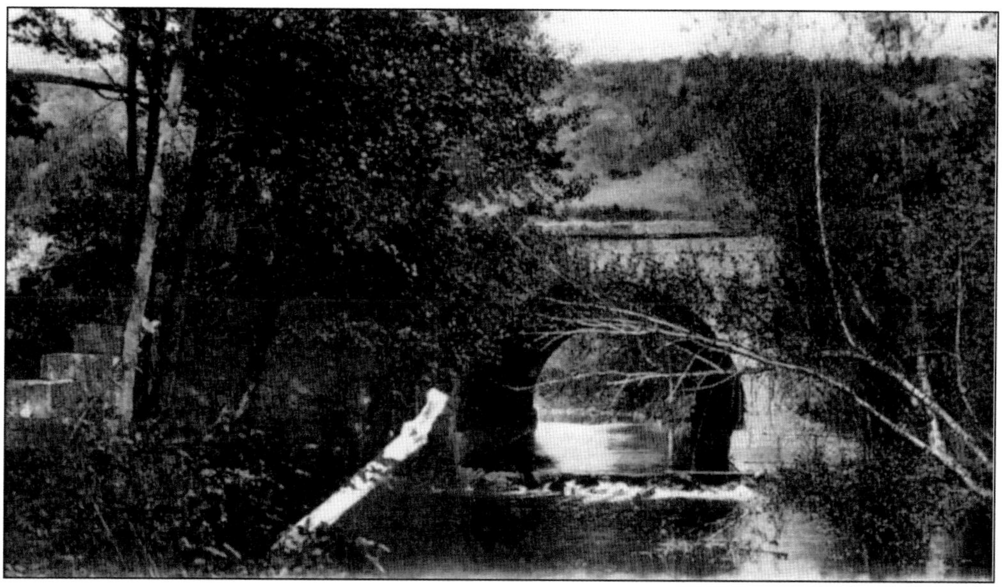

In 1848, the Manchester and Lawrence Railroad built this granite-block bridge to cross the Beaver Brook. While it is called "Lovers Leap," there is no evidence of any lovers having leaped off this bridge to their death in the mighty Beaver Brook. Since the mid-1990s, the Derry bike path has passed over the bridge.

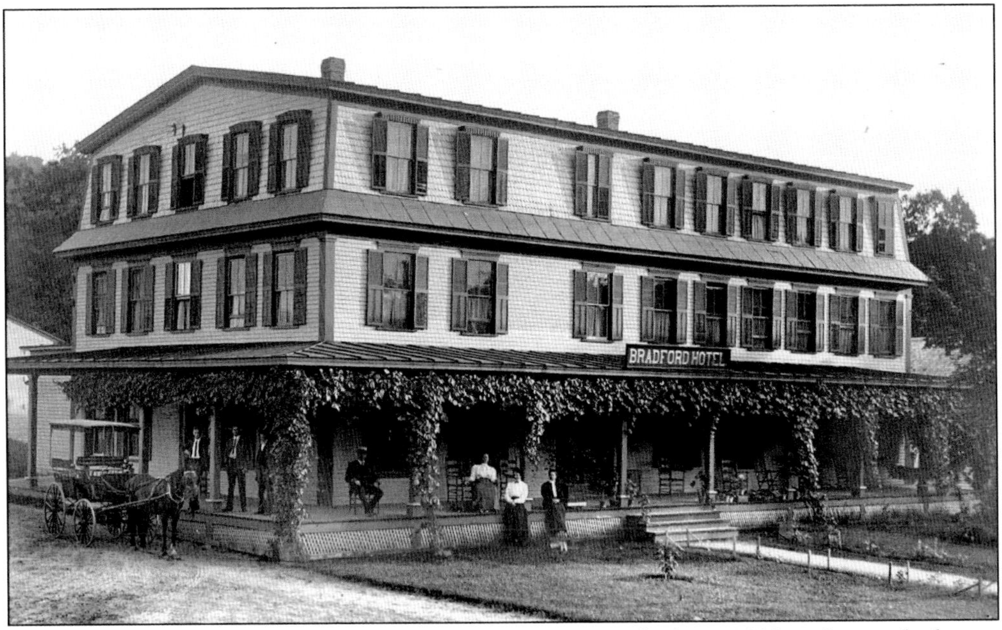

The Bradford Hotel, at Broadway and Martin Streets, was built in 1882 and named after its owner, Alden Bradford Smith. During the years when Derry was officially dry, the hotel was frequently raided by Prohibition officials searching for illegal liquor. The raids were usually successful. The greatly renovated structure is now an apartment building.

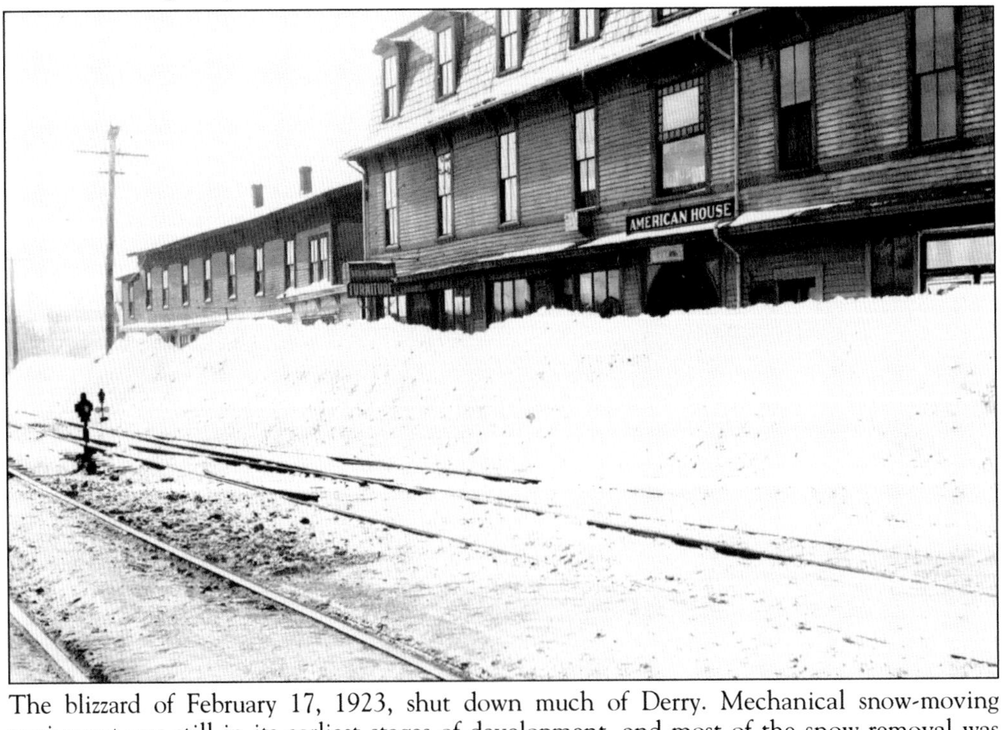

The blizzard of February 17, 1923, shut down much of Derry. Mechanical snow-moving equipment was still in its earliest stages of development, and most of the snow removal was still done by teams of men with shovels and horses. In the background are the American House Apartments. This block was destroyed in a fire during the 1970s.

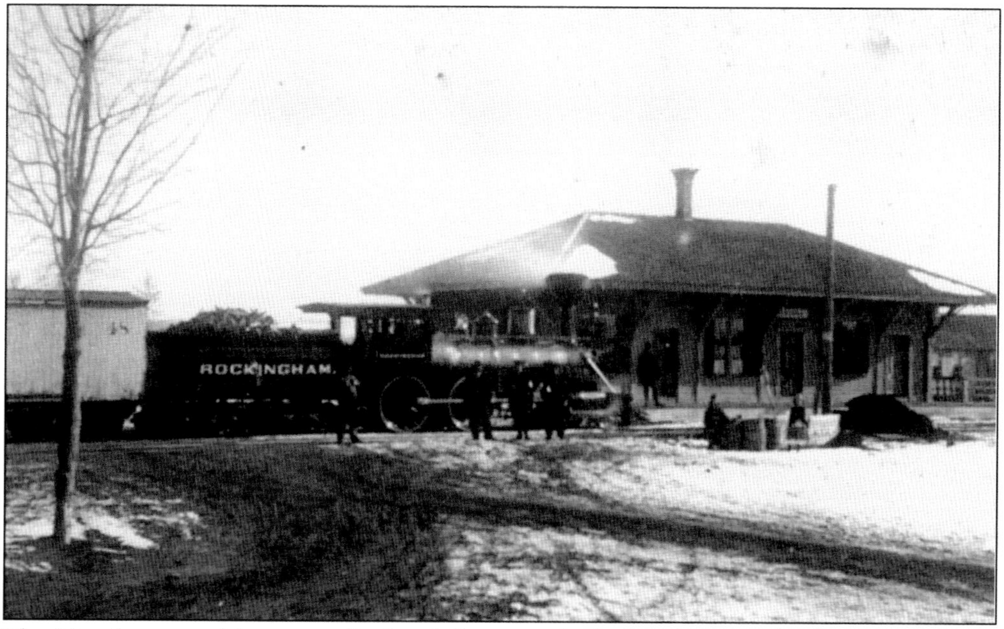

The Manchester and Lawrence Railroad Company built this depot in the farmland of West Derry in 1849. At that time, only three houses could be seen from the depot's front door. Slowly, a few stores, houses, a small shoe factory, a bank, and a hotel were built in the area. The great fire of 1882 leveled most of these buildings, including this railroad station. Within months the depot was rebuilt.

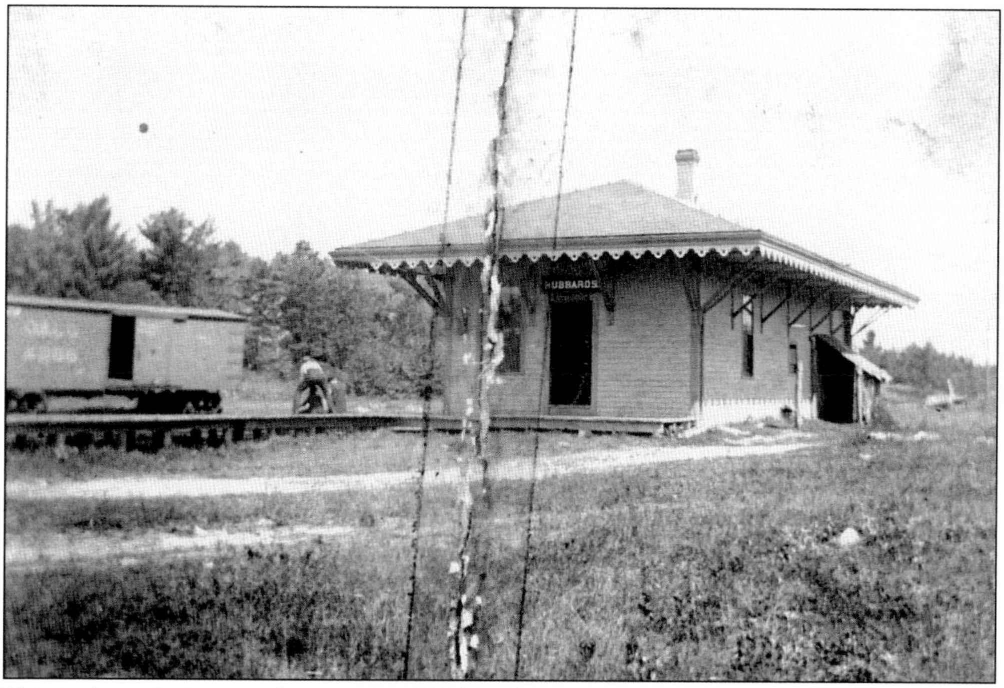

This is the only known photograph of Hubbards Station, on the side of Warner Road. The Nashua and Rochester Railroad built the station in 1873. It was never a profitable line and was closed by the Boston and Maine Corporation in 1934.

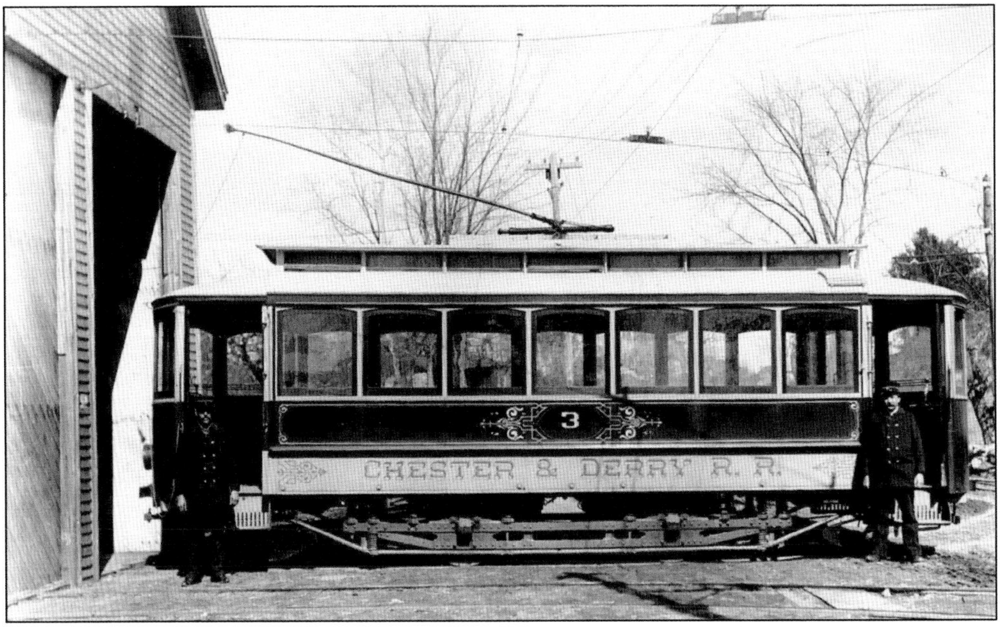

Pictured is the Chester and Derry Railroad trolley in 1896 at its East Derry Road car barn. Its entrance was just north of the former Chase Mill. On either side of the car are William West (left) and Edward Eastman. The green and yellow trolley could carry 28 passengers and was lighted and heated by electricity. The seven-and-three-quarter-mile-long street railroad was the shortest in New Hampshire.

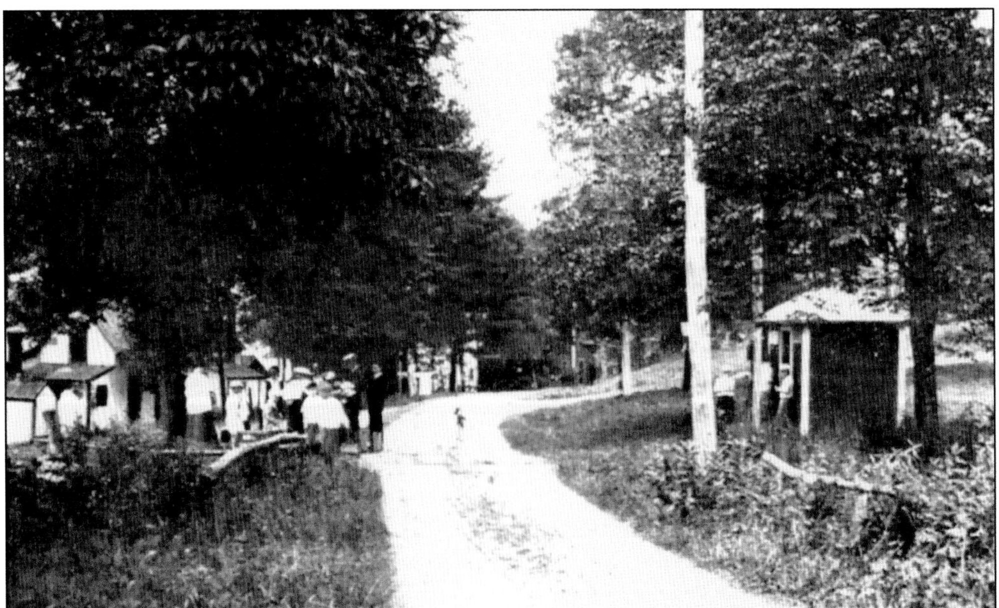

The Chester and Derry trolley circled around the north side of Beaver Lake on its way to Chester. On the right is the trolley waiting station, where the tracks cross North Shore Road. A few people are seen waiting for the next trolley.

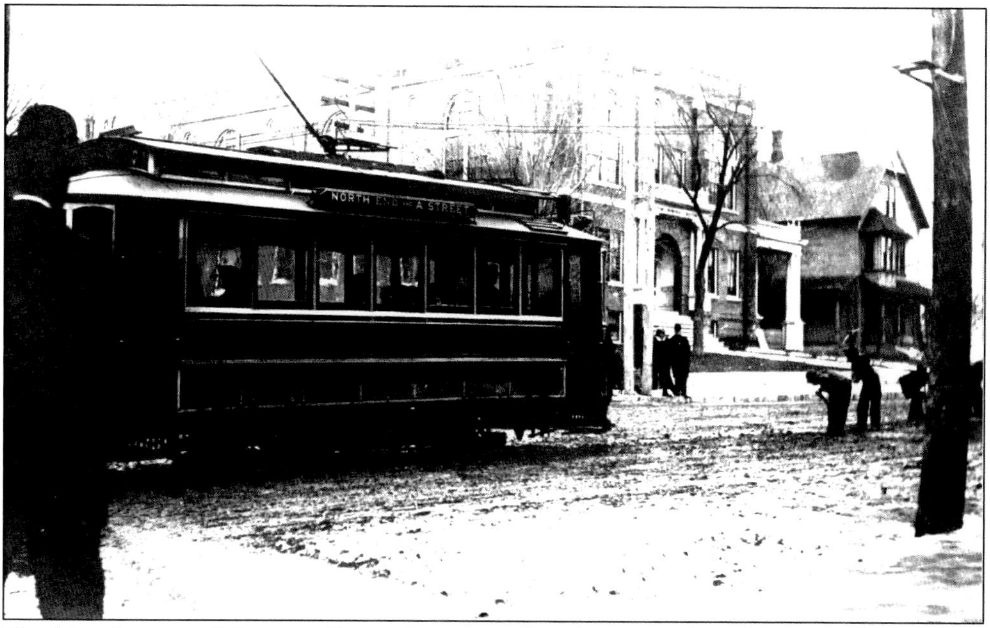
The Manchester and Derry trolley is shown traveling from Manchester and sloshing through the snow-covered road in front of the Adams Memorial Building. These workmen are clearing the tracks of snow and ice. This street railroad operated from 1907 to 1926.

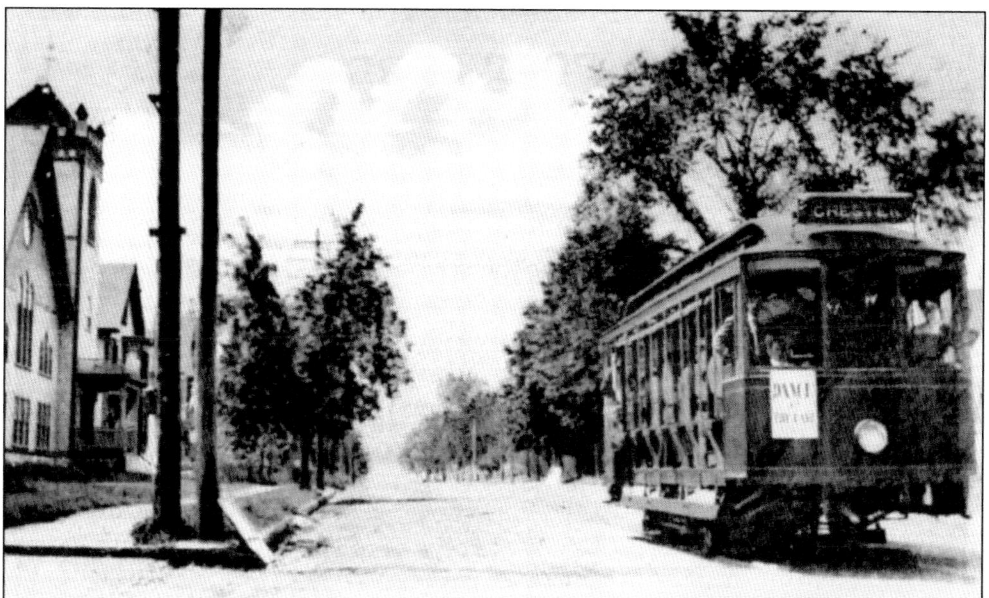

The Chester and Derry trolley carried passengers between the two towns from 1896 to 1928. St. Luke's Methodist Church is on the left. This trolley carries a sign advertising a dance at the Beaver Lake Pavilion. That pleasure palace had been built by the trolley company to attract riders on weekends.

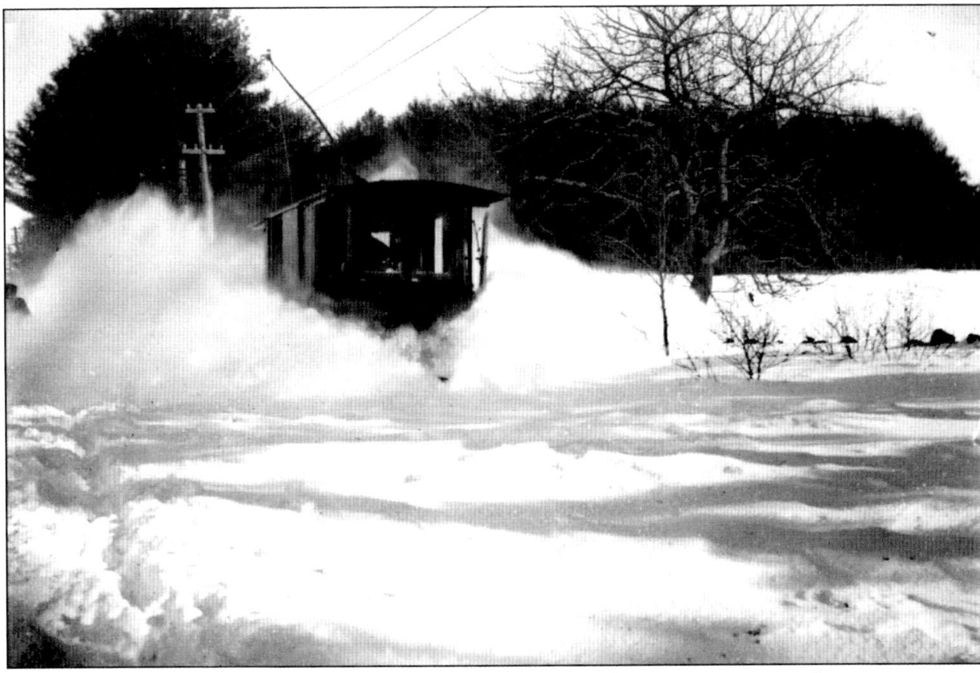

The plow of the Chester and Derry trolley is seen in February 1899, as it forces its way up Horse Hill toward East Derry. The driver has his head out the window, trying his best to figure where the rails are. On the left is the figure of a man being hit by trolley-thrown snow. (Bertha MacDougall photograph.)

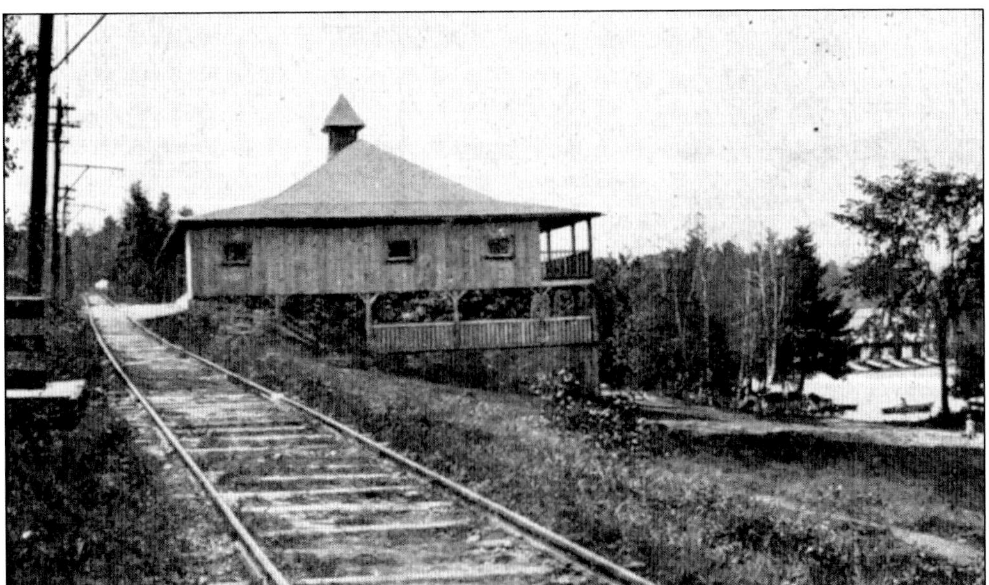

To encourage local residents to ride the street railroad, the Chester and Derry Railroad company built the Beaver Lake Pavilion. Here patrons could find a restaurant, dance hall, slot machines, and a sandy swimming beach. The pavilion was destroyed by fires in 1915 and 1960.

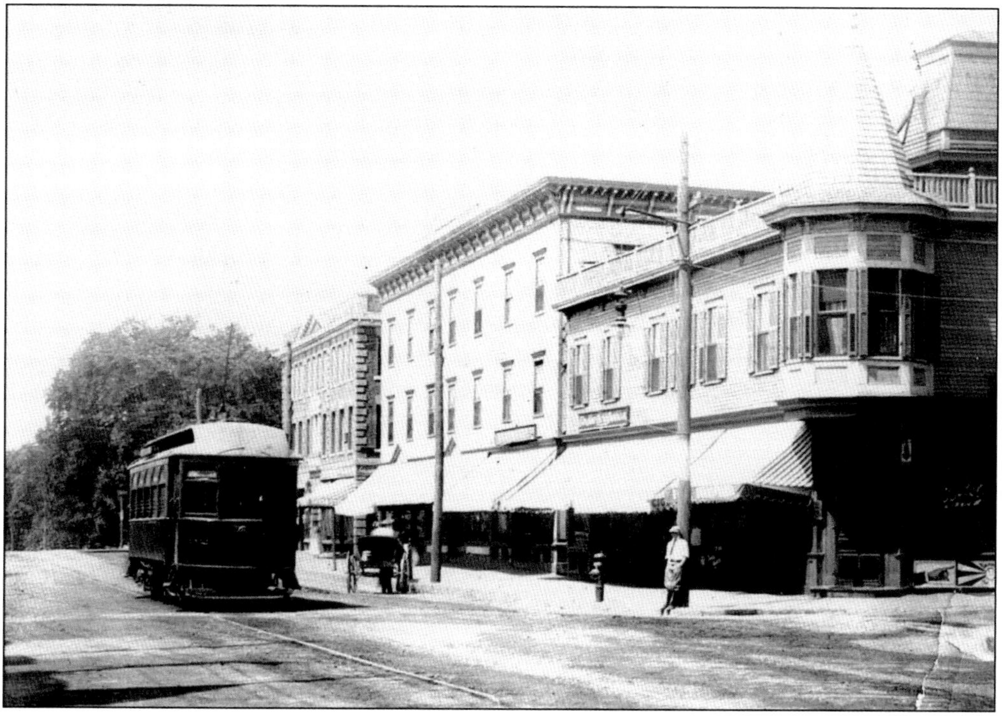

From 1907 through 1926, the Manchester and Derry trolley ran along West Broadway. It cost 15¢ to ride the 13 miles to city hall in Manchester. The ride took almost an hour. Competition from the railroad and automobile forced the line to close after only 19 years. This trolley car is now at the Seashore Trolley Museum in Maine.

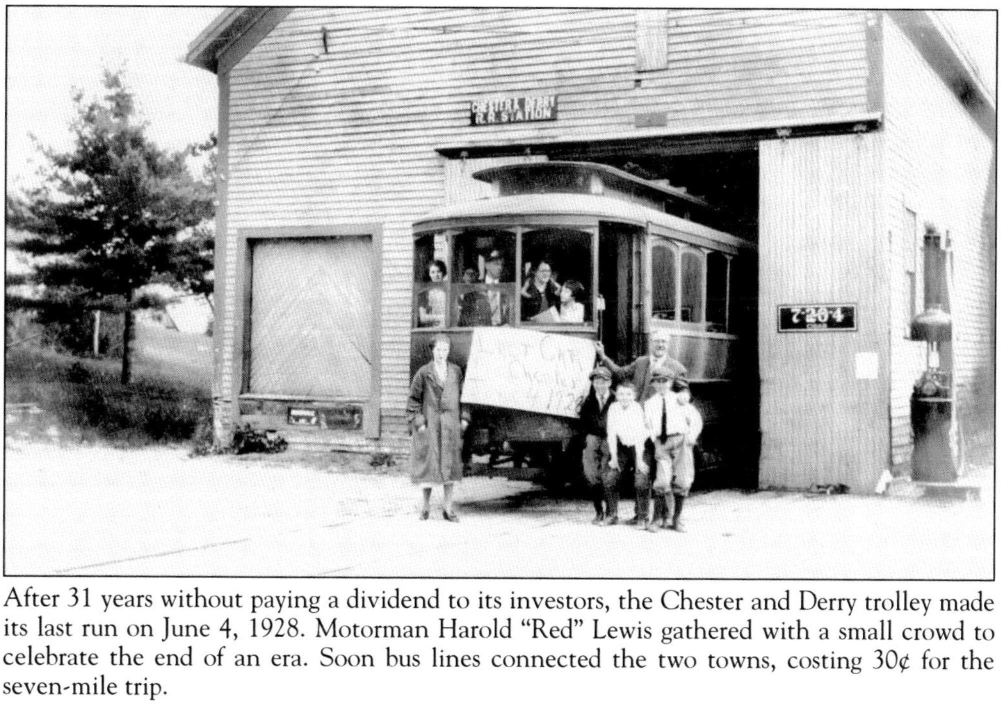

After 31 years without paying a dividend to its investors, the Chester and Derry trolley made its last run on June 4, 1928. Motorman Harold "Red" Lewis gathered with a small crowd to celebrate the end of an era. Soon bus lines connected the two towns, costing 30¢ for the seven-mile trip.

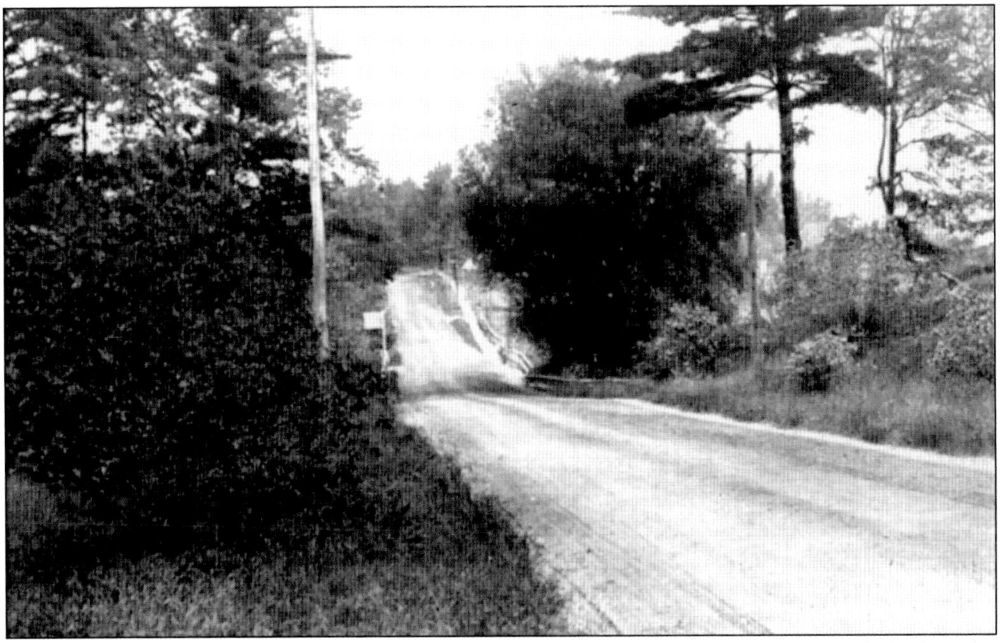

This photograph of Birch Street around 1930 shows the gentle slope immediately before the Beaver Brook bridge. The area has changed greatly in the last 75 years. The open fields and forests are now crowded with apartments, gas stations, stores, homes, and healthcare facilities.

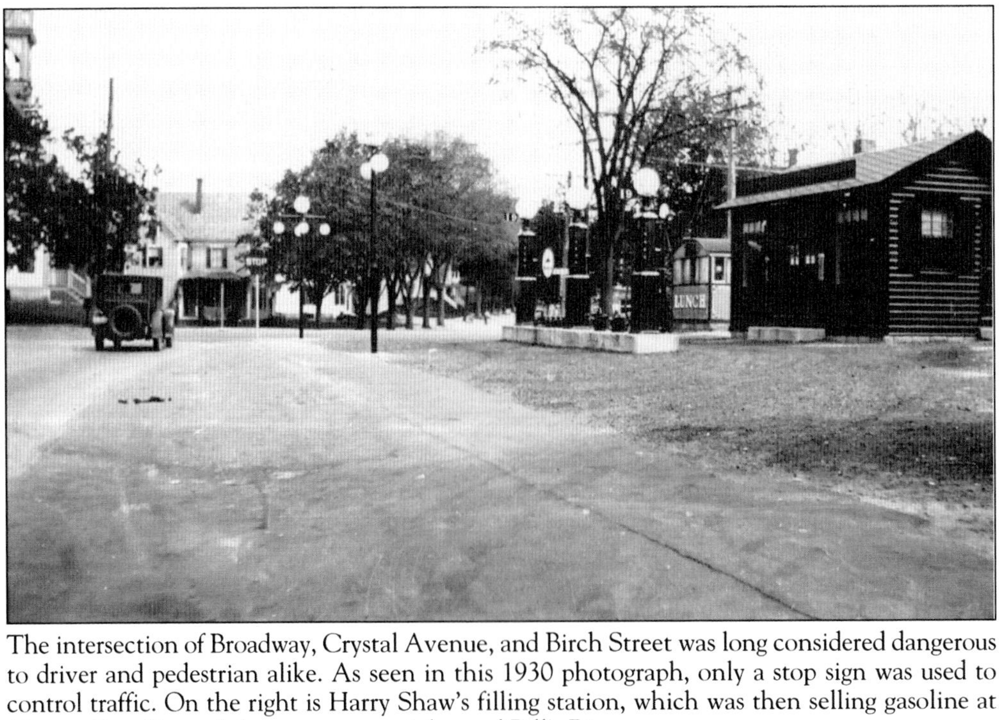

The intersection of Broadway, Crystal Avenue, and Birch Street was long considered dangerous to driver and pedestrian alike. As seen in this 1930 photograph, only a stop sign was used to control traffic. On the right is Harry Shaw's filling station, which was then selling gasoline at 19¢ a gallon. Beyond that one can see John and Bill's Diner.

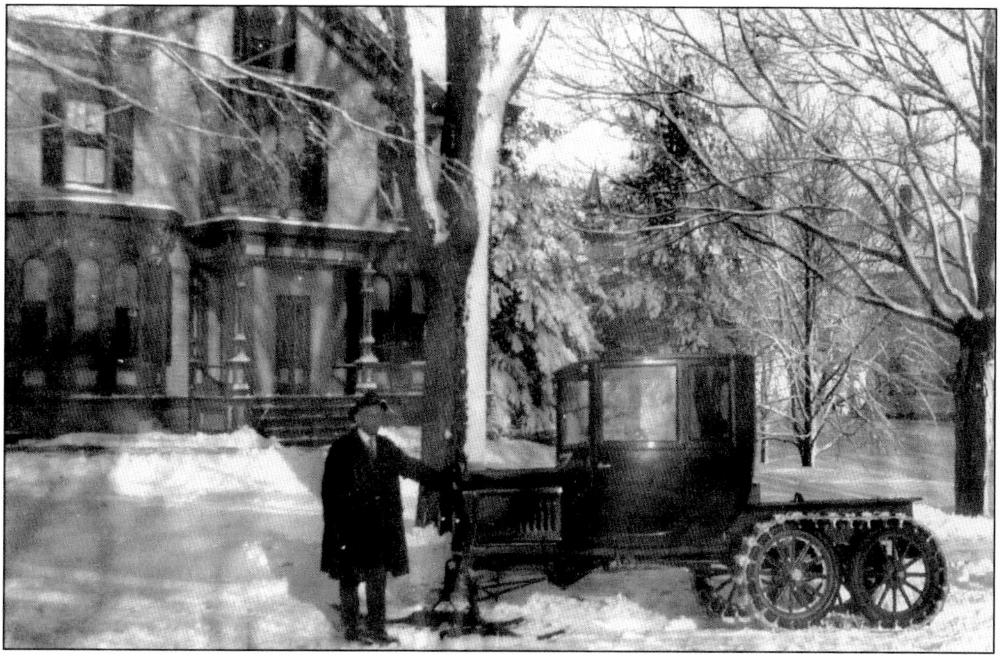

In 1922, Dr. Charles Newell found it difficult to make house calls during the long Derry winters. His solution was to purchase a half-track Fordson truck with skis on the front instead of tires. Thereafter, the mother in labor, the child with mumps, and the victim of influenza could be assured that Doc Newell would come to their bedside.

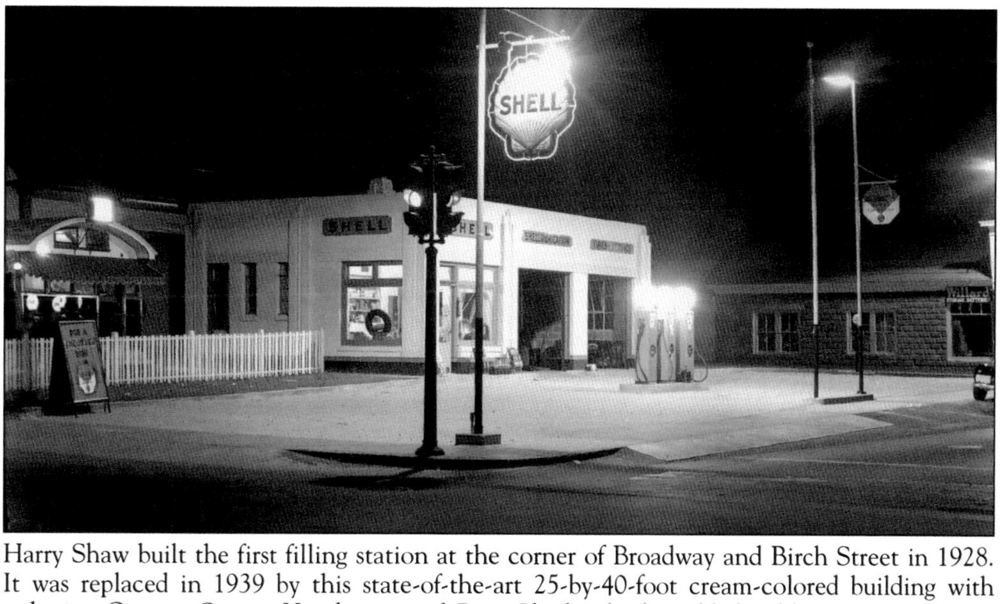

Harry Shaw built the first filling station at the corner of Broadway and Birch Street in 1928. It was replaced in 1939 by this state-of-the-art 25-by-40-foot cream-colored building with red trim. Owners George Henderson and Pete Chadwick also added public restrooms and a "lubritorium." The building was bought by Frank DiMarzio around 1947, and in the early 1990s it became the site of Dandi-Lyons Ice Cream Store. (Arthur Lear photograph.)

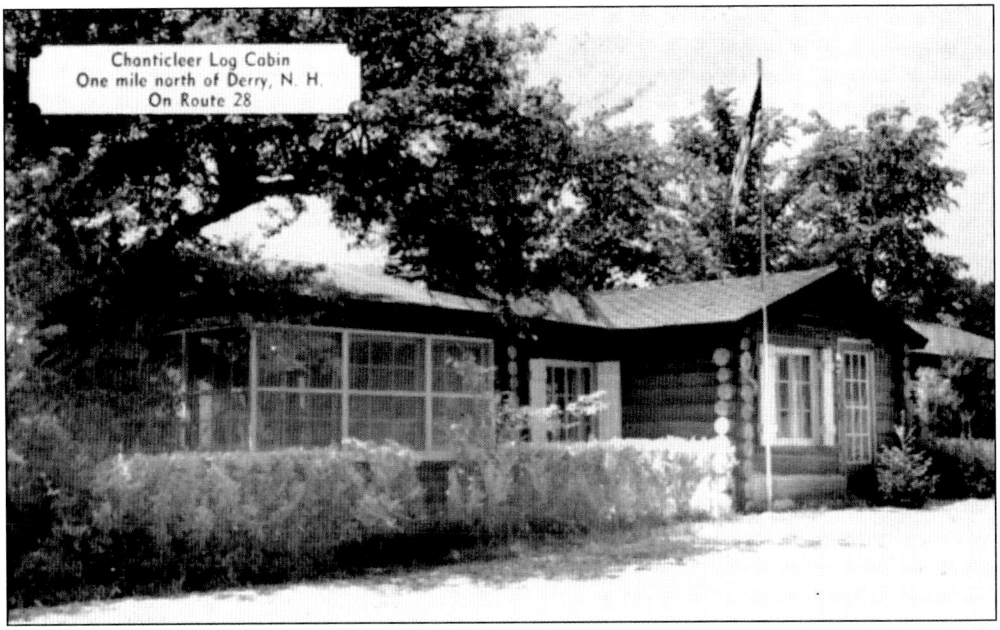

The Chanticleer Log Cabin Restaurant, on Route 28, was established in 1925 and usually only opened during the summers. It specialized in fried chicken meals for a dollar. In 1939, patrons ate 5,000 chickens. After a few sad years as a nightclub, the property was sold to Trinity Assembly of God, who used the buildings as its Christian Life Center. It was razed in 1998.

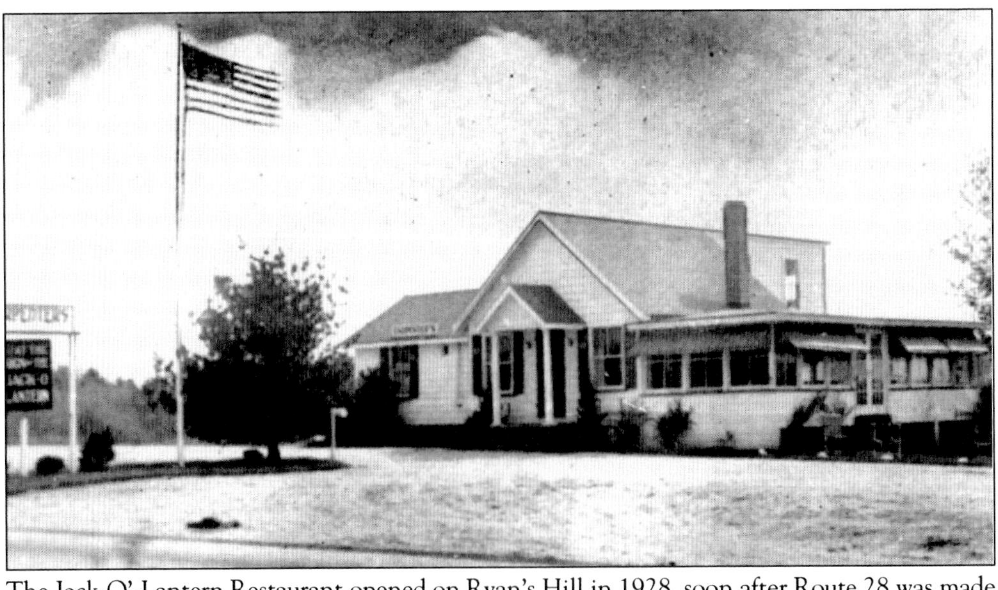

The Jack-O'-Lantern Restaurant opened on Ryan's Hill in 1928, soon after Route 28 was made into a cement-paved road. Owner W. H. Carpenter tried to get speeding cars to stop at the restaurant by advertising free croquet and tennis courts. In 1932, the Jack-O'-Lantern offered chop-suey for 25¢ a plate, club sandwiches for 65¢, and a five-course meal for $1. Dinner patrons were entertained by radio shows playing from the public-address speakers.

Six

MILLS

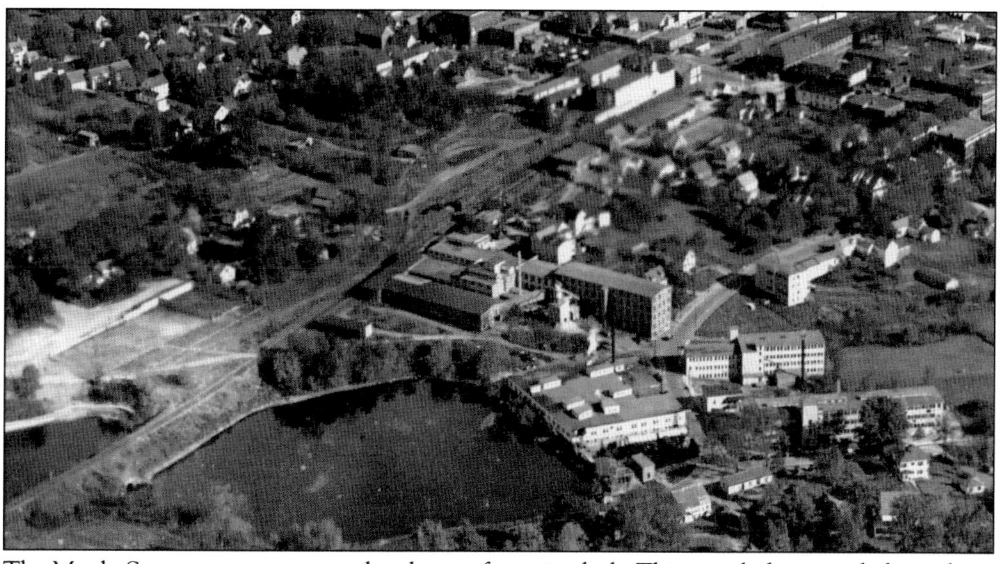

The Maple Street area was once a local manufacturing hub. This aerial photograph from about 1940 shows that the area around Horne's Pond was the location of a mattress factory, a poultry slaughterhouse, an electrical plant, and several massive shoe factories. All that survives today is the former Klev-Bro Shoe Company factory at lower right.

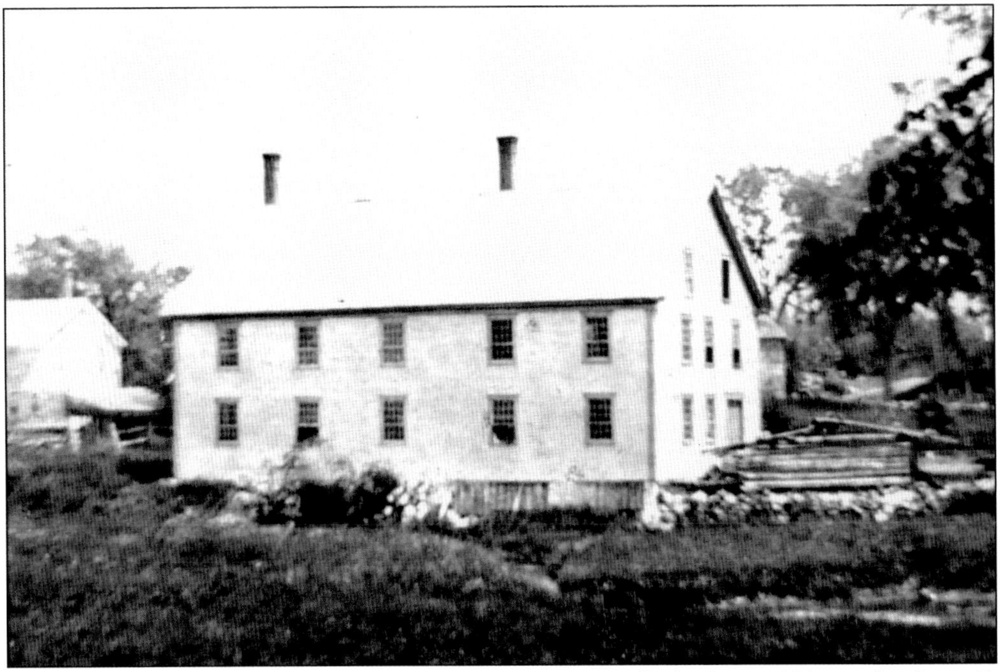

The Gregg-Underhill mill on Thornton Street was originally built in 1831 as a lumbermill. From 1869 to 1882, when this photograph was made, it was the Benjamin Chase factory, which produced nursery labels and harness shafts. For the next 20 years, the Underhill Edge Tool Company manufactured axes and hatchets there.

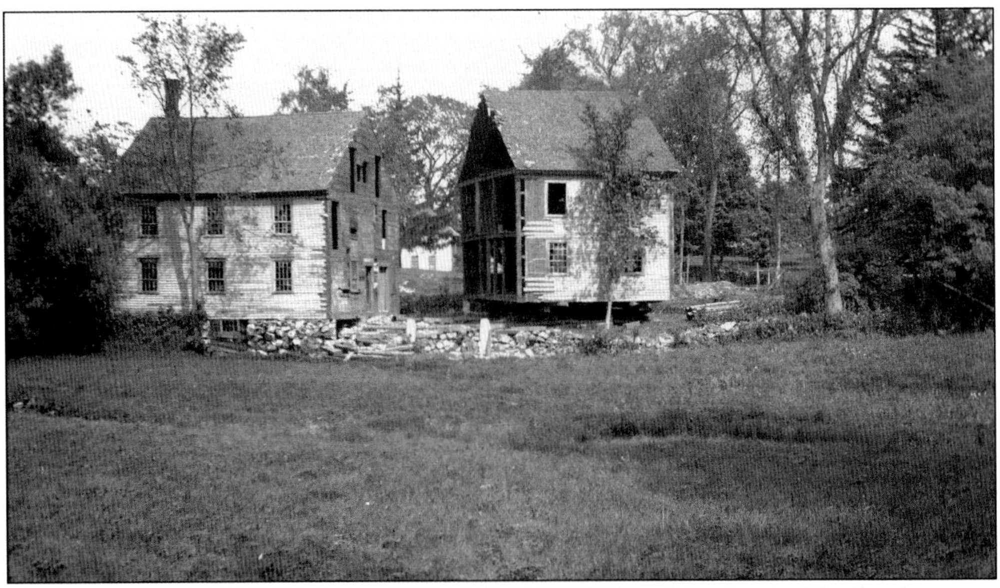

In 1908, the Gregg-Underhill factory was purchased by the Dearborn family. The Dearborns cut the building into two sections, and with a team of draught animals dragged one section along Thornton Street. There it was set on a new foundation and converted into a two-family home. The other section of the mill was made to serve as a barn for the new house.

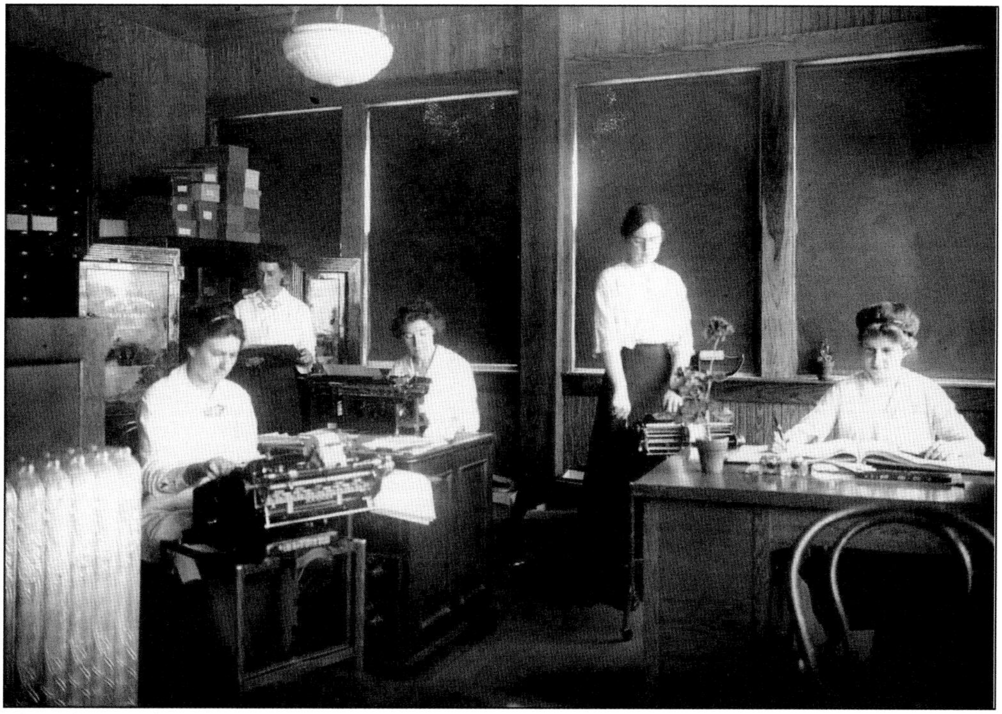

The office of the Derry Shoe Company was state of the art in 1918. All bookkeeping was done by hand. Letters were written on a manual typewriter. The young woman standing in the center is Helen Bachelder (1898–1988), a future Derry school board member and teacher. She is operating an adding machine here. (The other women pictured are not identified.)

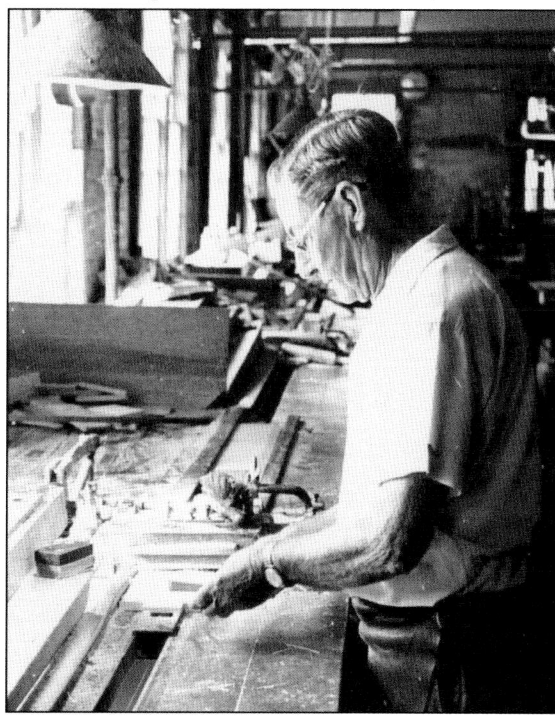

Raymond Butterfield (1903-1985) is shown in 1975 working at a saw, cutting garden labels at the Benjamin Chase Company. The factory was filled with rows of unshielded saws. Very few longtime Chase employees retired with all their fingers. The company hired many elderly men who worked each year until they earned the exact maximum amount allowed before they would lose any of their Social Security benefits. (*Derry News* photograph.)

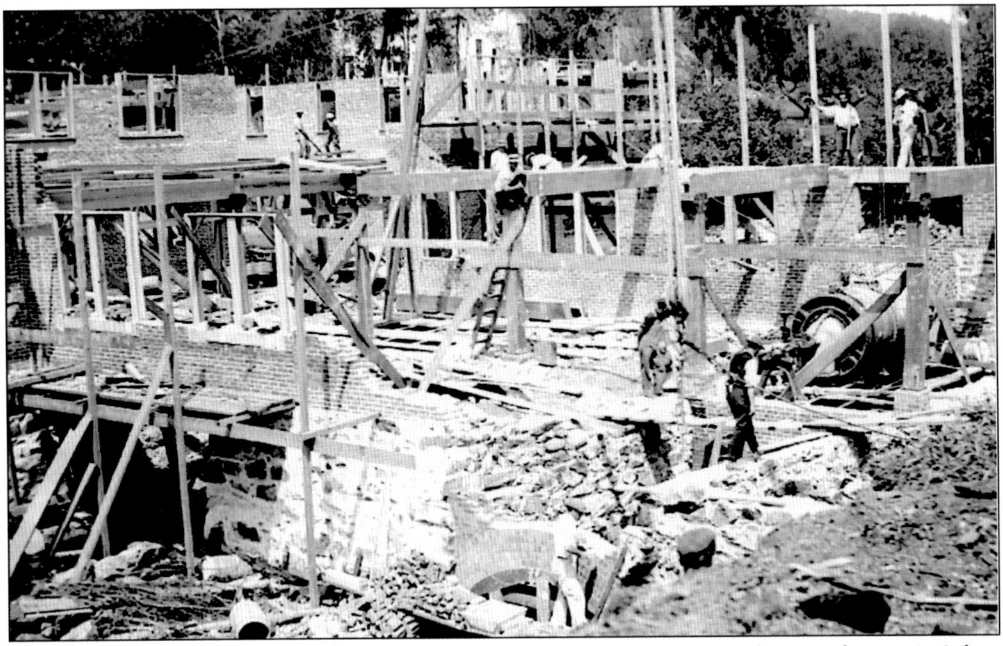

The original 1867 wooden Benjamin Chase mill on Chester Road was destroyed in a 1910 fire. The new mill is seen here, being built of fireproof brick. On the right is the huge turbine that provided electricity to power the saws and planers in the woodworking mill.

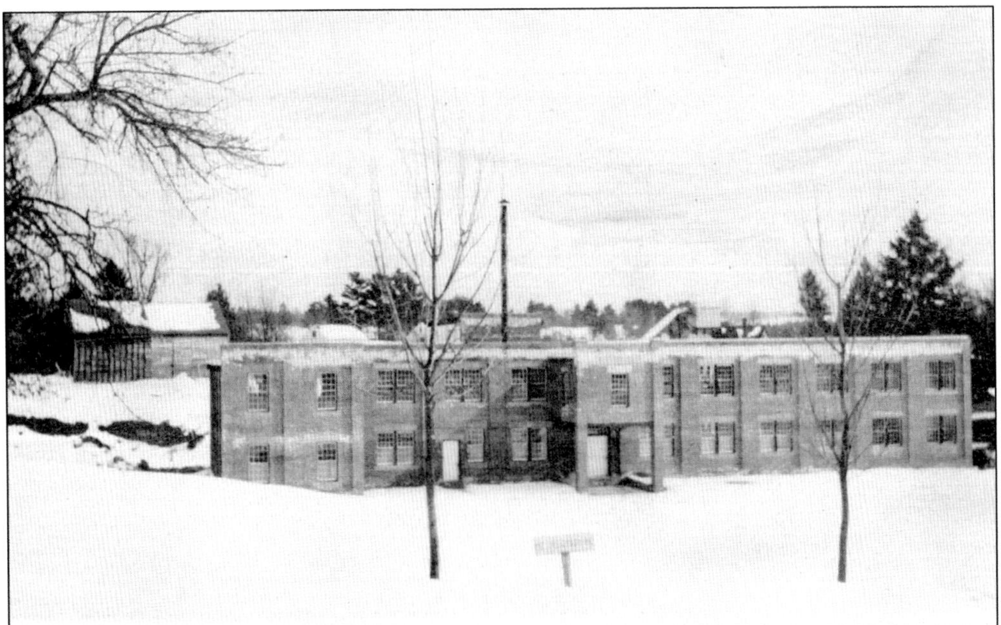

In 1912 the newly built Benjamin Chase mill in Derry Village was the world's largest manufacturer of wooden nursery labels. The Beaver Brook flowed directly beneath the building and generated electricity. In 1998, the mill operations moved to more-modern facilities. The building is presently being converted to luxury apartments.

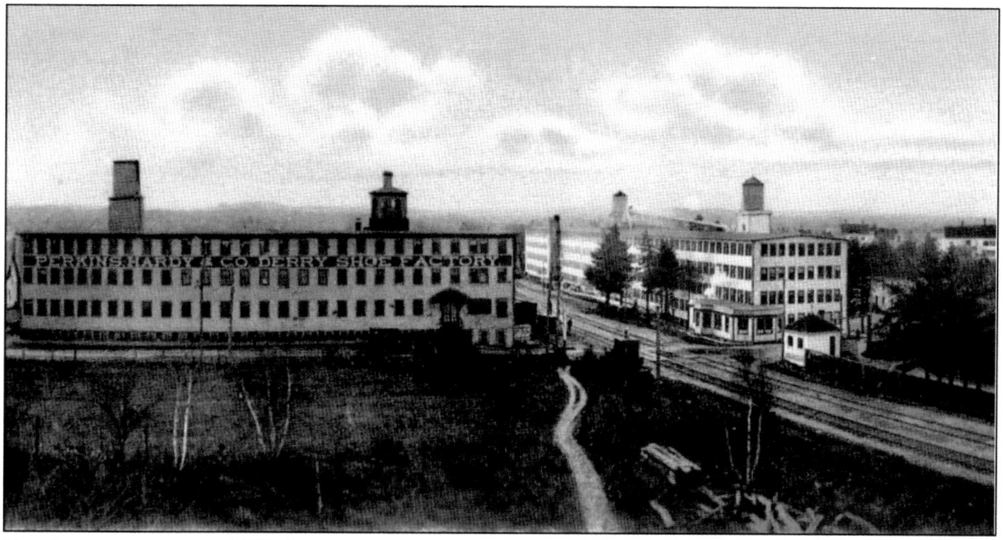

South Avenue around 1910 was a very active commercial area. On the right is the H.E.H. shoe factory that had been built in 1902. At 582 feet long, it was claimed to be the largest wooden factory in the world. On the left is the Perkins, Hardy and Company factory that was destroyed in a 1915 fire. The H.E.H. factory was torn down around 1939.

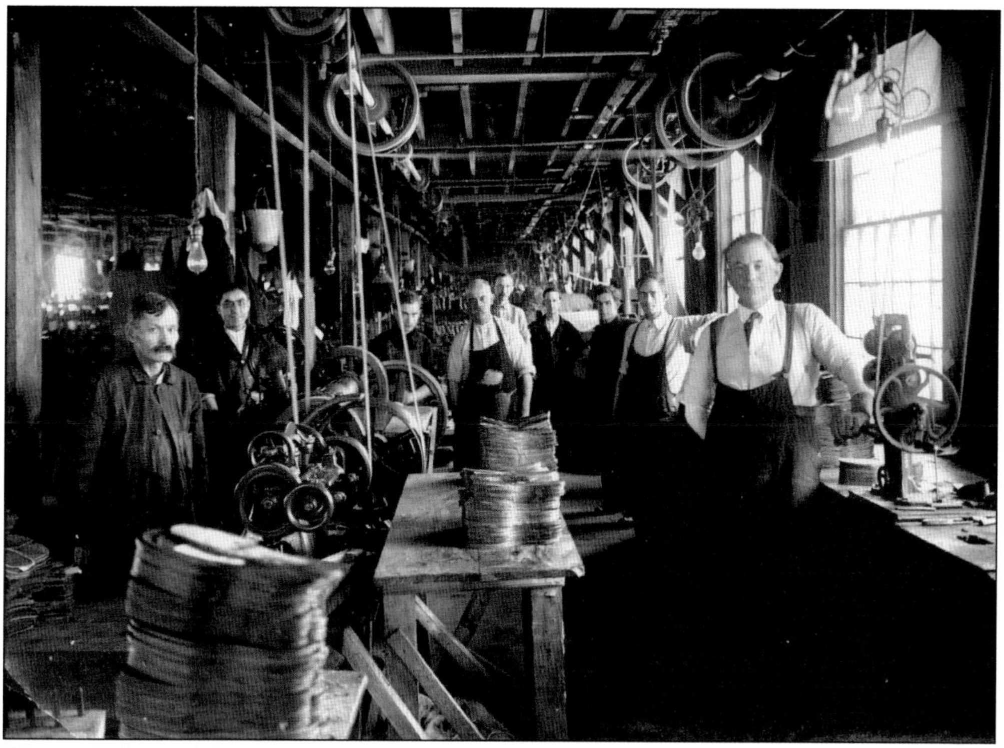
The work floor of the Derry Shoe Company c. 1918 was lined with unshielded pulleys that could easily snag a worker's shirt or arm. Work-related accidents were very common. The light bulbs dangling from cords were only allowed to be turned on during cloudy days.

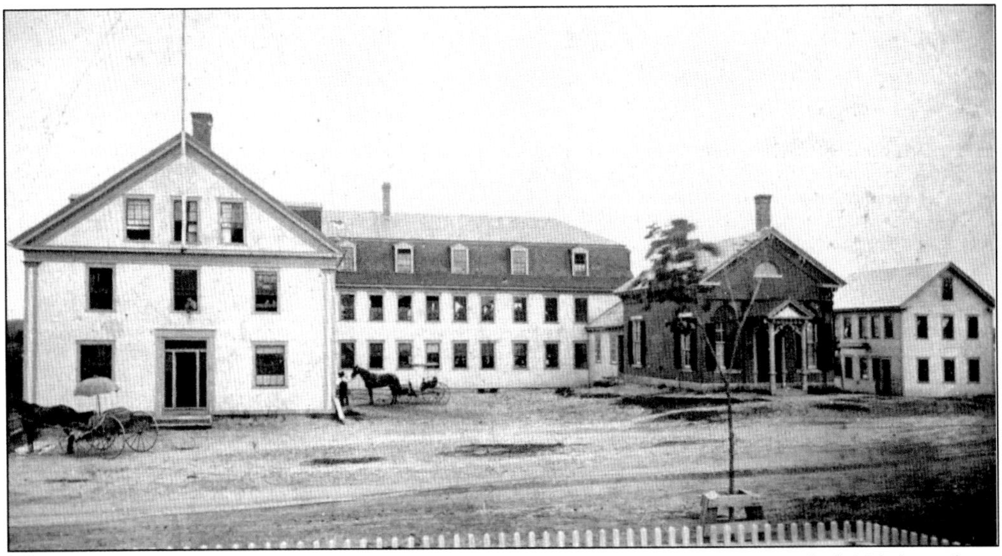

The W. S. and R. W. Pillsbury Shoe Company's facility in the 1890s extended 200 feet along West Broadway. The small brick building toward the right was built in the 1850s as the area's first bank and later housed the area's first school. By 1892, it was the office of the Pillsbury factory. The complex was later made into stores and apartments, which were destroyed in a 1979 fire.

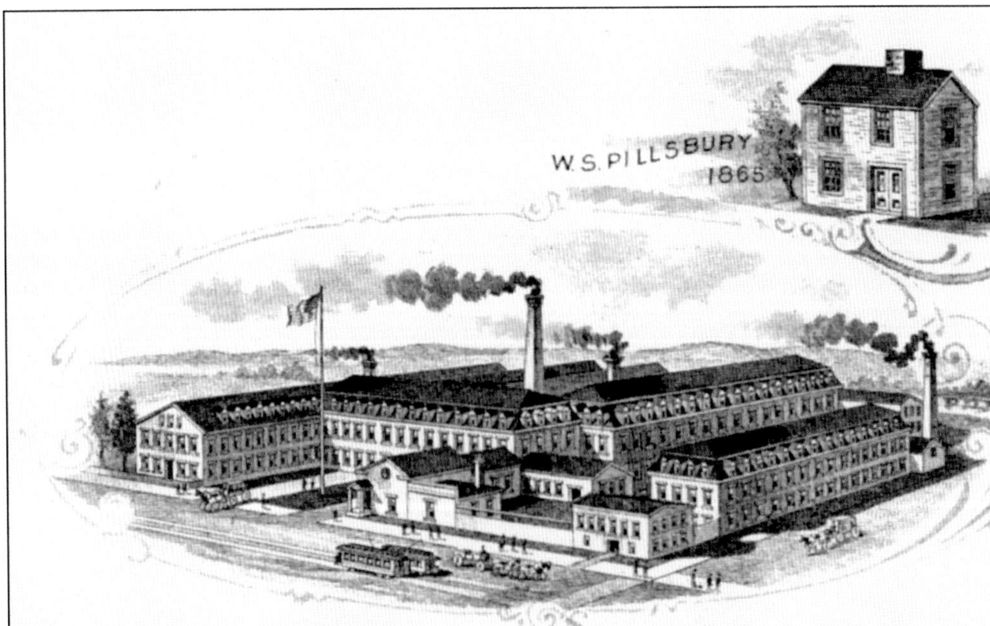

In this 1901 engraving of the W. S. and R. W. Pillsbury Shoe Company factory, an artist has presented a slightly exaggerated view of the complex. The small hut at the top right is Col. William S. Pillsbury's first shoe shop. The Manchester and Derry trolley line on Broadway is, in reality, a single track, not a double track as the artist drew.

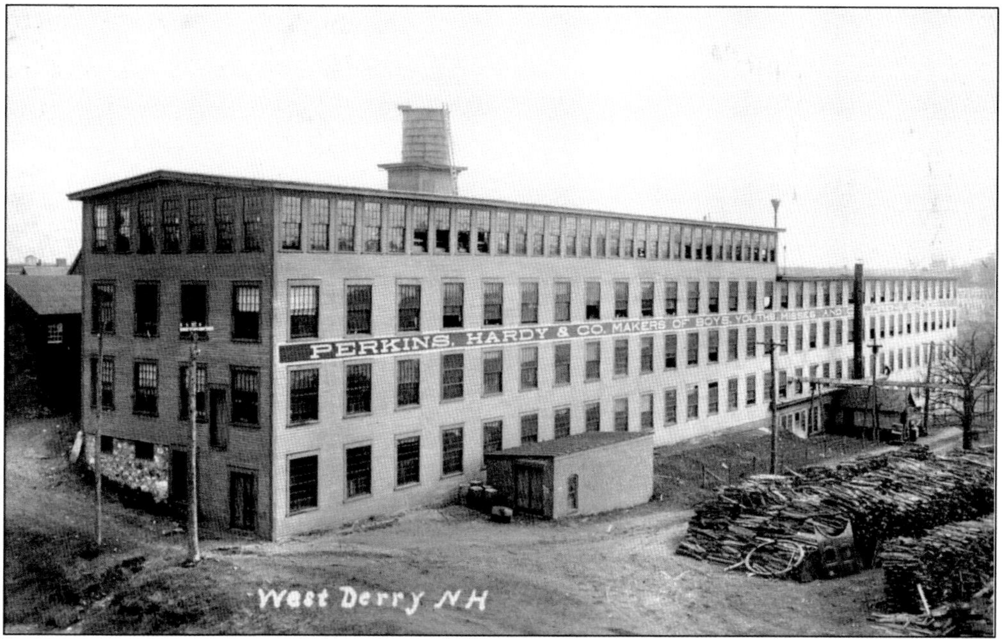

The Perkins, Hardy and Company shoe factory on Maple Street was built around 1900 by local investors. The company manufactured "boys, youths, misses and children's shoes." The Klev-Bro Shoe Company tore down the factory after 1939. The piles of wood seen here are from the nearby Horne's sawmill.

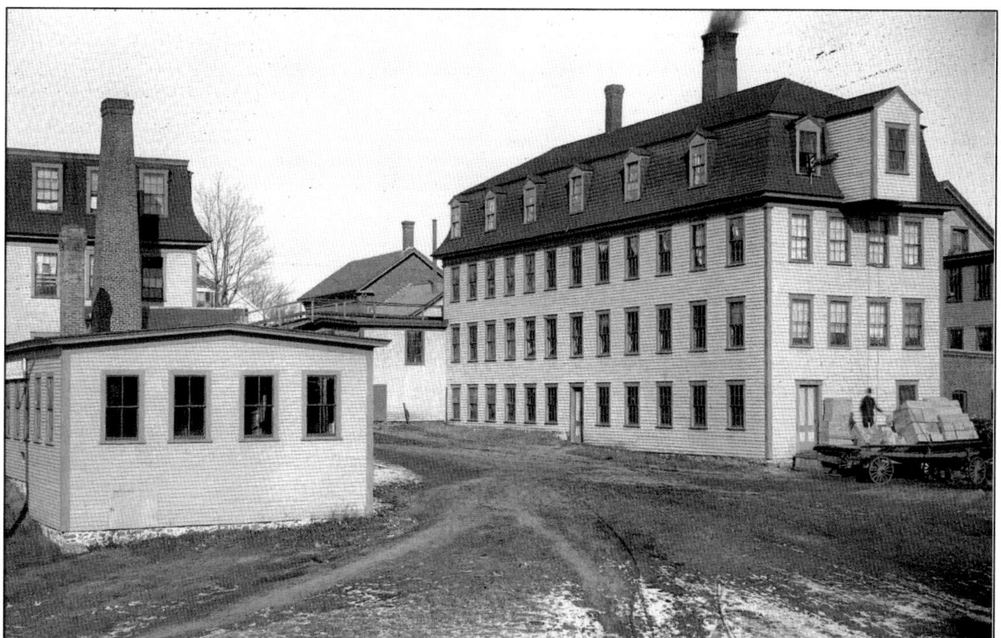

The Pillsbury Shoe Company factory extends several blocks deep off Broadway. By the time of this photograph in 1890, it was employing 650 workers. These workers averaged $1.50 pay for a 10-hour day. Colonel Pillsbury's company was manufacturing 300 varieties of shoes and boots that were distributed all over the world.

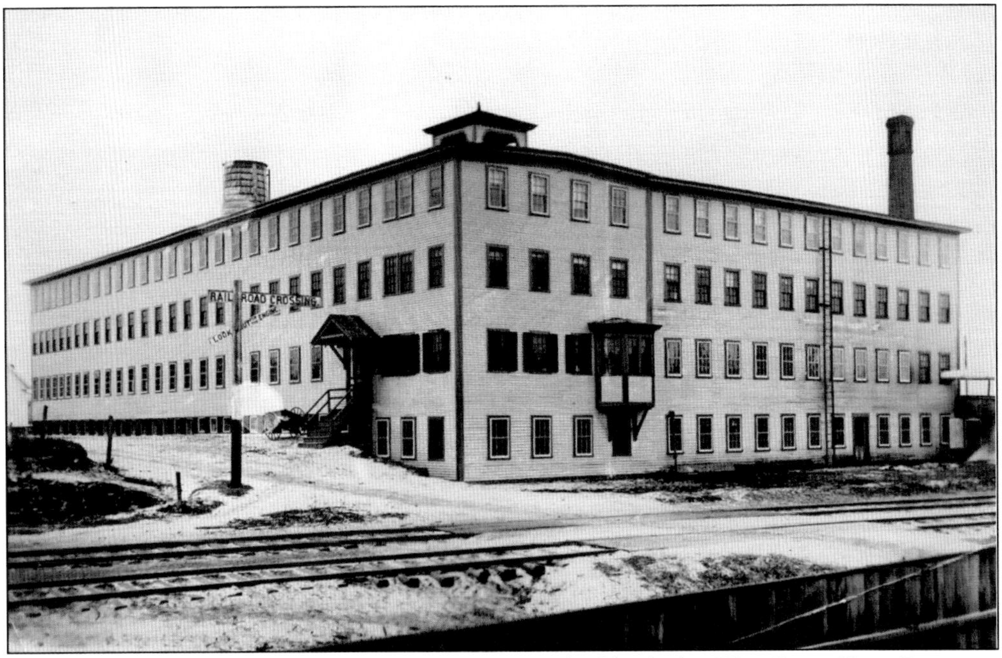

Col. William Pillsbury's Derry Building Association had built the Woodbury Shoe Company factory around 1885. It extended 176 feet along South Avenue. While it had been rented to several different firms during the years of its existence, the facility was usually remembered as the local factory of the Woodbury Shoe Company of Beverly, Massachusetts.

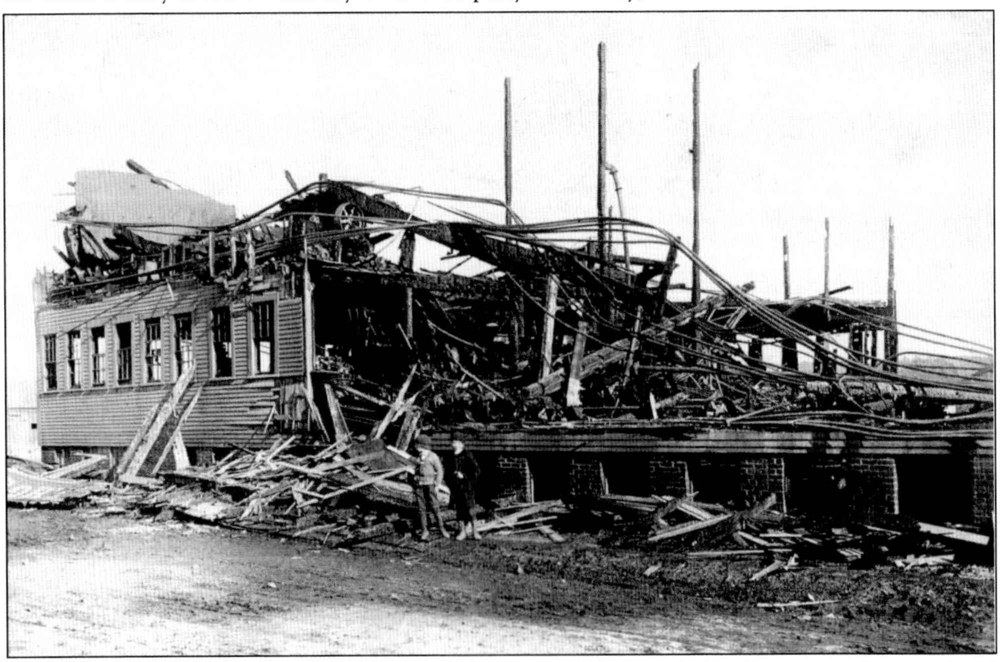

The fire at the Woodbury Shoe Company factory on March 17, 1915, put hundreds of local men and women out of work. Within a year, a new factory had been rebuilt on the site by the Citizen's Building Association. They were bankrolled by local businessmen who knew Derry's prosperity depended upon the shoe factories staying in Derry.

Seven

Upper Village

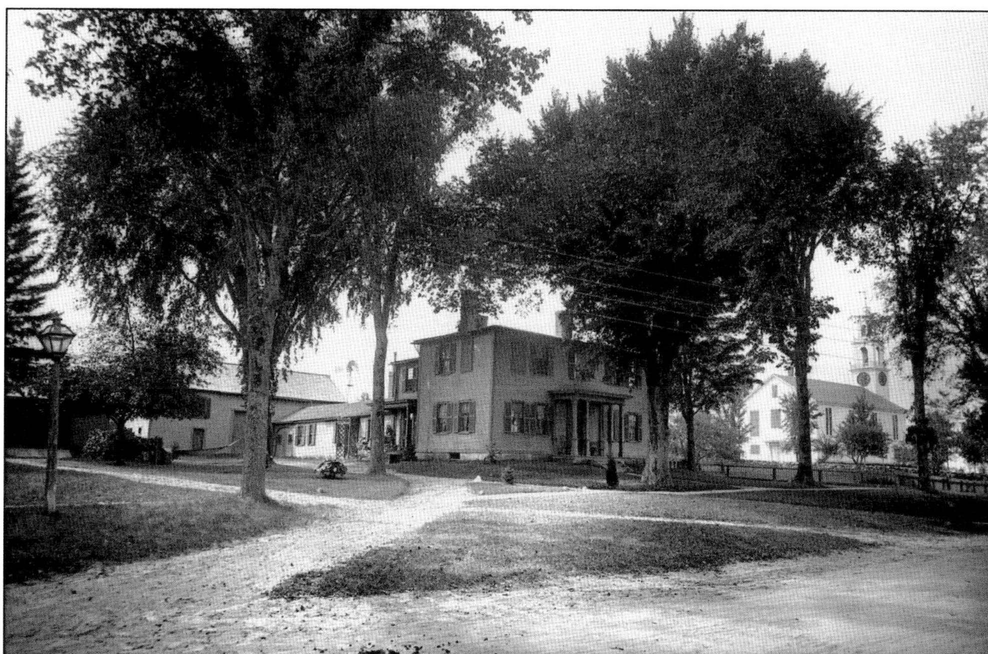

Around 1810, Rev. Edward L. Parker built this stately home on East Derry Hill. His next-door neighbor was the church where he preached for 40 years. After a brief period of ownership by the town, the house became a private residence. The Taylor Library was built to the right of the house in 1929.

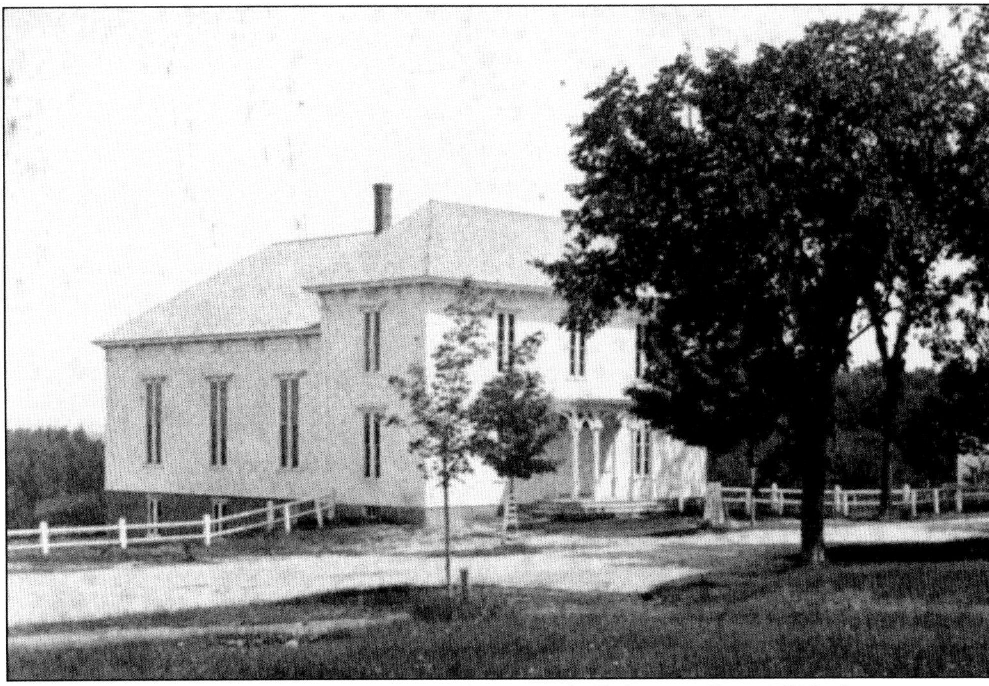

After years of deliberation, Derry built its first town hall (pictured) in 1876 after receiving a bequest from Pamela Newell and a gift of land from Sarah Parker. The building cost nearly $8,000. It remained the town hall until the Adams Memorial Building was constructed in 1904. The old town hall is now home to the local Headstart Program and the Red Star Twirlers. This Charles Bartlett photograph was made in 1882.

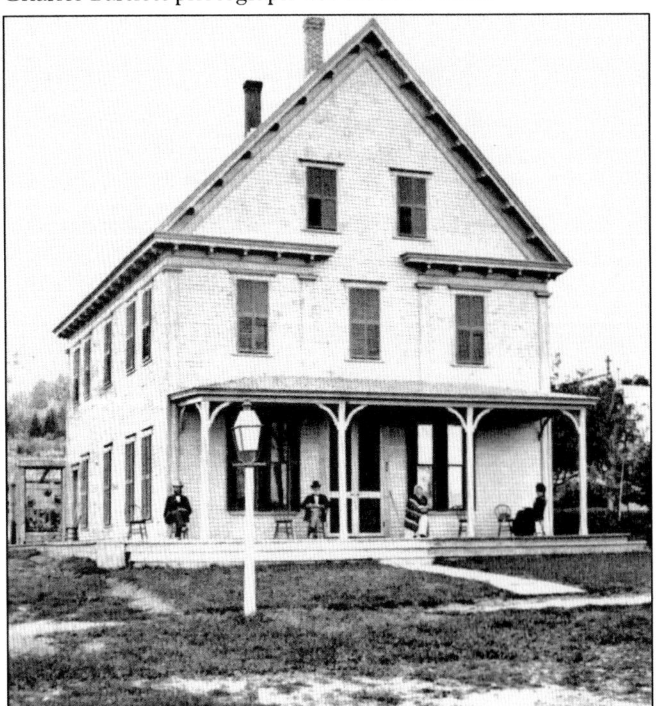

This Civil War–era photograph shows the East Derry Store at its original site on Island Pond Road. It was dragged to its current site by teams of oxen around 1865. The upstairs hall was home to many groups, including the Nutfield Grange and the local Masonic Lodge. The building has housed the East Derry post office since 1870.

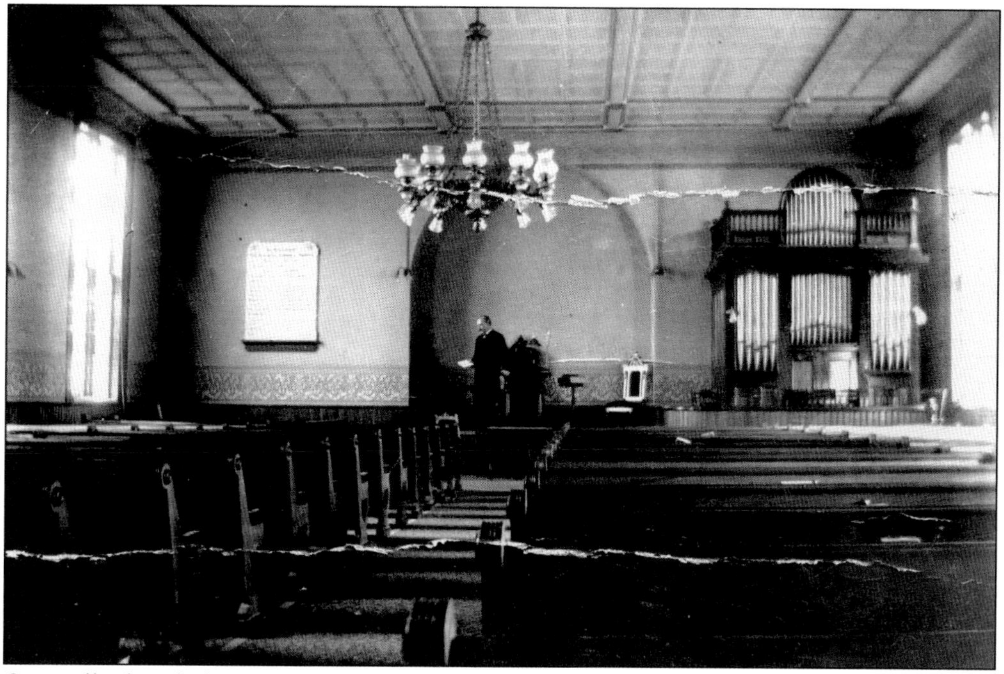

Originally the whole interior of the First Parish Church was a single room with a second-floor balcony. In 1845, a floor was built across the building at the balcony level. The new second floor became the sanctuary, while the lower area was used as the church hall. The memorial plaque on the wall at left honors Rev. Edward Parker (1785–1850), the town's first historian.

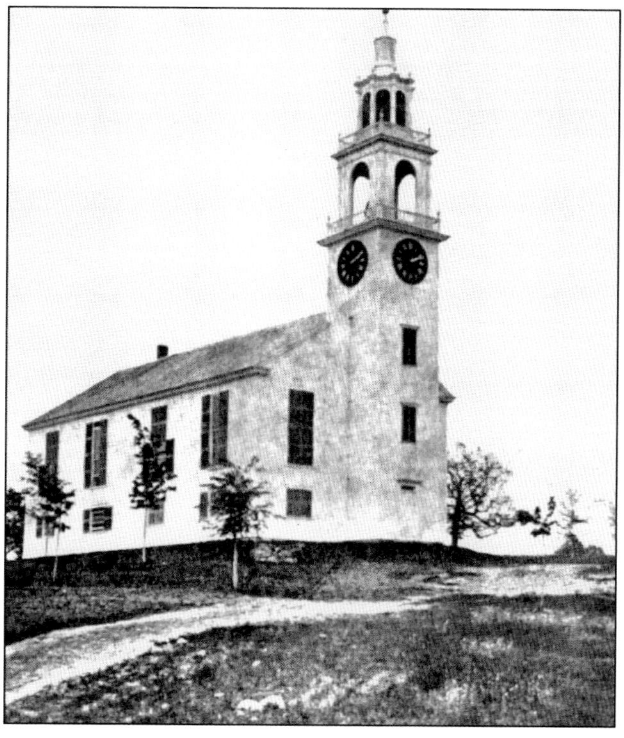

At the time of this 1882 photograph, the First Parish Church was already 113 years old, having been erected in 1769. A 24-foot center portion had been added in 1822, and the steeple clock had been installed in 1880. The Civil War monument was constructed near the front of the church in 1889. (Charles Bartlett photograph.)

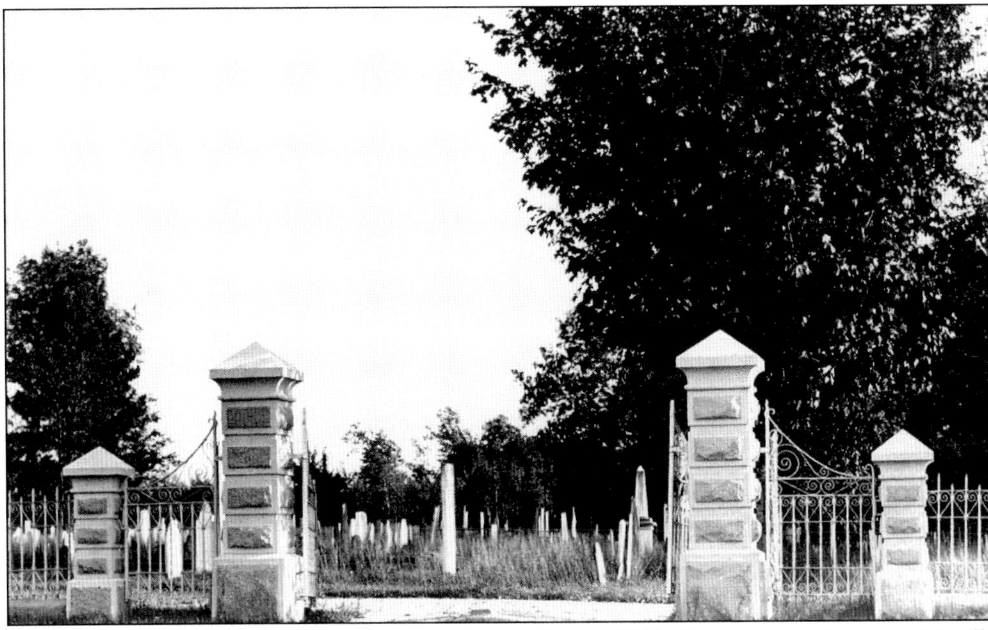

This *c.* 1900 photograph shows the entrance to Forest Hills Cemetery as it was originally designed. Later it was decided that the opening was too narrow for modern vehicles. The entrance was made wider by moving one of the massive granite posts further to the side. One of the curved side gates was removed and lost in this redesign.

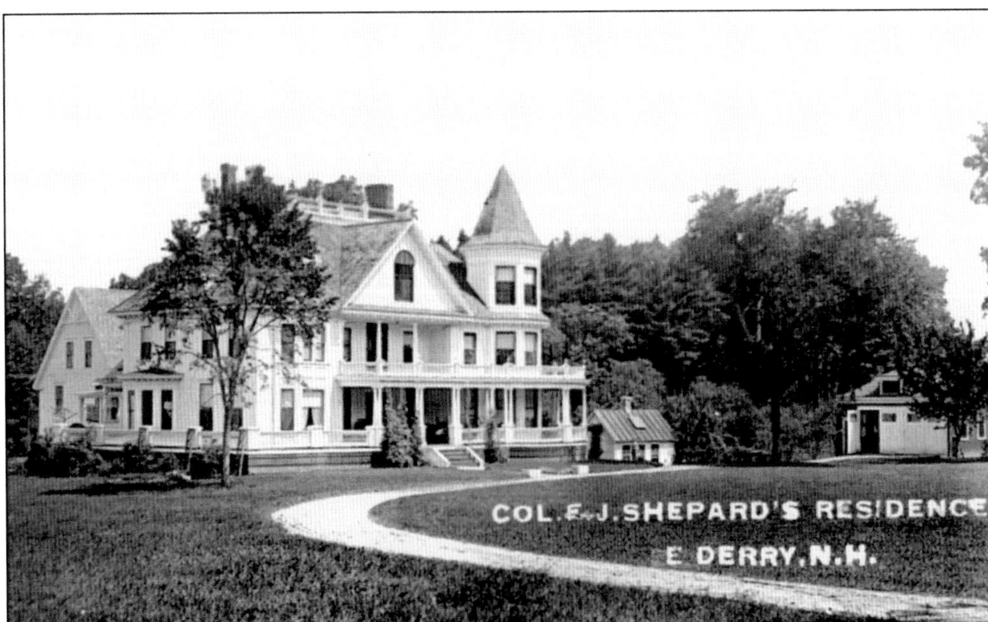

This impressive mansion in East Derry was built between 1863 and 1896 by William and Frederick Shepard. It was the showplace of the town and included a real ballroom. After the death of Frederick's widow, the building was razed in 1952. The large house lot was recently given to the town by the Shepard family as a public park.

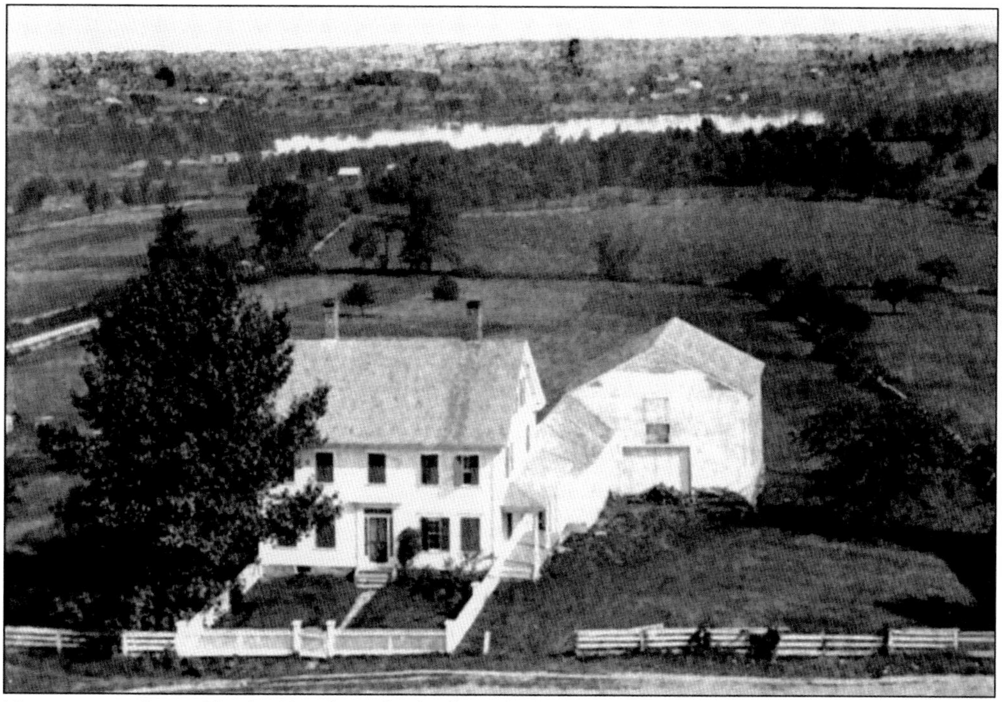

Newspaper editor Charles Bartlett climbed to the belfry of the First Parish Church in 1881 to take this photograph. In the foreground is the David Bassett House, built in the 1870s on the site of Stephen Holland's tavern. Bassett was the town's leading Tory before the Revolutionary War. In the distance is Beaver Lake.

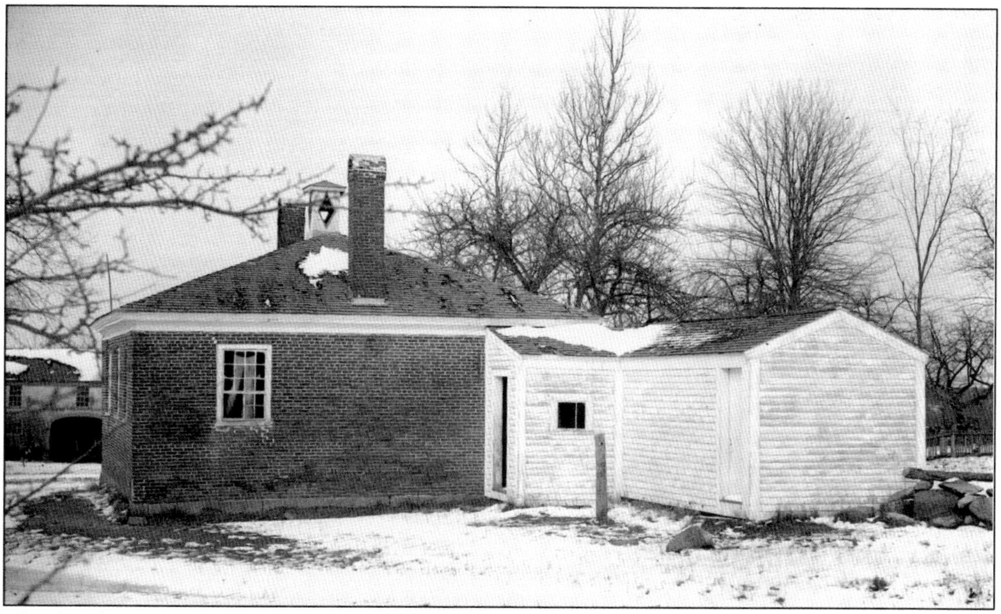

This brick, one-room schoolhouse was built in 1823 at the junction of Warner Hill Road and Hampstead Road. The land, building construction, and schoolhouse furniture cost the district taxpayers $620 in total. In 1887, the former Adams Female Academy replaced this site as the district school. This old brick school was sold and demolished in 1892.

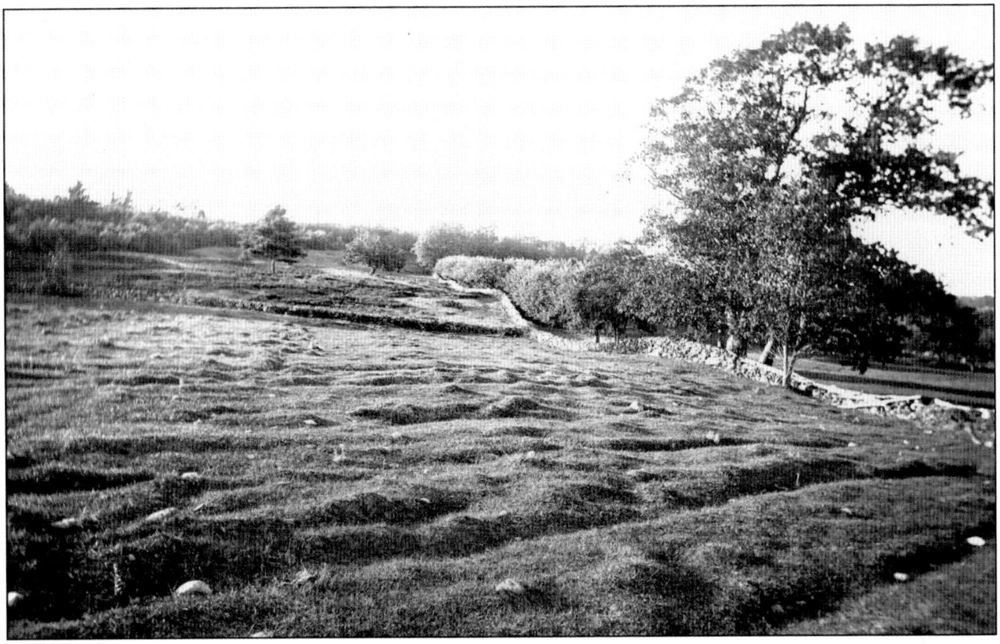

This Kilrea Road potato field was photographed soon after the harvest of 1890. Derry became "NH's place to be" in the 1960s. With the beginning of the building boom, the area has greatly changed. The once-rural landscape is now cut up into house lots. The area is only two miles from where America's first potato crop was planted in 1719.

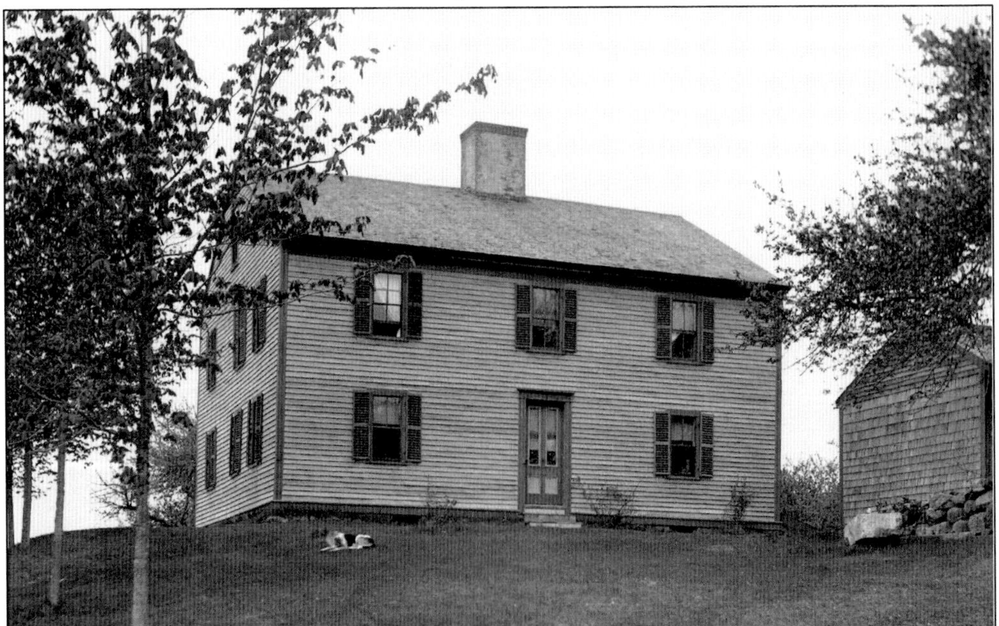

Gen. George Reid (1735–1815) fought in the Revolutionary War, from the Battle of Bunker Hill to the British surrender at Yorktown. During his six-year absence from Derry, he entrusted his wife, Molly, to oversee the construction of this farmhouse. Gen. John Stark said, "If ever there is a woman in New Hampshire fit to be governor, 'tis Molly Reid." The local DAR chapter is named in her honor.

Eight

Lower Village

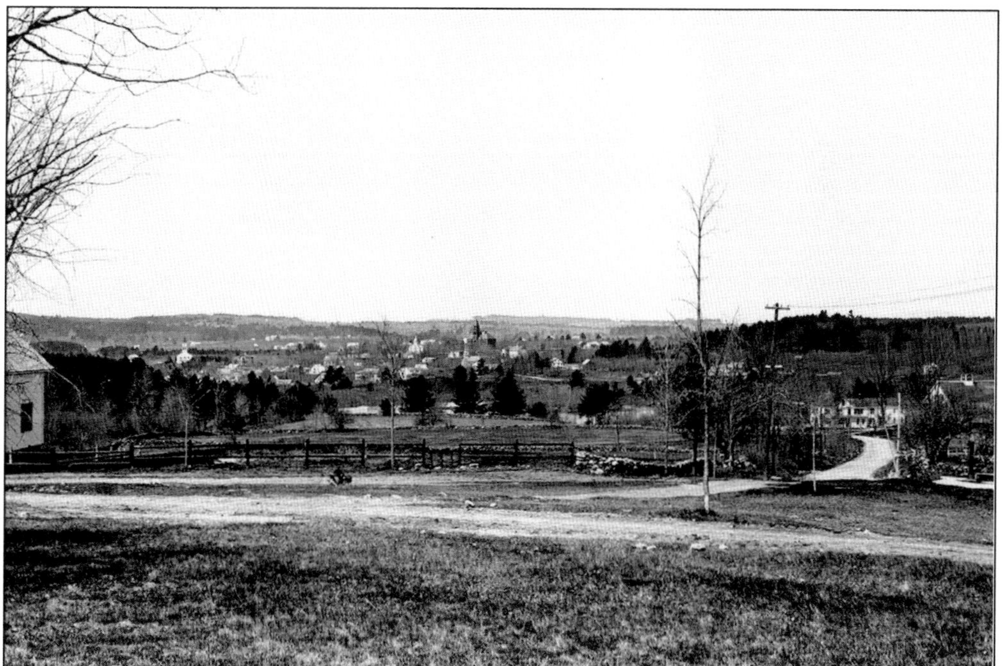

This 1890 view from Cemetery Road in East Derry, captures almost all of the Lower Village. On the far left is the steeple of the Central Congregational Church. In the center is the brick tower of the Pinkerton Building, and in front of that is the former First Methodist Church on Nesmith Street that was torn down in the 1920s.

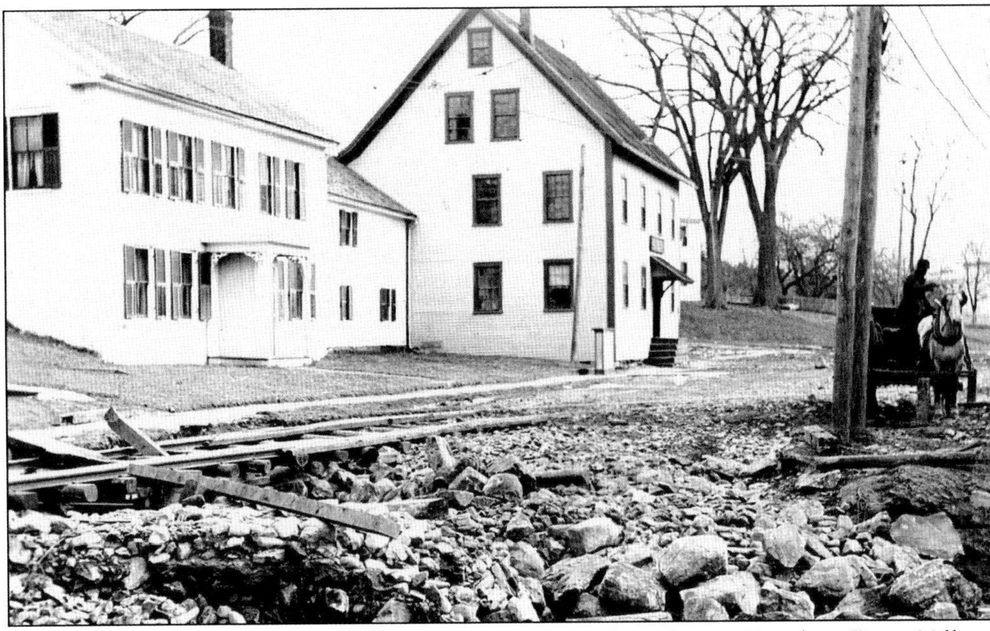

On February 13, 1900, a freshet, or sudden flood, swept down Beaver Brook in Derry Village. Several bridges were destroyed. Most of the area resembled a wide pond. This photograph shows the area around Hardy's gristmill on Thornton Street. The tracks of the Chester and Derry trolley can be seen on the top of the pile of rubble.

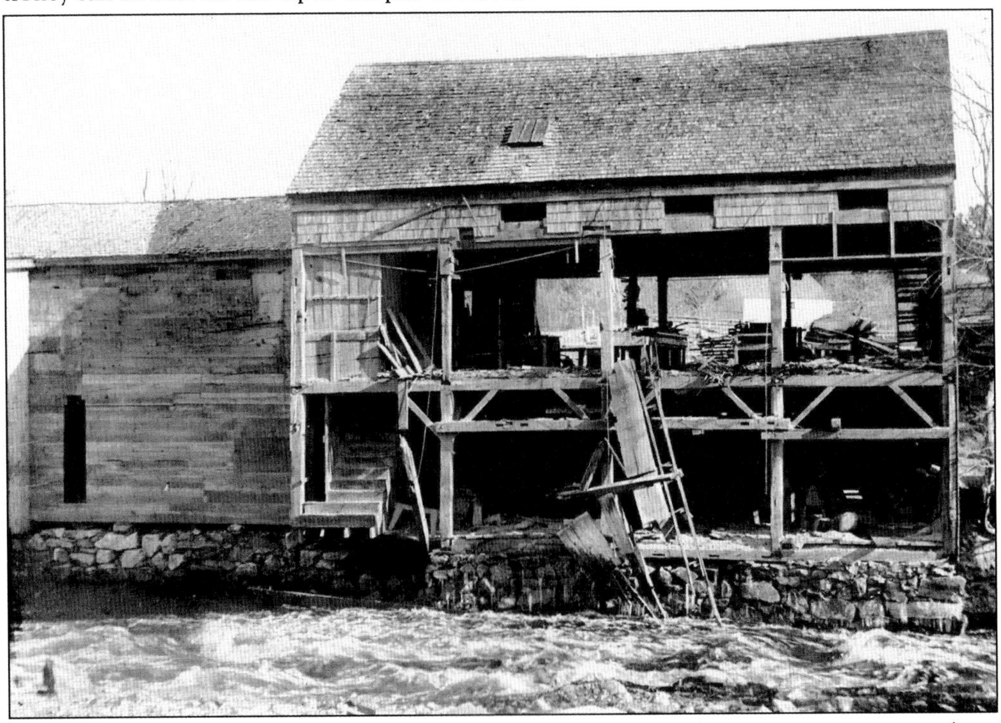

The great freshet (flood) of 1900 came roaring down Beaver Brook, sweeping away everything in its path. The Benjamin Chase lumbermill had its southern half ripped off by the rushing water. The mill was soon repaired but was later destroyed in a 1910 fire.

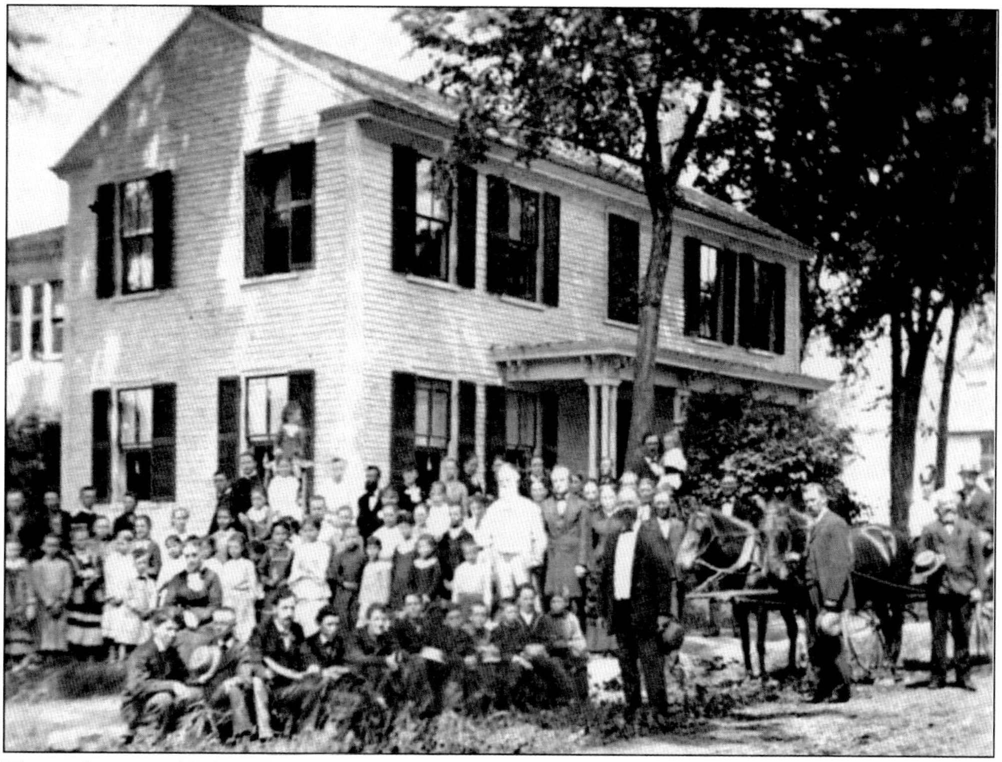

This gathering is likely in honor of George Adams's 60th birthday in 1884. This early-19th-century residence was disassembled in 1926 and carted to Lane Road, East Derry. There it was reassembled by the Rutter family. This house lot is now the site of Hood Park. (Charles Bartlett photograph.)

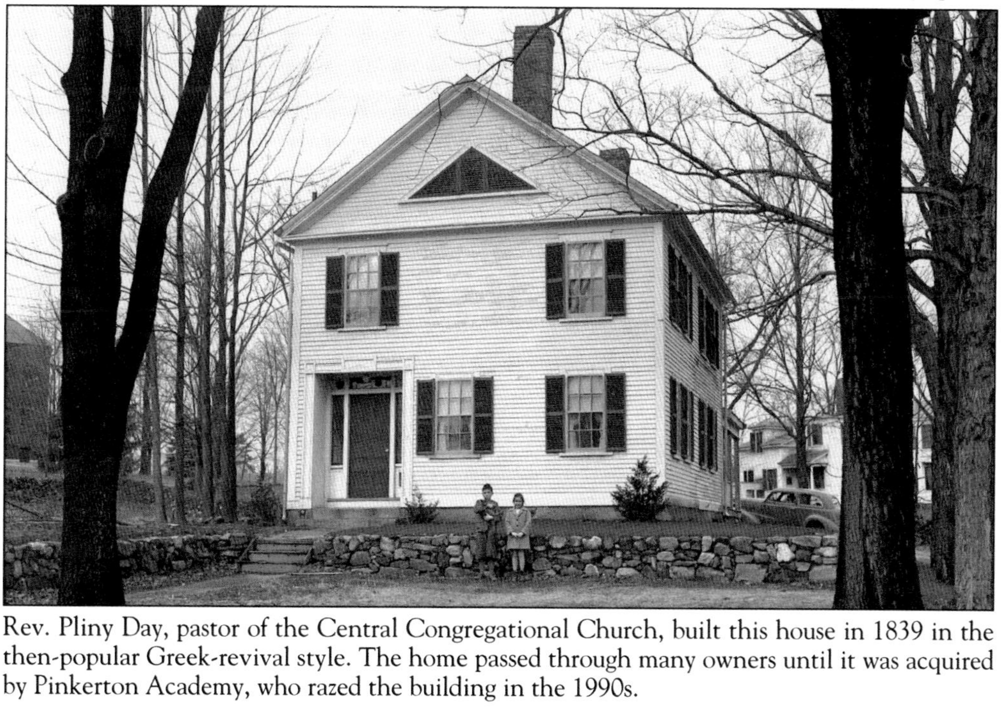

Rev. Pliny Day, pastor of the Central Congregational Church, built this house in 1839 in the then-popular Greek-revival style. The home passed through many owners until it was acquired by Pinkerton Academy, who razed the building in the 1990s.

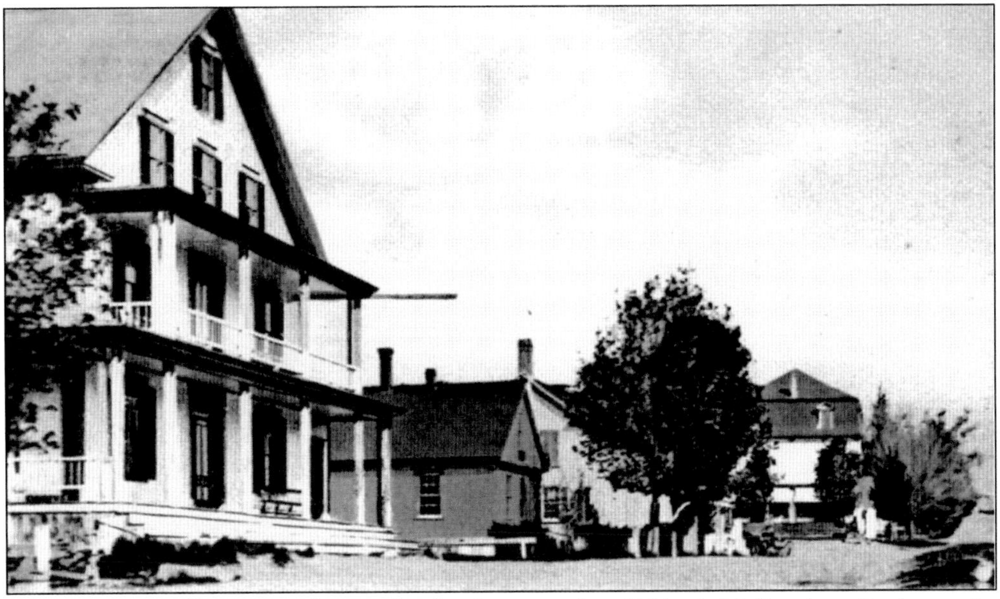

Here is Derry Village around 1904. In the foreground is Hildreth Hall, a boardinghouse for Pinkerton Academy. Next along the line is the former law office of Charles Bartlett and the Bartlett House, the home of the local DAR chapter from 1936 to 2004. The Association Hall is at the top of the village.

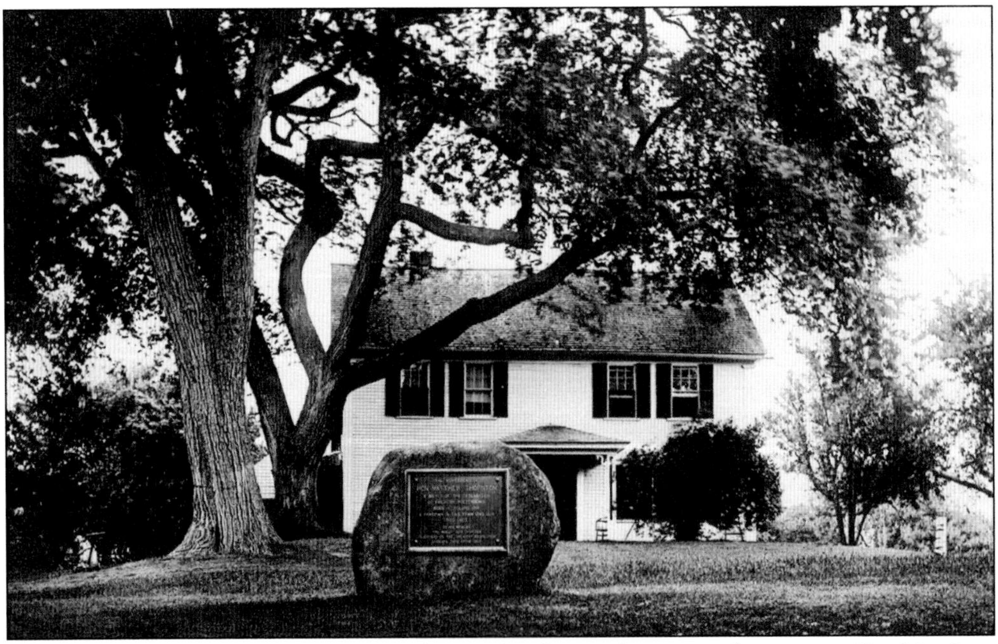

Thornton Square gets its name from being the former home to the patriot Dr. Matthew Thornton. This signer of the Declaration of Independence lived here from 1757 to 1779. It is one of the few Declaration signers' homes in America still in private ownership. The monument was erected by the Molly Reid DAR Chapter in 1909.

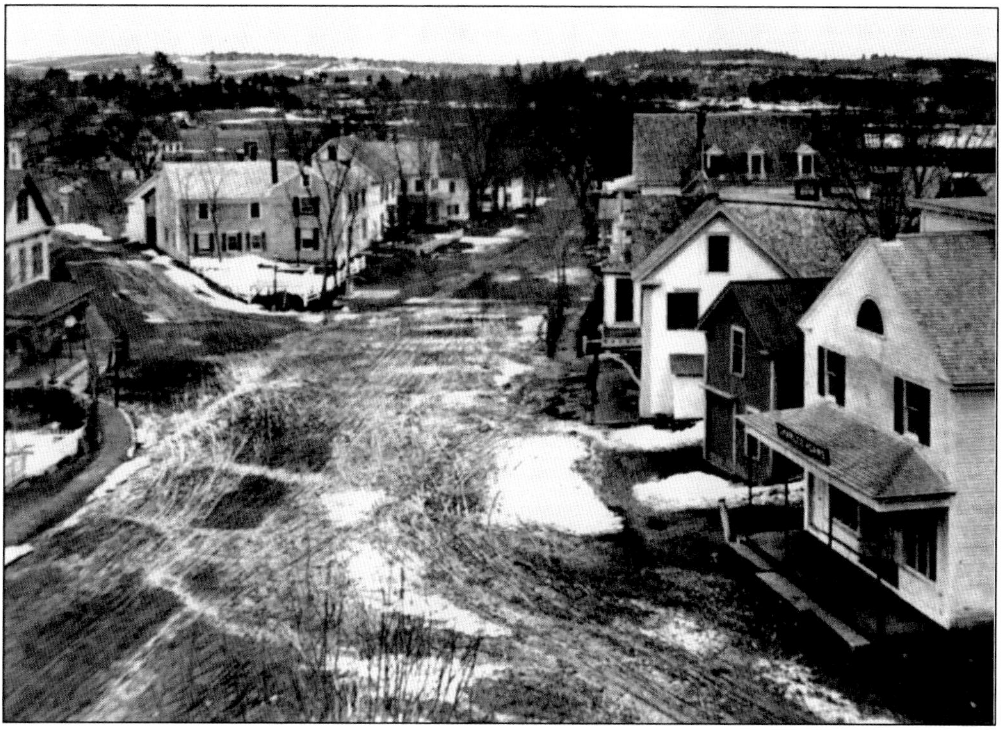

This photograph was taken in 1882 from the top of the Association Hall. The view looks south toward the site of the future traffic circle. At the far left is Couch's General Store. Across Thornton Street is a small point of land lined with kerosene streetlights that is the site of the town's first bandstand.

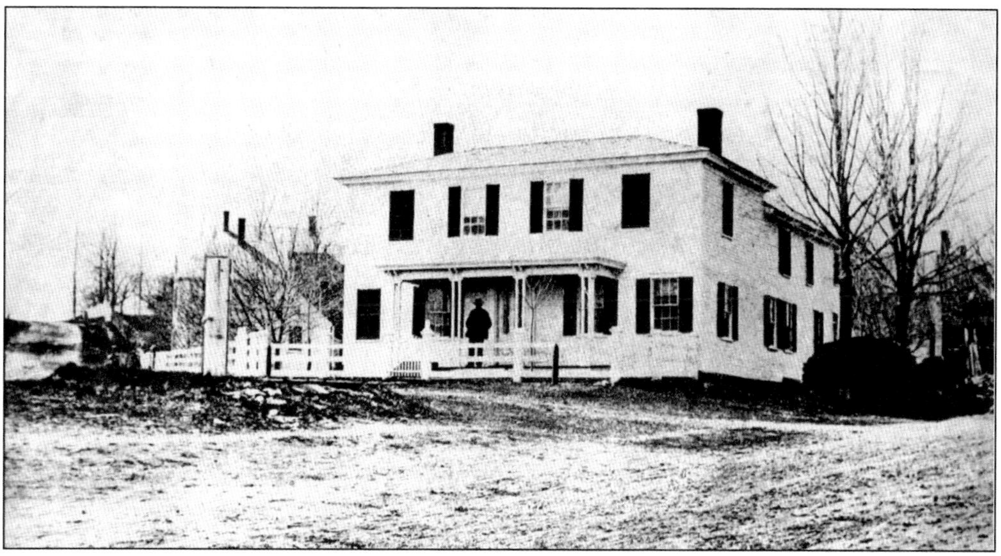

This grand Federal-style home at 1 Pinkerton Street was built around 1820 and was destroyed in an 1870 fire. Note the town's hay scale and the town pump to the left of the building. The Association Hall was built on this lot in 1876 by the Derry Building Association. Later it was called Proctor Hall, while it was the headquarters of the Ladies Benevolent Society. It is now the home of Academy Antiques.

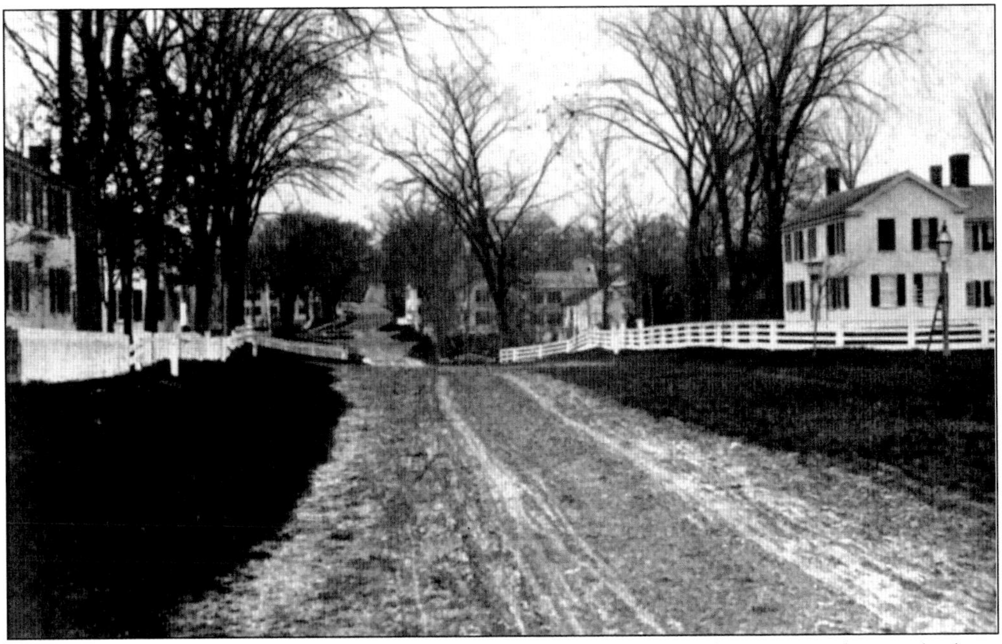

This photograph from 1882 shows the approach to Derry Village on the Route 28 bypass, looking north toward the site of the future traffic circle. The Federal-style homes on the side were built throughout the decade following 1805, when the road was constructed. The Londonderry Turnpike was a privately owned toll road that connected central New Hampshire with the market cities of Massachusetts.

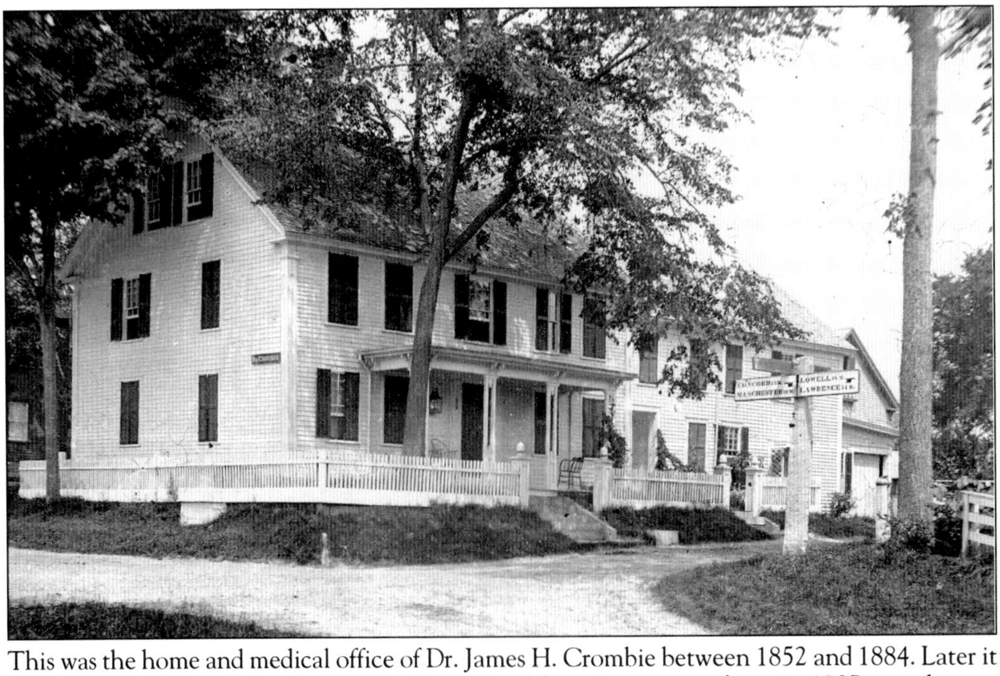

This was the home and medical office of Dr. James H. Crombie between 1852 and 1884. Later it was a boardinghouse for workers of the H. P. Hood farm. It was torn down in 1937 to make way for the traffic circle. Route 102, which leads to Chester, is in the center of the picture, passing the doctor's front porch.

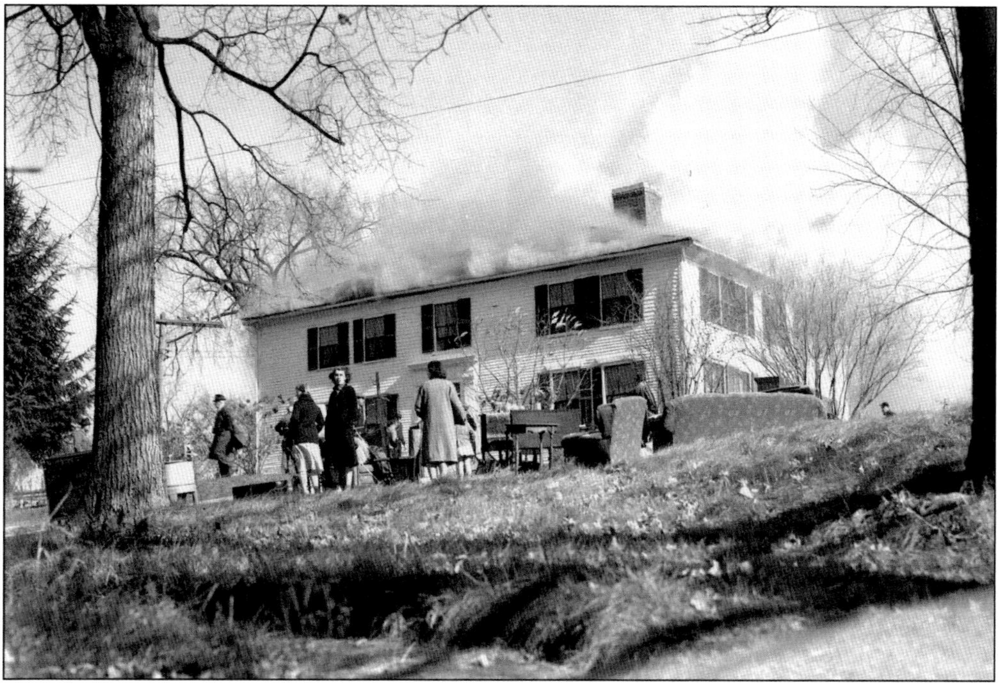

This house at 27 Thornton Street was built *c.* 1810 on the site of a Colonial garrison. In November 1939, a fire broke out in the kitchen. Locals rushed to the house to save the antique furniture. While much damage was done to the interior of the house, quick work by local firemen saved the structure from ruin. (Arthur Lear photograph.)

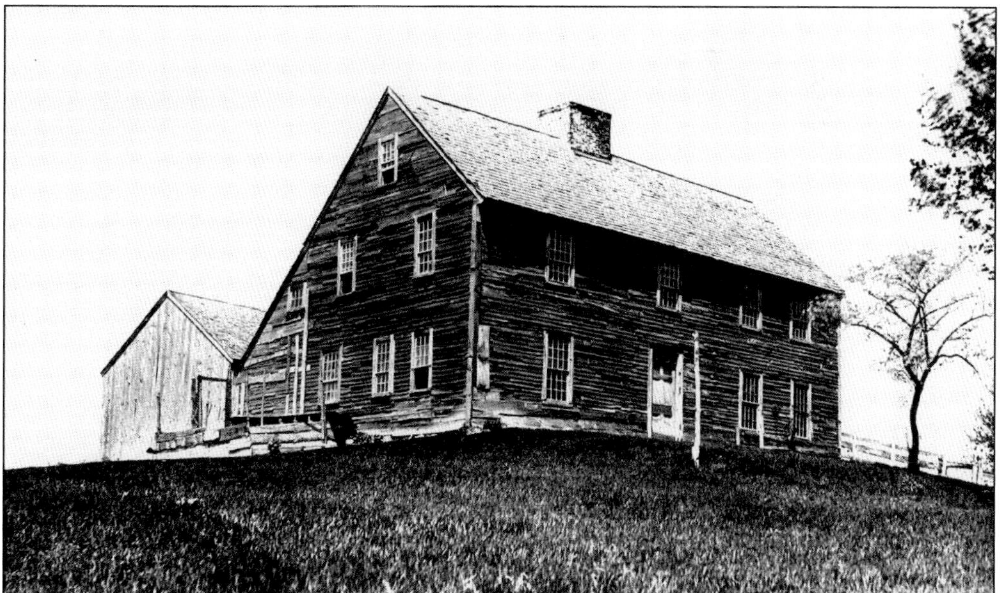

This house at 49 South Main Street is claimed to be the oldest residence in Derry, having been erected *c.* 1730. It was likely built by pioneer James Gregg on the site of the log hut he built in 1719. The much-enlarged and improved building is now the home of Circle of Friends School and Day Care.

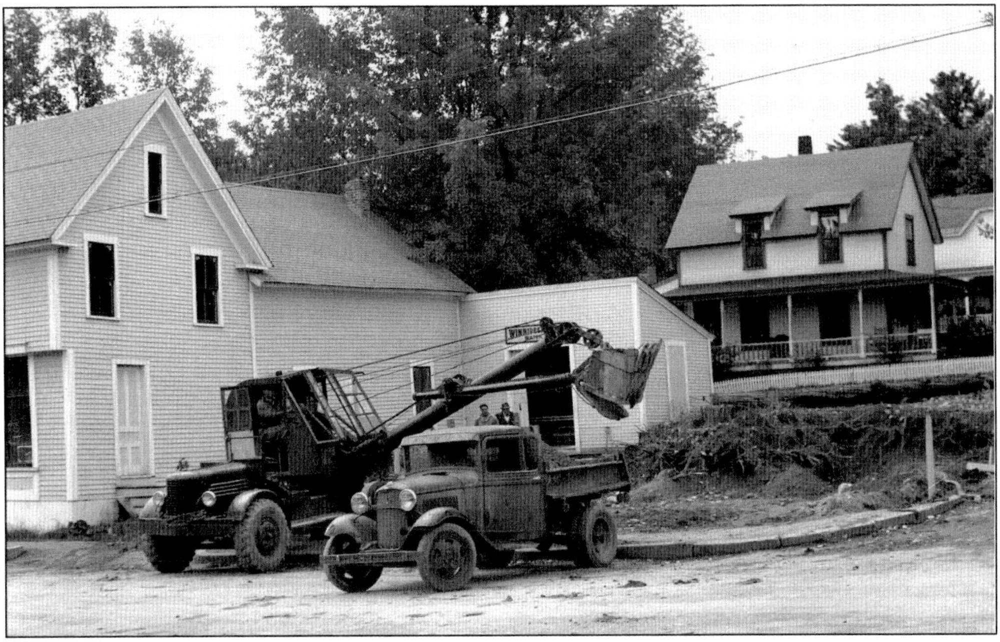

From 1936 through 1940, the federal government greatly improved the Route 28 bypass. The road was extended to 25 feet in width and given stabilized shoulders. In 1940, the actual reason for the work was finally disclosed: the road was to be used by the military to connect Grenier Airfield with Fort Devens in the event of war.

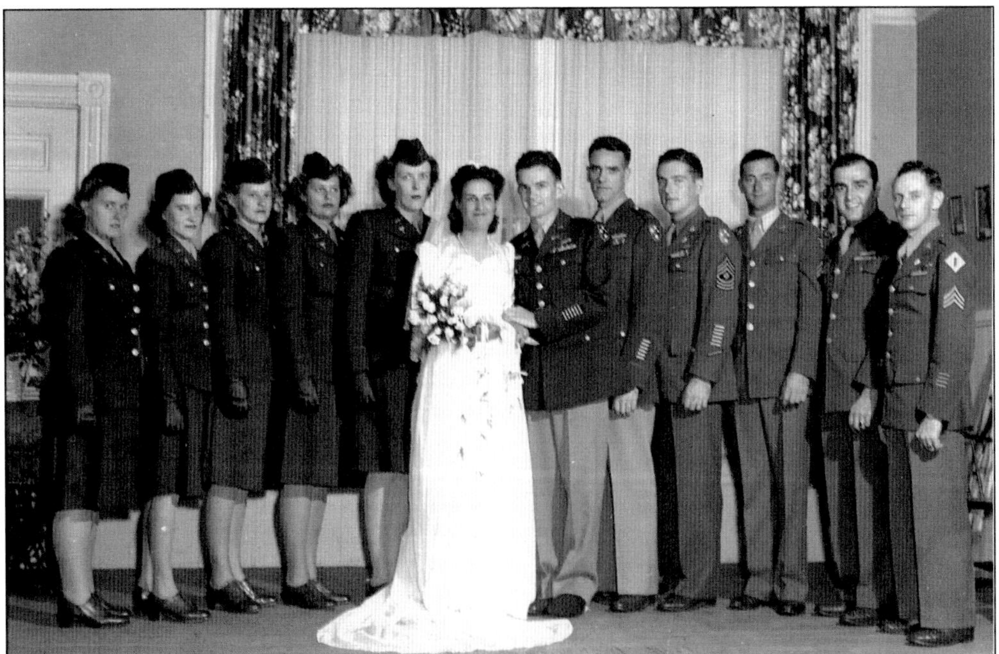

The wedding of Elizabeth Pitman and John Potter took place at the Central Congregational Church in 1945. Every member of the wedding party was in active military service, including the bride, who was a WAC lieutenant. The groom, best man, and ushers all had earned the Purple Heart. The organist was Lt. Col. Alan B. Shepard Sr.

Nine

BROADWAY

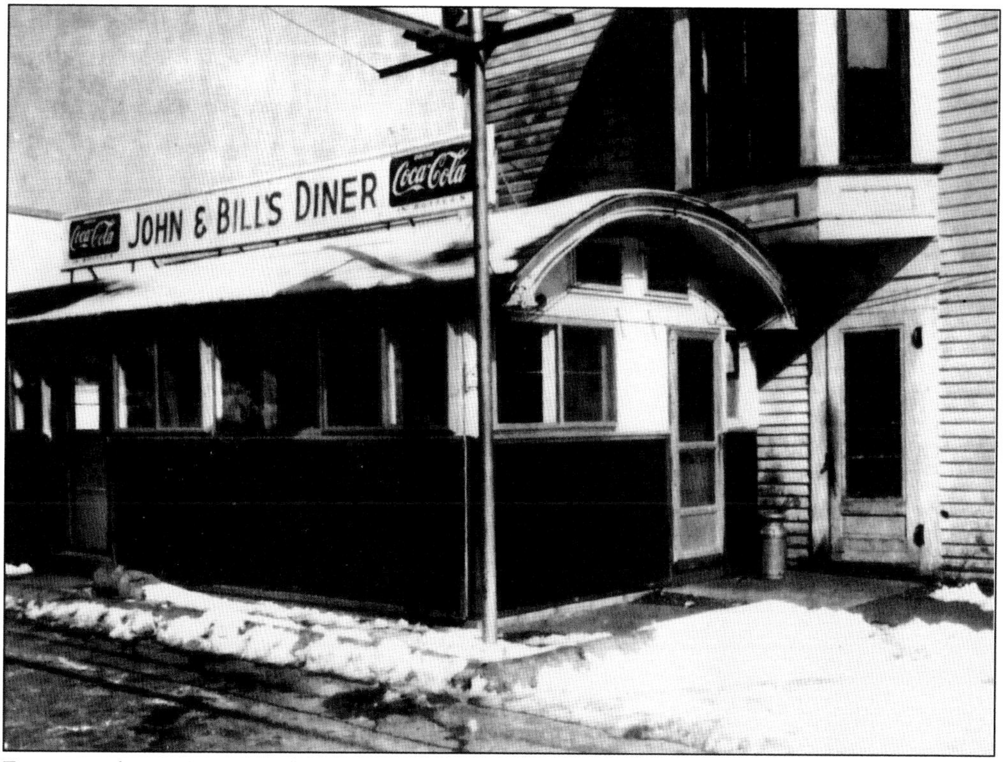

For more than 35 years, John and Bill's Diner was where Derry's elite met to eat. Owned by John Bellaveau and Bill O'Hara, it was originally at 51 East Broadway. In 1959, the diner was moved to Crystal Avenue. The restaurant opened at 6:00 a.m. every morning and closed at 2:00 a.m. It was famous for its hot dogs and custard pie with dates. The diner closed in the 1960s, and the lot was sold to Dunkin' Donuts.

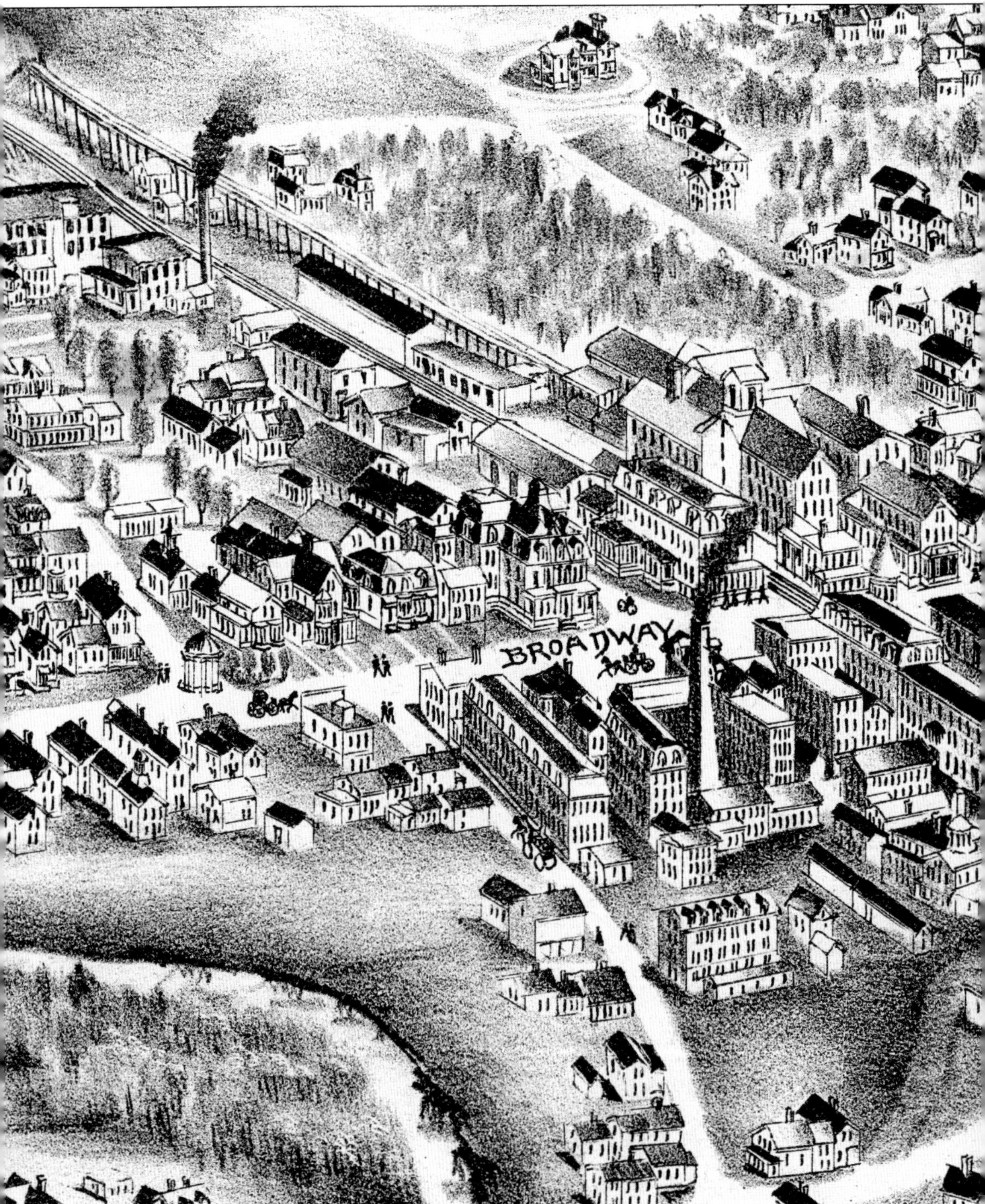

In 1898, local publisher Charles Bartlett commissioned an artist to draw West Derry. For a month, the man walked the streets sketching into his notepad. At the end of the four weeks, he had produced a bird's-eye view of the tour. He had to imagine how the local scenery would look if he were floating over Derry in a hot-air balloon. He drew the town from Elm Street on the west end

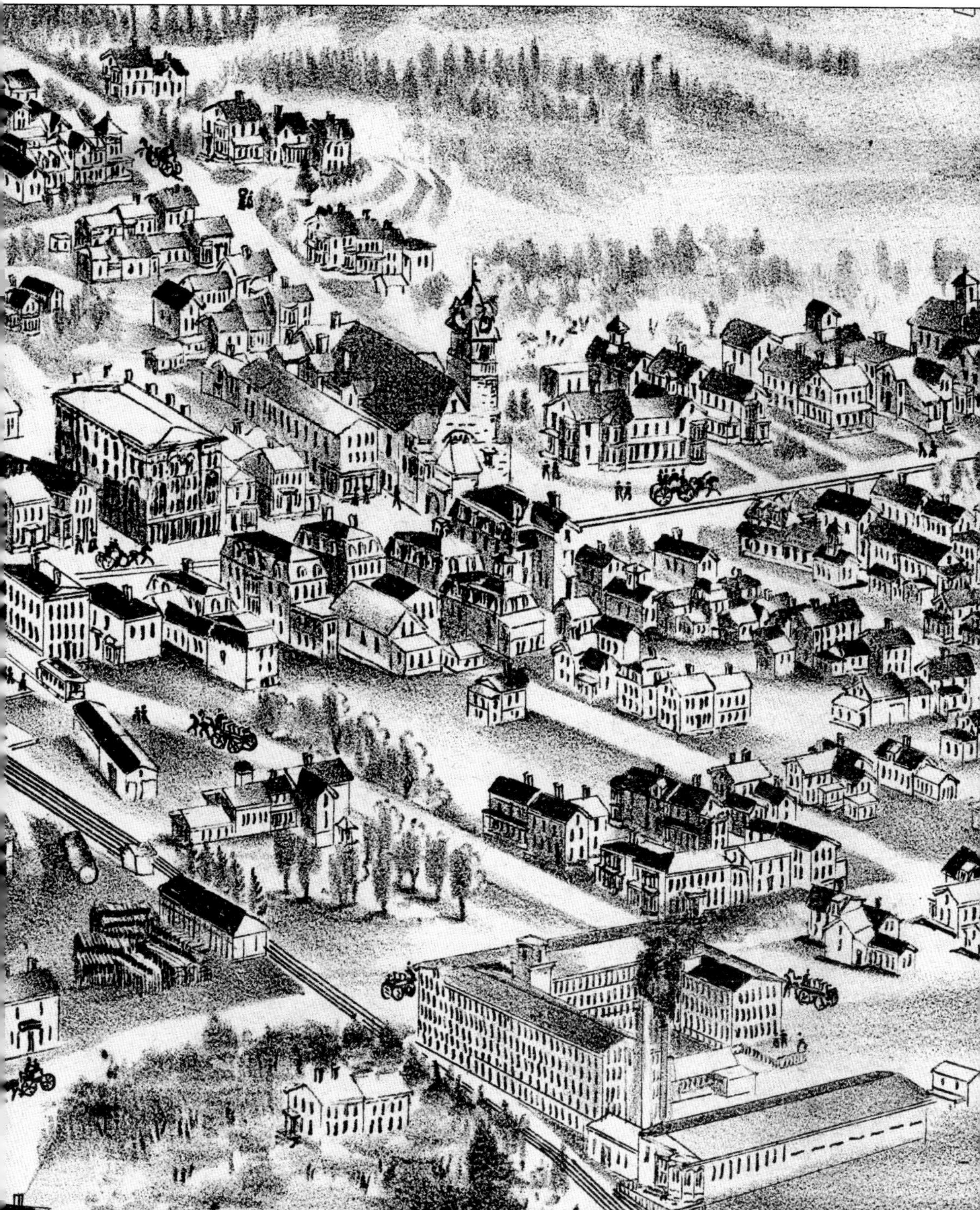

to Beaver Lake on the east. Around the edge, the artist drew renderings of 29 Derry institutions, stores, and homes. Most likely, those who were so honored had paid to be included. It is believed that about 500 of the bird's-eye views were printed and sold for a dollar each. These and similar artistic renderings of Derry in 1877 and 1887 can be found at the town museum.

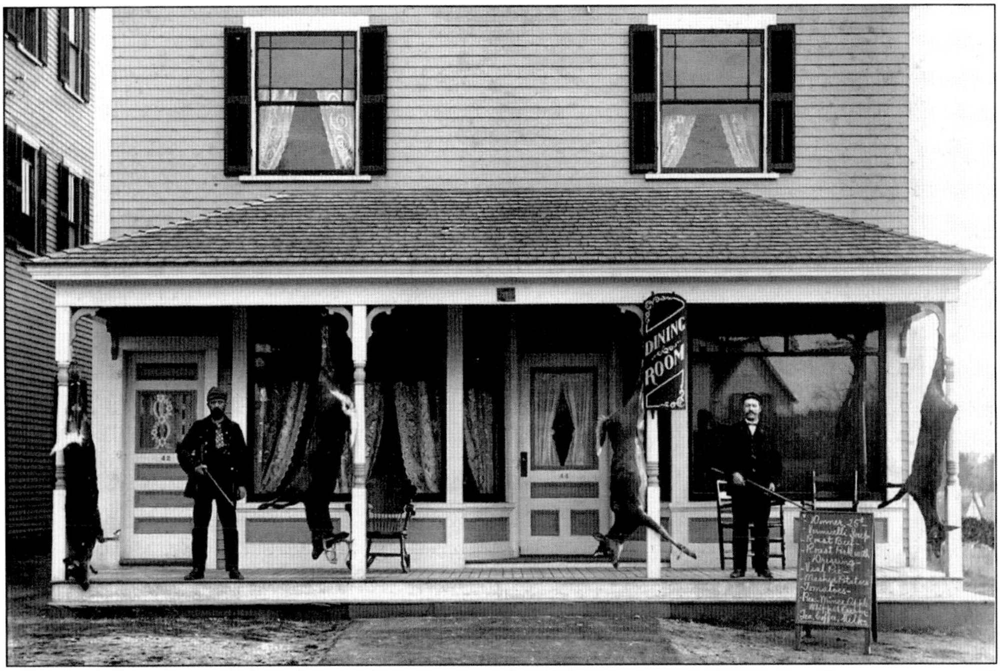

The shoe factory workers of West Derry around 1910 frequented the Depot Restaurant at 42 West Broadway. The four deer hanging on the porch were likely to be on the menu soon. The chalkboard advertises a complete roast beef or pork dinner for 25¢. The building is now the law office of attorney John Skoko. (Rand photograph.)

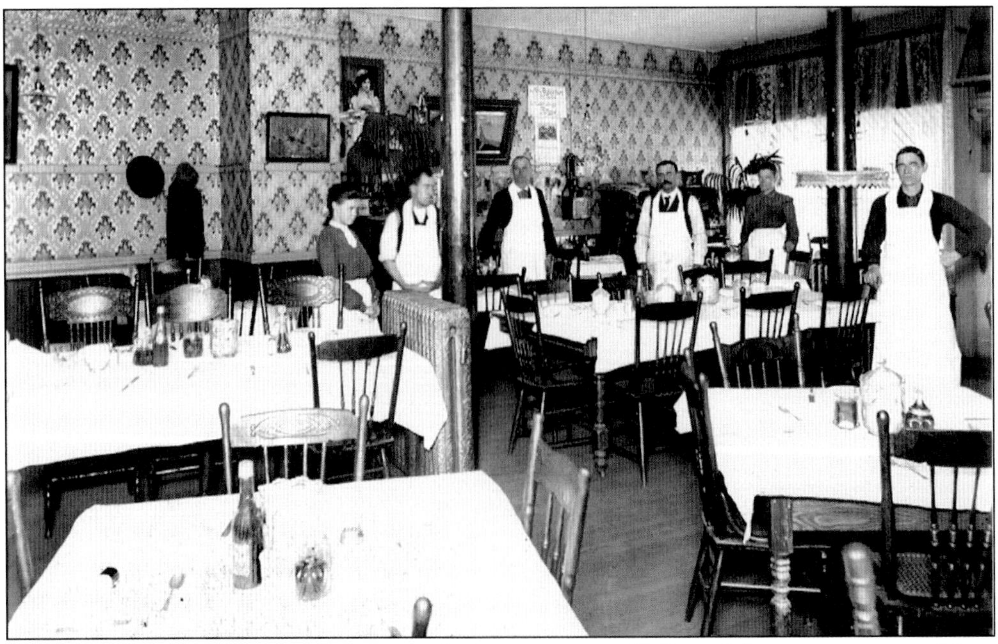

Patrons at the Depot Restaurant enjoyed an attentive staff. Potted ferns, a piano, and lace curtains indicate an attempt at small-town chic. Workers could buy monthly meal tickets entitling them to three meals a day at a bargain rate. The sign on the wall announced there were no refunds for missing meals.

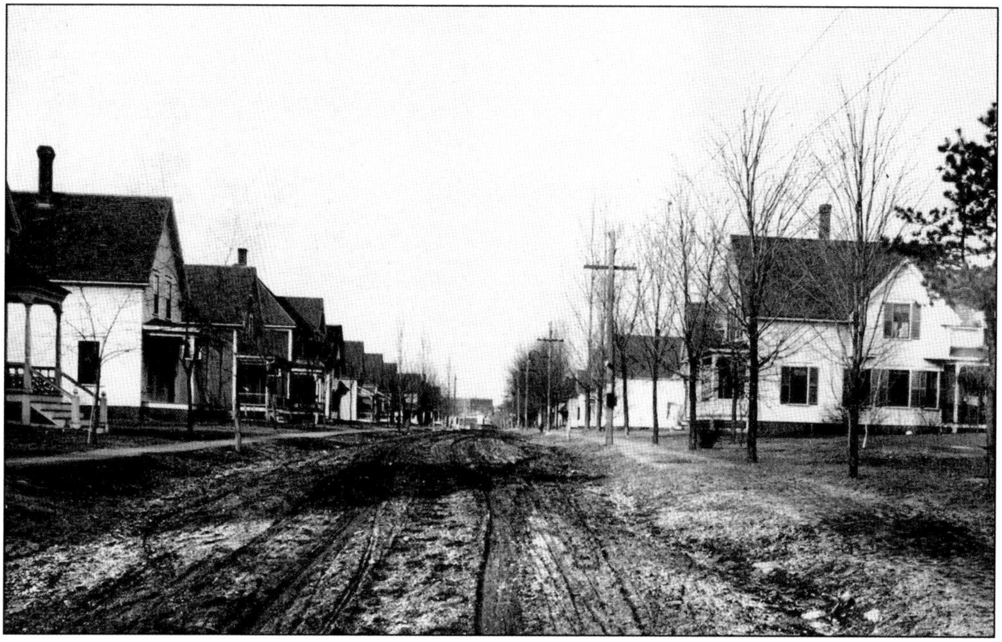

The side roads in West Derry are lined with single-family homes built early in the 20th century for shoe factory workers. This 1910 view of Highland Avenue shows an area that only a decade before was an open field used as a racetrack.

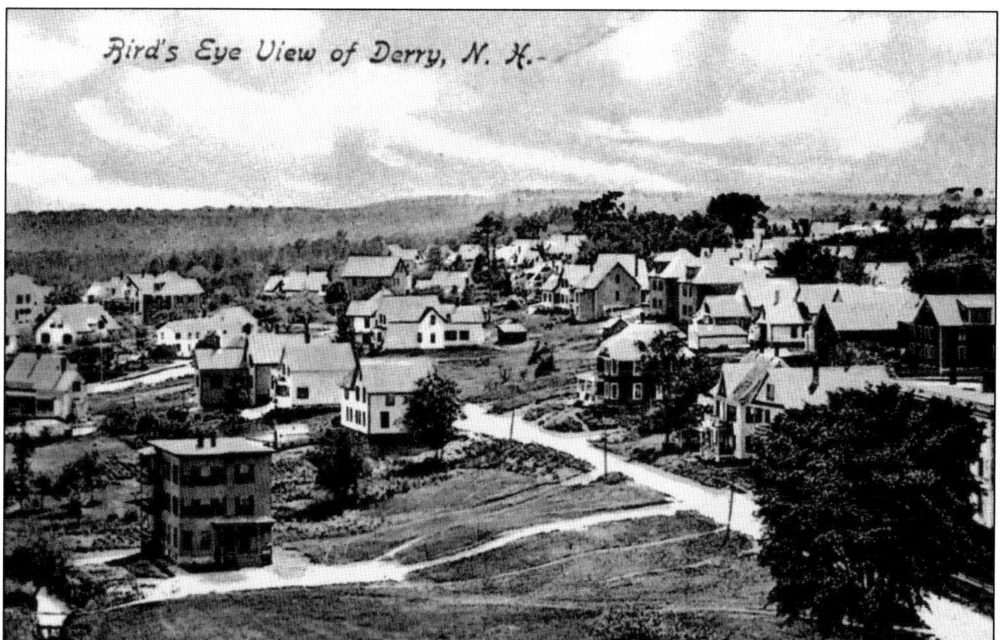

In order to record this view of Elm Street in 1907, the photographer Leon W. Rand climbed the 100-foot chimney of the Derry Electric Company. Today there are many more houses, roads, and trees in this area. On the lower left is the three-decker apartment building at 25 Elm Street. Within a few years it was moved up the hill to the immediate side of Elm Street.

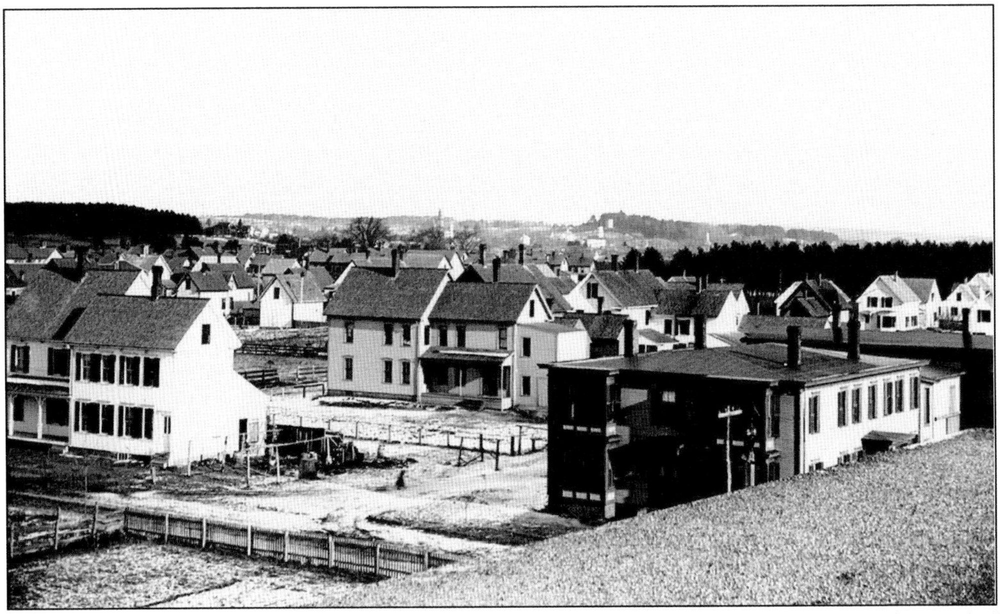

This photograph shows the area of South Avenue around 1890, looking east from the roof of the Woodbury Shoe Company factory. A decade before, the area had been empty fields and wood lots. In 1885, Col. William Pillsbury formed an investment group to build workers' homes and tenements. Many of these buildings were destroyed in the 1960 fire at the Chelmsford Shoe Company factory.

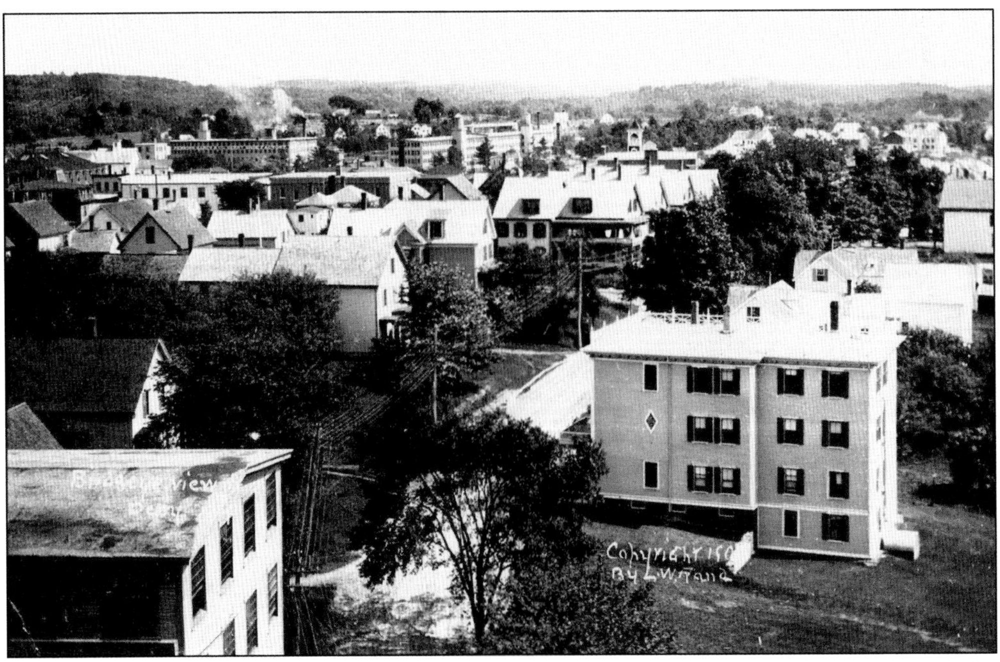

To achieve this view of Maple Street in 1907, photographer Leon W. Rand climbed up the staging of the newly constructed 100-foot chimney of the Derry Electric Company. In the distance, several buildings of the large shoe factory complex on South Avenue can be seen.

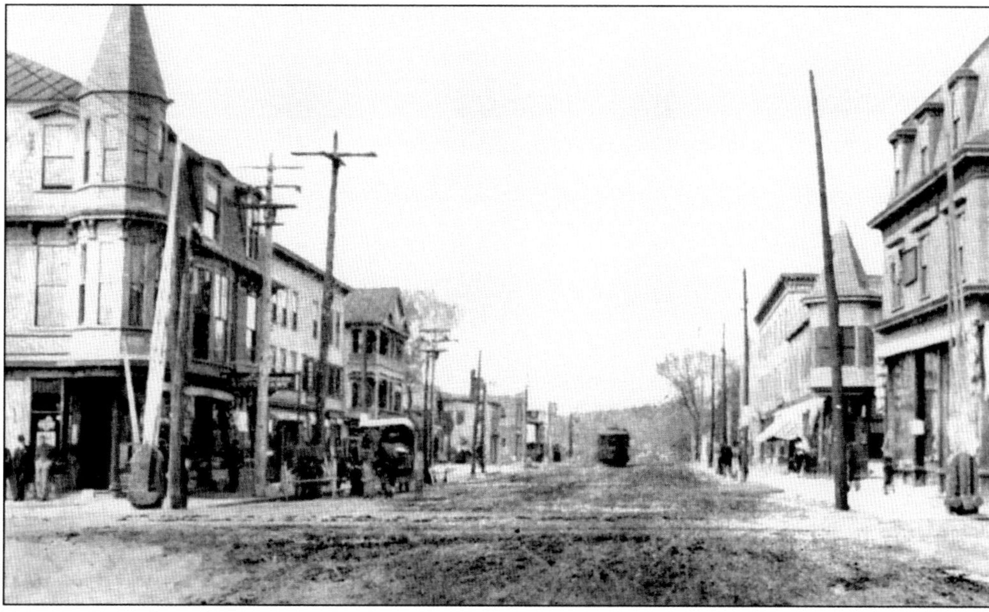

Here is West Broadway in 1908. This area was still unpaved during the early years of the 20th century. On the left and right are the twin traffic gates that were lowered to close off the street when the dozens of trains rushed through each day. Notice the Manchester and Derry trolley coming down the middle of the street.

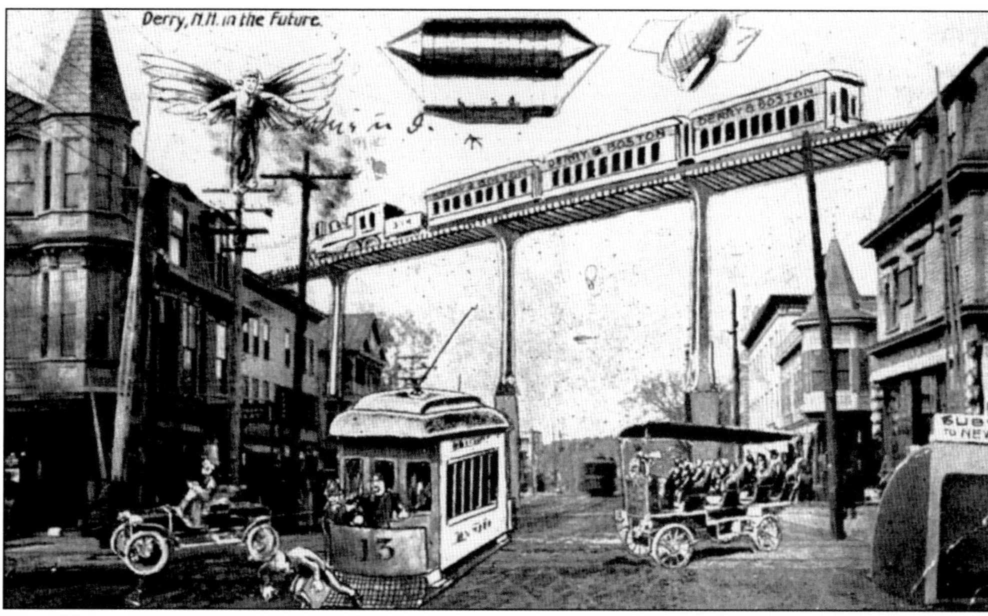

The illustration for this postcard—captioned "Derry, N.H. in the Future"—shows Derry as the artist imagined it would become. In the sky are a variety of great airships. Curiously the artist added a man with wings, but included no airplanes. A subway line would run between Derry and New York City, and there would finally be a Derry Bypass in the form of an elevated railroad bridge. The artist certainly underestimated the number of cars that would be traveling on Broadway.

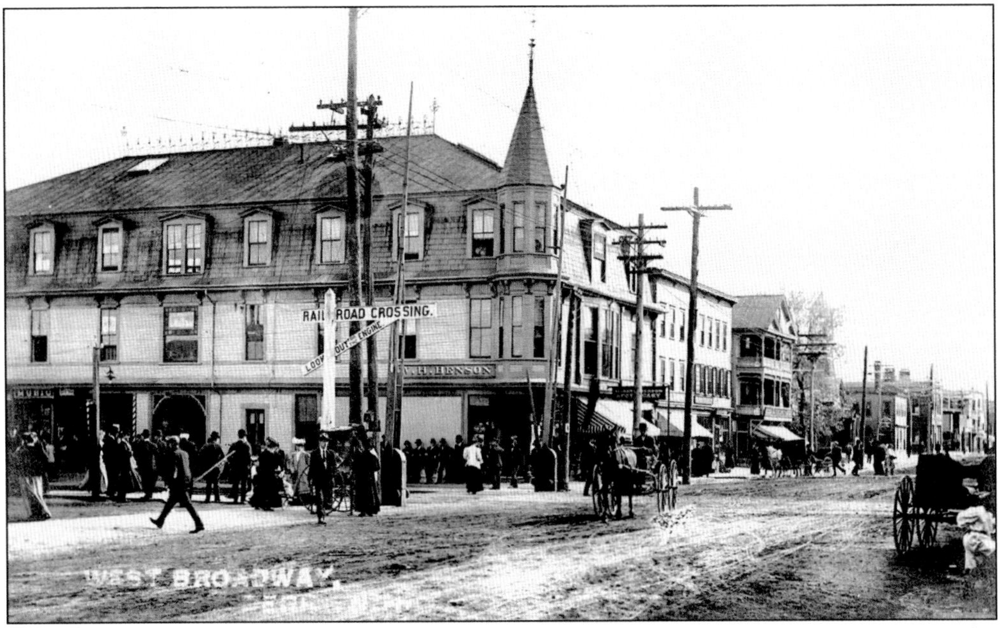

In the years around the First World War, Depot Square was the busiest place in Derry. The building with the turret held the American House apartments, Benson's Drug Store, the Derry Bank, a barbershop, a restaurant, and the town's first music store.

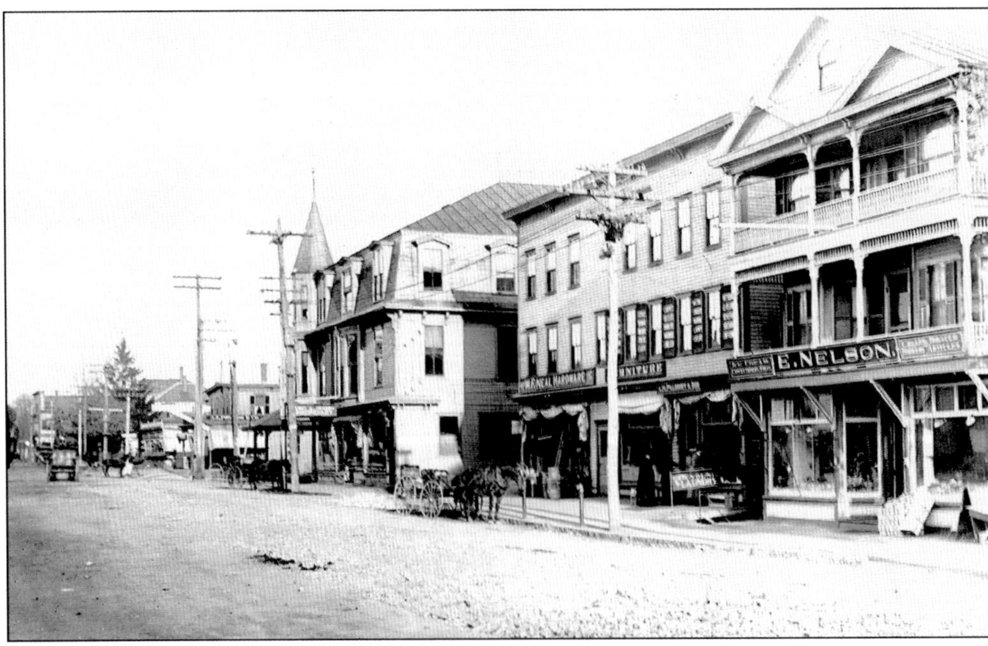

Around 1915, Derry housewives could do all their shopping on Broadway. There never seemed to be a vacant store. Notice the horse hitches in front of some of the stores. At the left is a horse drinking from the water trough in front of the depot. Nelson's fruit store, on the right, claimed to be the birthplace of the ice-cream sundae.

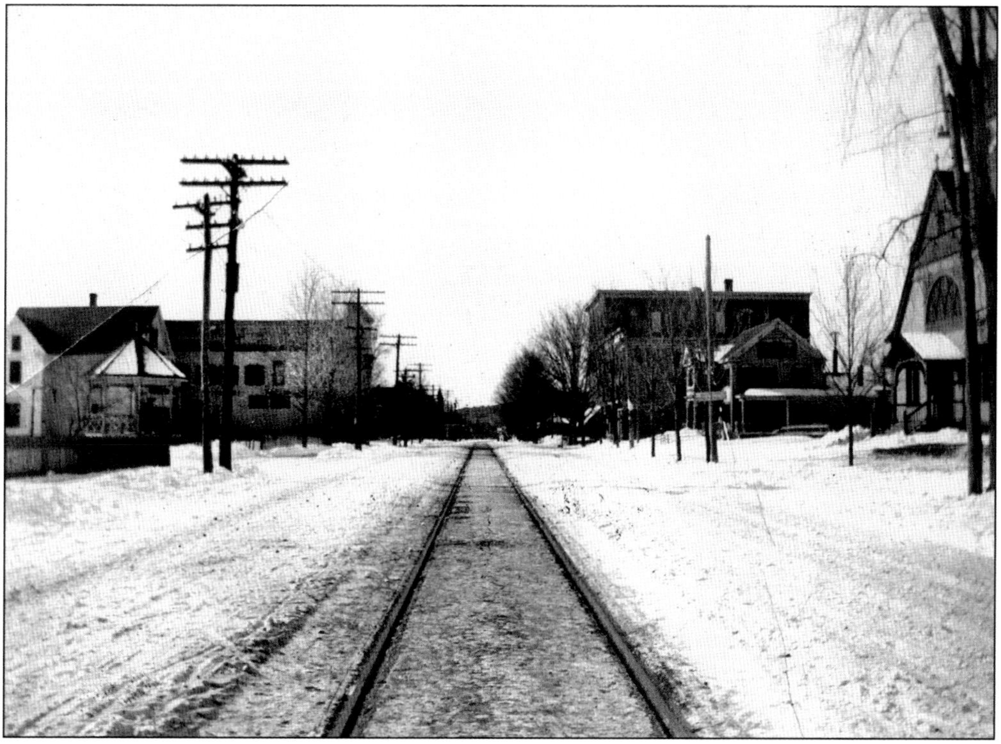

This view shows the tracks of the Chester and Derry trolley extending to the west down Broadway. On the left is Derry's bandstand, and overhead an electric arc streetlight.

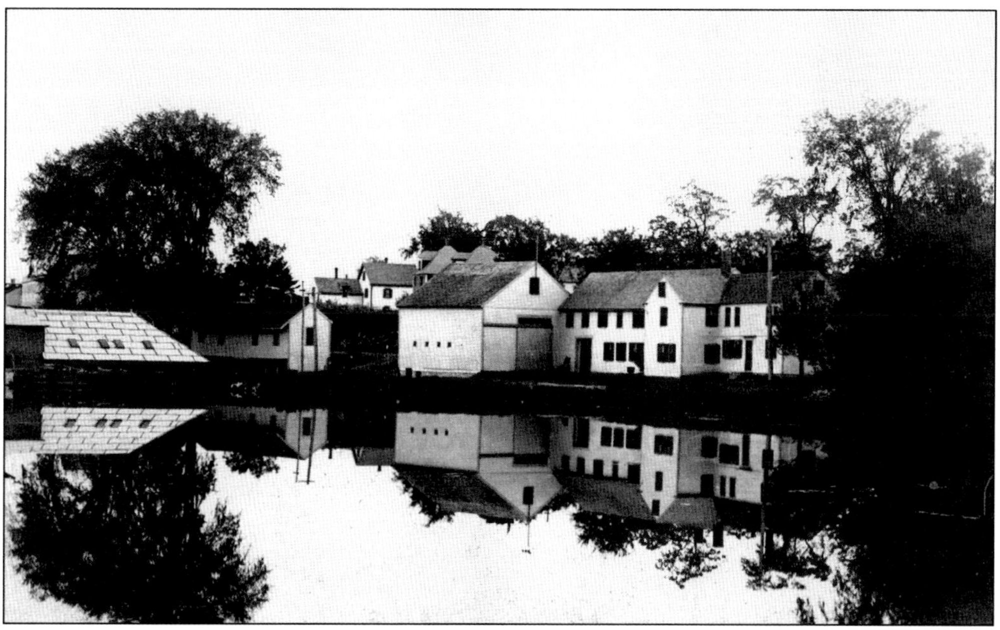

The Horne Homestead on Maple Street was built in the early 19th century. The pond was created in the 1720s when the river was dammed to create a power source for a water-powered sawmill. In 1848, a railroad causeway divided the pond into two separate bodies of water.

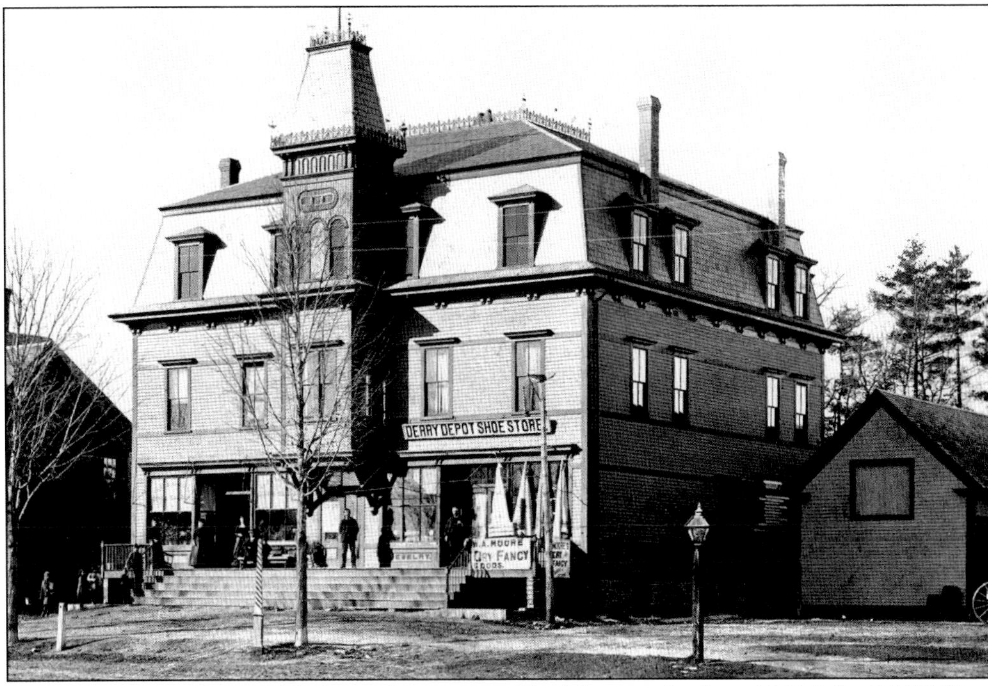

This combination fraternal lodge and commercial building was built in 1884. The Odd Fellows met in the upper floors. The street level contained a restaurant-saloon, barbershop, shoe shop, and dry goods store. The building was destroyed in an 1897 fire. Its replacement was destroyed in a 1963 fire. The site is now occupied by a strip mall at 24 East Broadway.

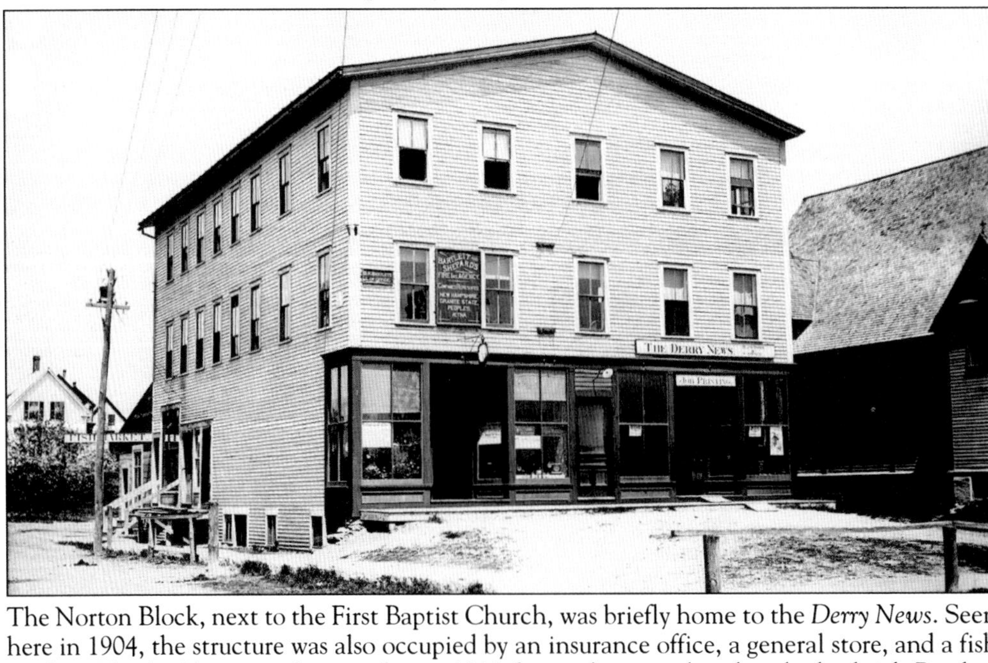

The Norton Block, next to the First Baptist Church, was briefly home to the *Derry News*. Seen here in 1904, the structure was also occupied by an insurance office, a general store, and a fish market. The building was destroyed in a 1915 fire and was replaced with the brick Bartlett Block, which housed the Derry Electric Company. The site is presently home to the Salvation Army's outreach programs.

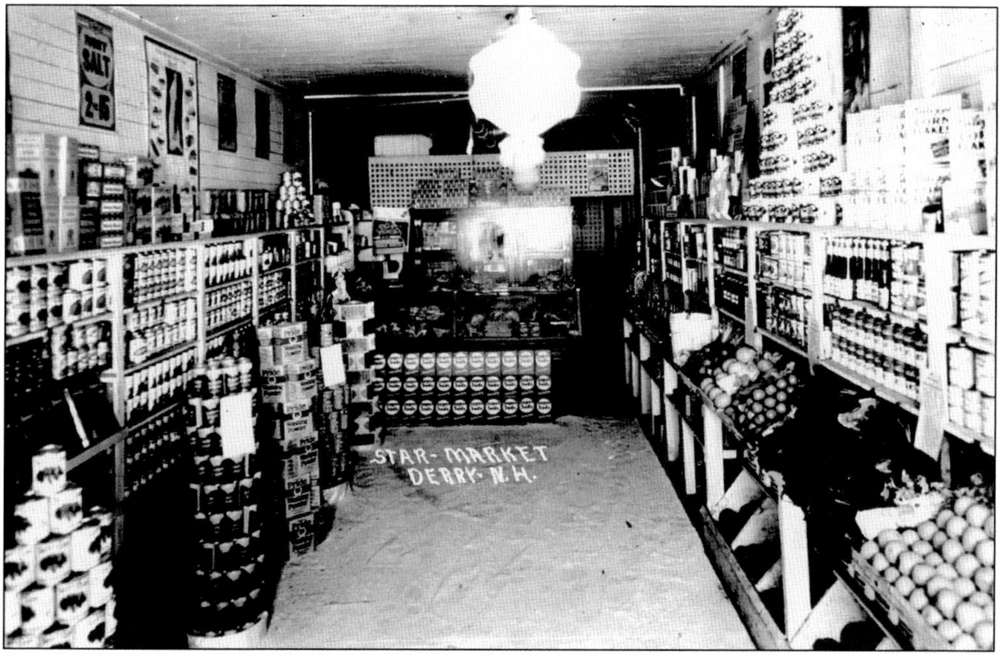

During the 1930s, one of the most popular grocery stores was the Star Market at 41 East Broadway. It operated on the modern, self-service method. Customers could get their own cans and produce rather than waiting for the storekeeper to take items off the shelves.

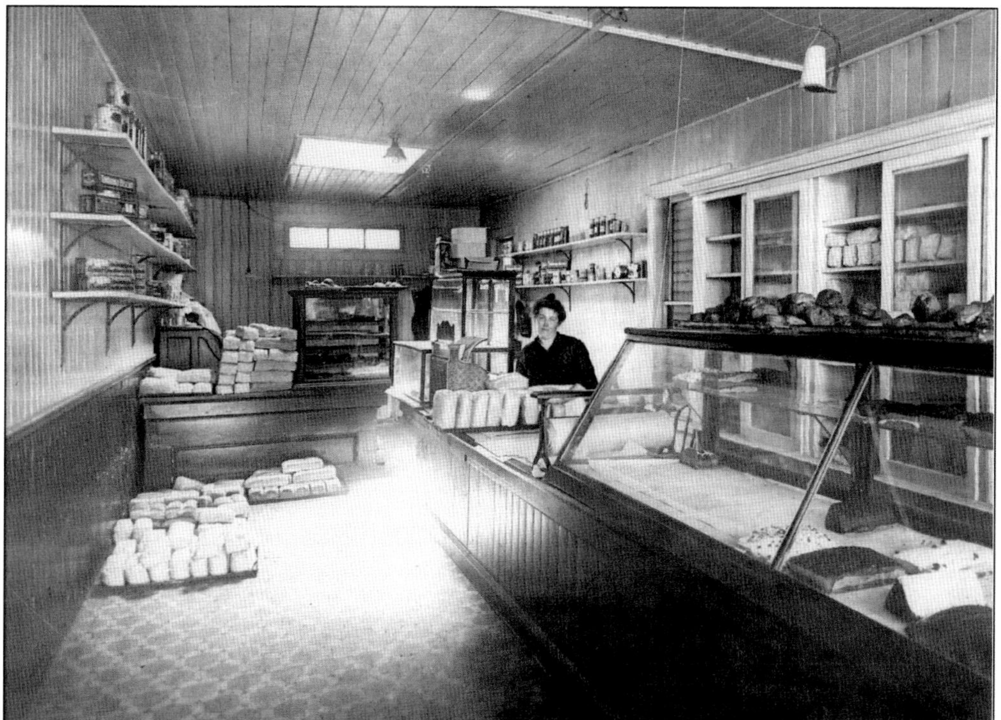

Jennie Hanks Hatch is shown around 1920 in her bakery at 19 East Broadway. Most of her customers were the families of shoe workers, whose population dominated this area of town.

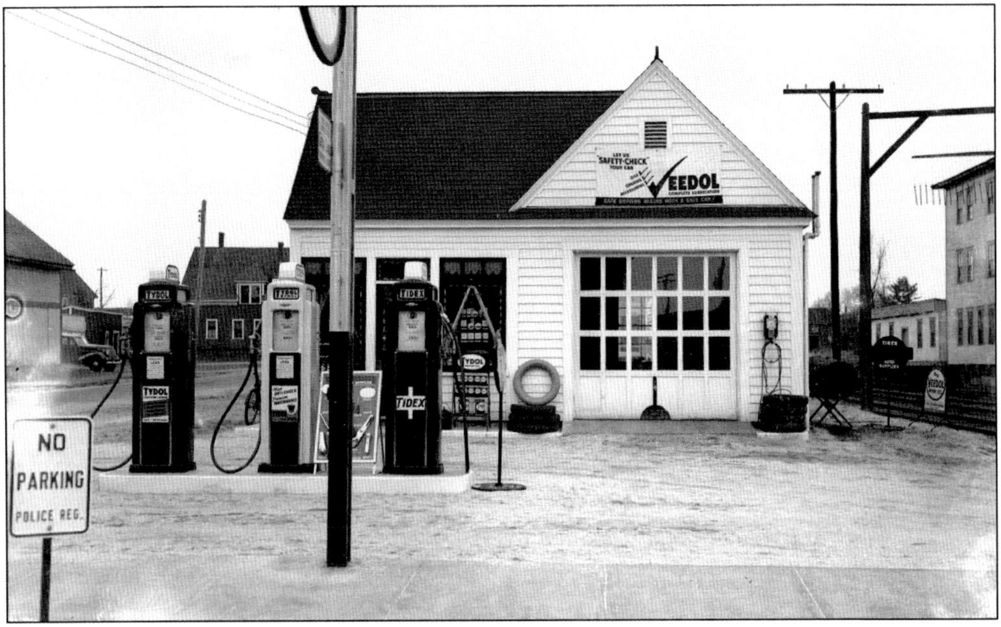

Albert Dion Jr. (1895–1961) built this 1 West Broadway garage. In 1961, the whole building was lifted off its foundation and moved down Broadway to a new site in Londonderry. In its place, Dave Hicks erected an ultra-modern, cement filling station. It is now D & J Automotive.

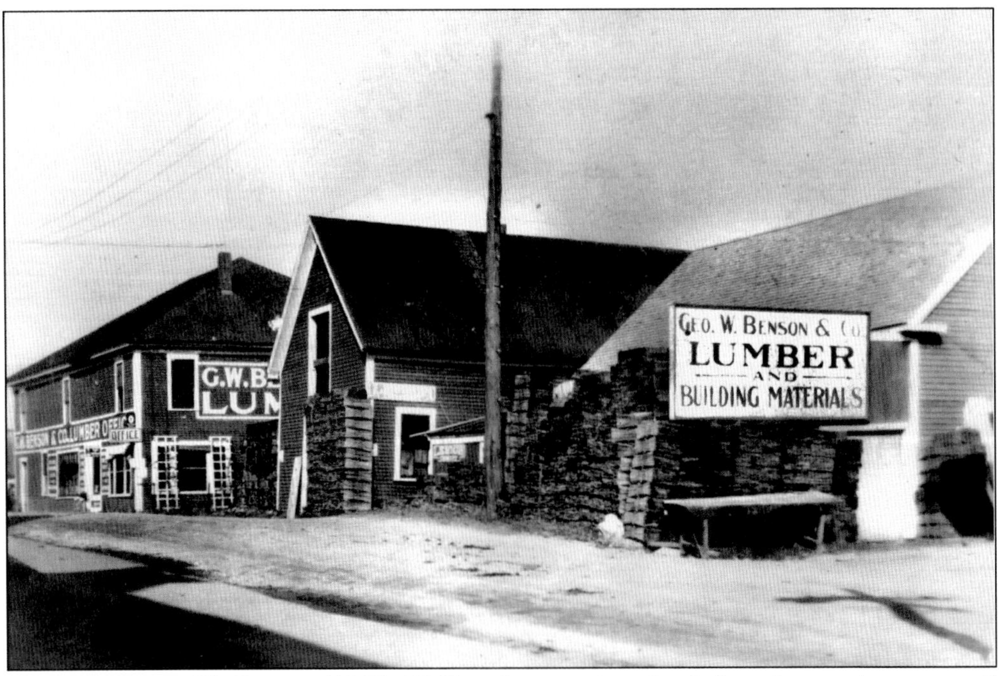

In 1913, George W. Benson (1867–1923), a foreman in a local shoe factory, began to sell lumber on Martin Street. By 1922, locals could buy everything from "sills to saddle boards" at his store. The business is now run by members of the fourth generation of the Benson family.

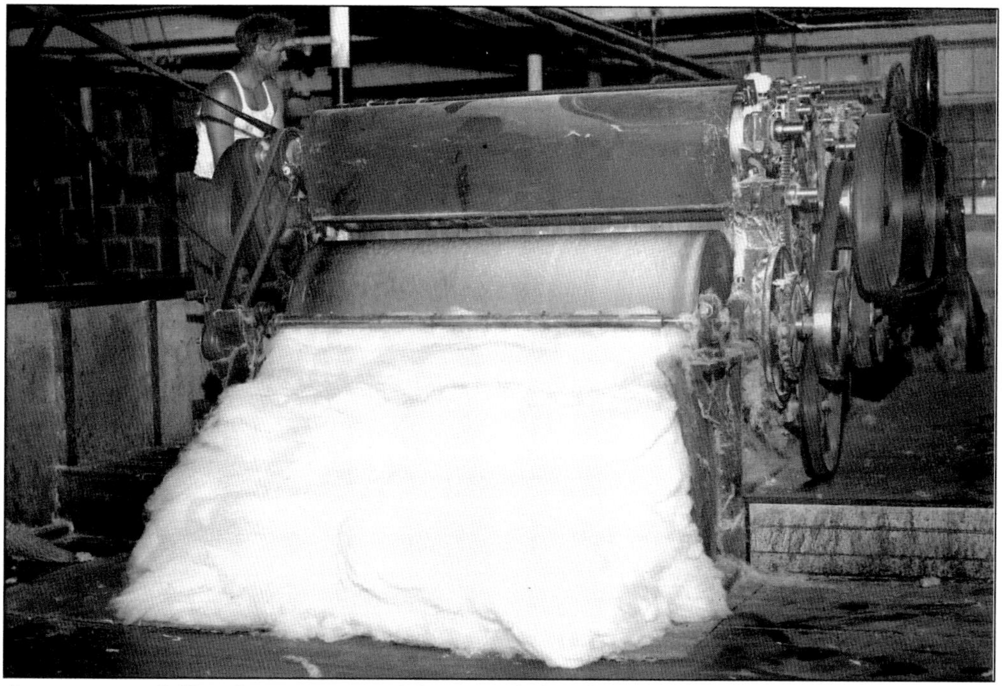

A mattress and fiber factory operated for several decades on Martin and Maple Streets. The company's slogan was, "You never awake until the crowing of the cock." At the time of this photograph in 1938, the company advertised that it would pick up your old mattress and refurbish it with new stuffing.

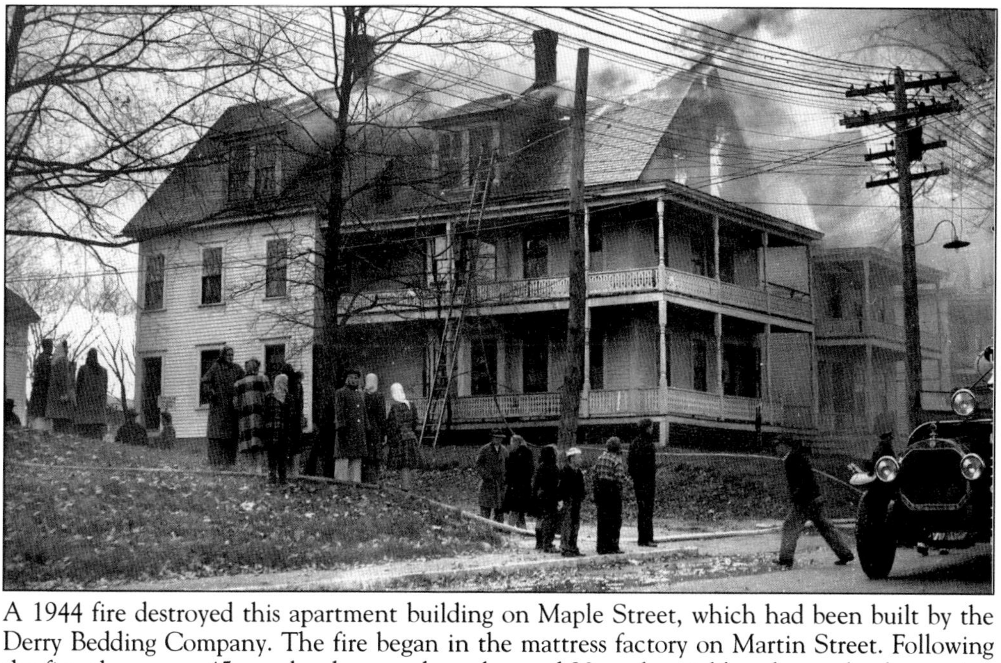

A 1944 fire destroyed this apartment building on Maple Street, which had been built by the Derry Bedding Company. The fire began in the mattress factory on Martin Street. Following the fire, there were 45 people who were homeless and 30 workers jobless due to the destruction of the large two-story Derry Bedding Company building. The company did continue to operate for a dozen more years in a smaller building.

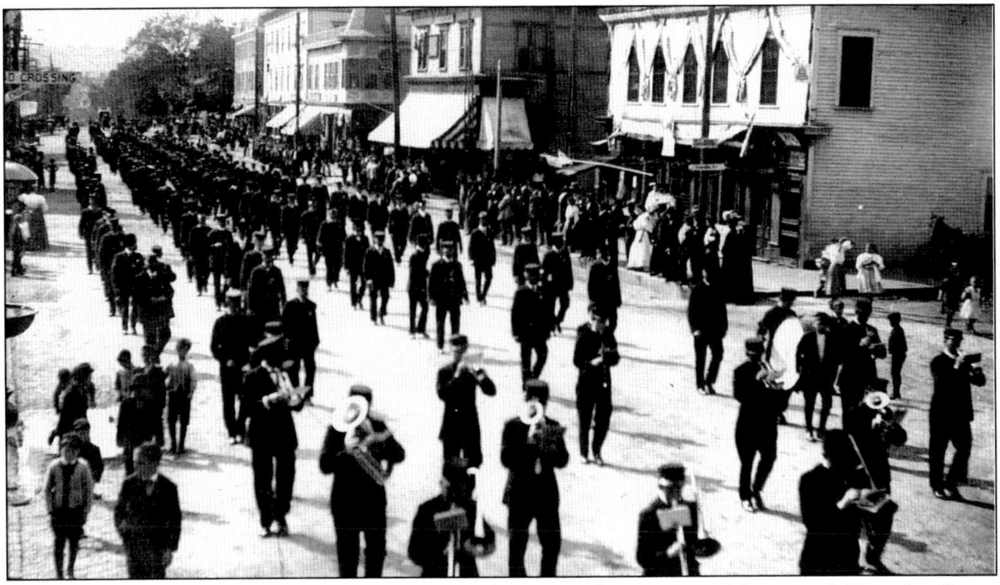

Broadway was the usual route for Derry's parades. Here, long lines of firemen follow the Derry Brass Band. The block on the immediate right is Wilson's Market, which was torn down by the town around 2000 and replaced with a small park. To the left of the market is the Central Block that was destroyed in a 1934 fire.

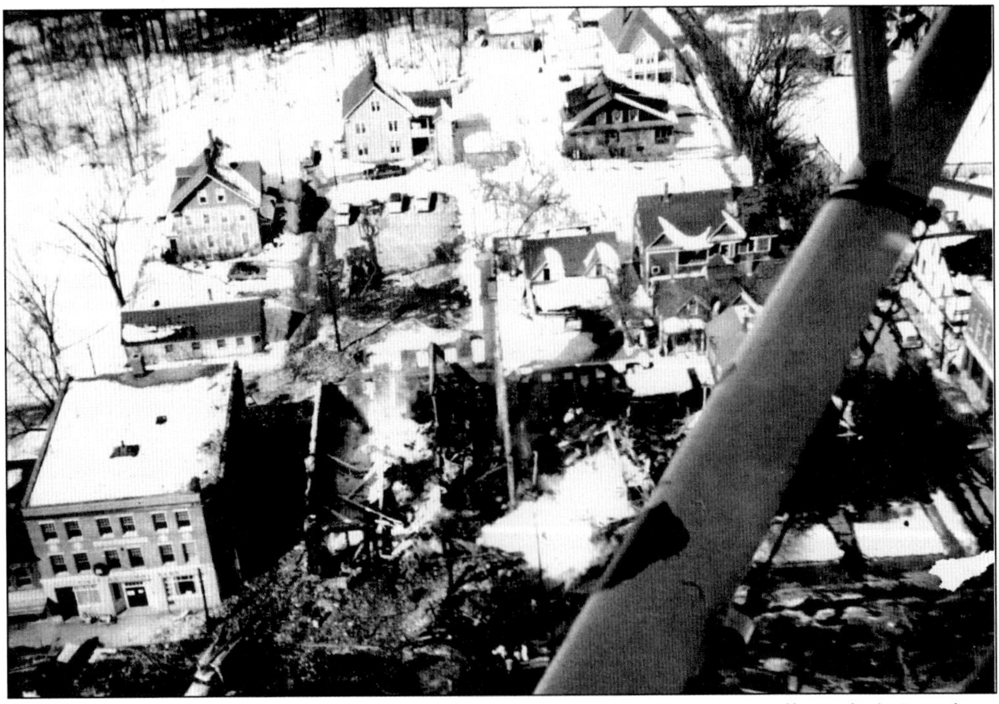

This aerial photograph was taken from a plane piloted by Judge George Grinnell. A whole Broadway block was lost in this 1963 fire, which extended from McAllister Court to Franklin Street. Two people died in the blaze. Included in the fire's destruction were the Odd Fellows Lodge and J. J. Newberry's Store ("the dime store"). The far upper left of this image depicts the site of today's Derry Municipal Center.

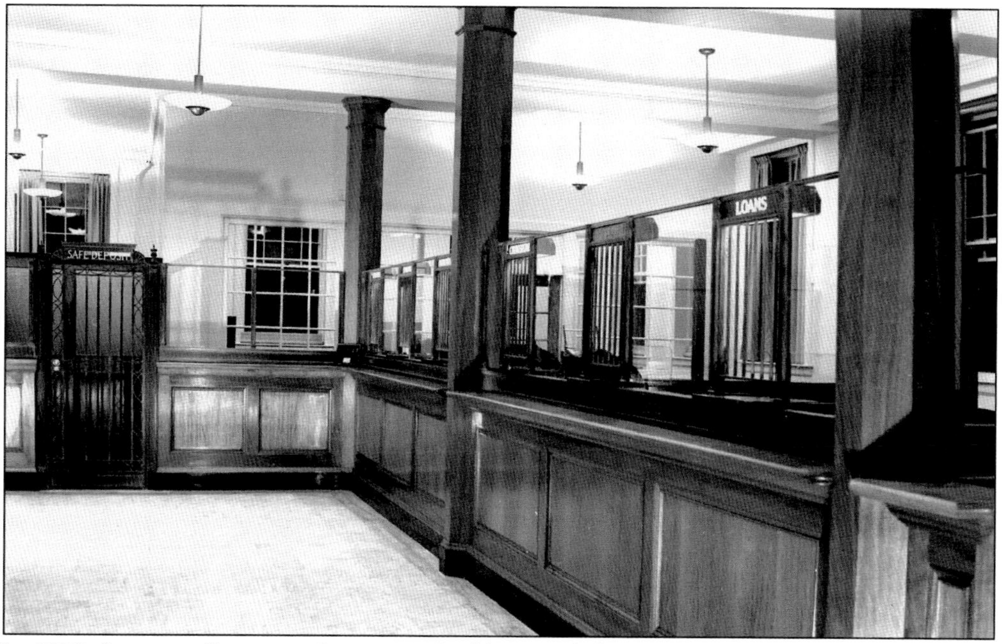

In 1939 the post office moved to a new building, and the First National Bank took over the entire first floor at 20 East Broadway. The expanded area was renovated in a style that was described in the *Derry News* as "light, airy, and roomy." The moving of the vault required round-the-clock police guard for 12 days and nights. (Arthur Lear photograph.)

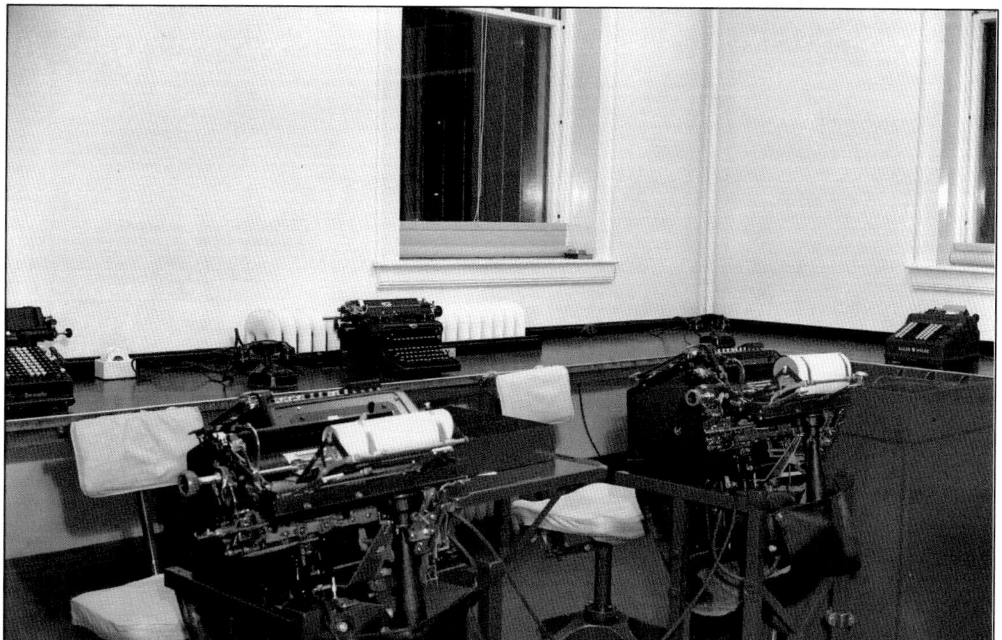

Before the post office relocated in 1939, the First National Bank felt its half of the building at 20 East Broadway was intolerably crowded. After the move, the bookkeepers, secretaries, and tellers had ample room to work. This photograph shows the state-of-the-art office equipment in the pre-computer era. (Arthur Lear photograph.)

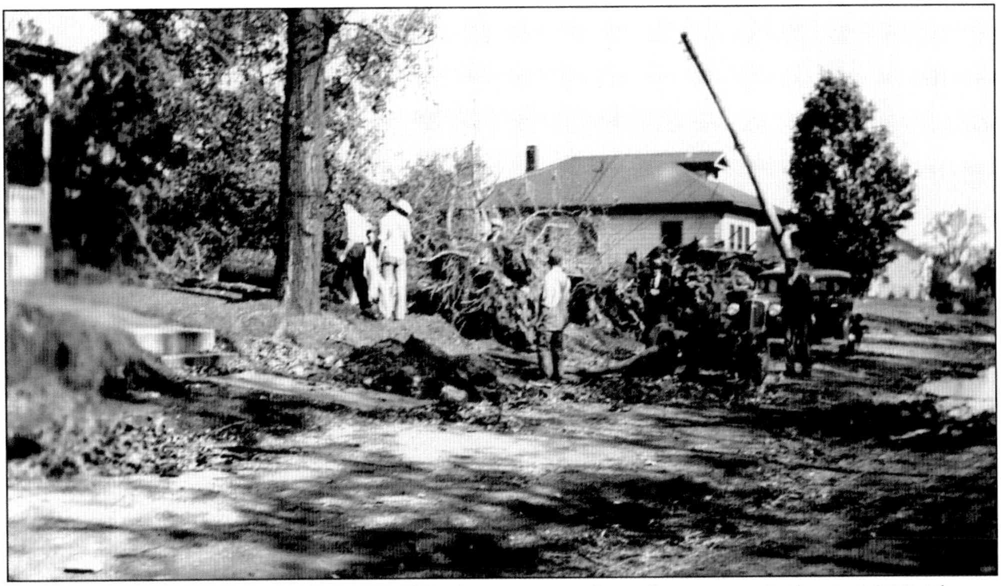

Thunder, torrential rains, and wind suddenly interrupted a calm summer's day in 1948. Shown here is the storm damage at 109 West Broadway. A two-foot-high sand bar blocked Nesmith Street. Derry was hit again in September 1979, by a "microburst" that sheared 500 trees and blocked 14 roads.

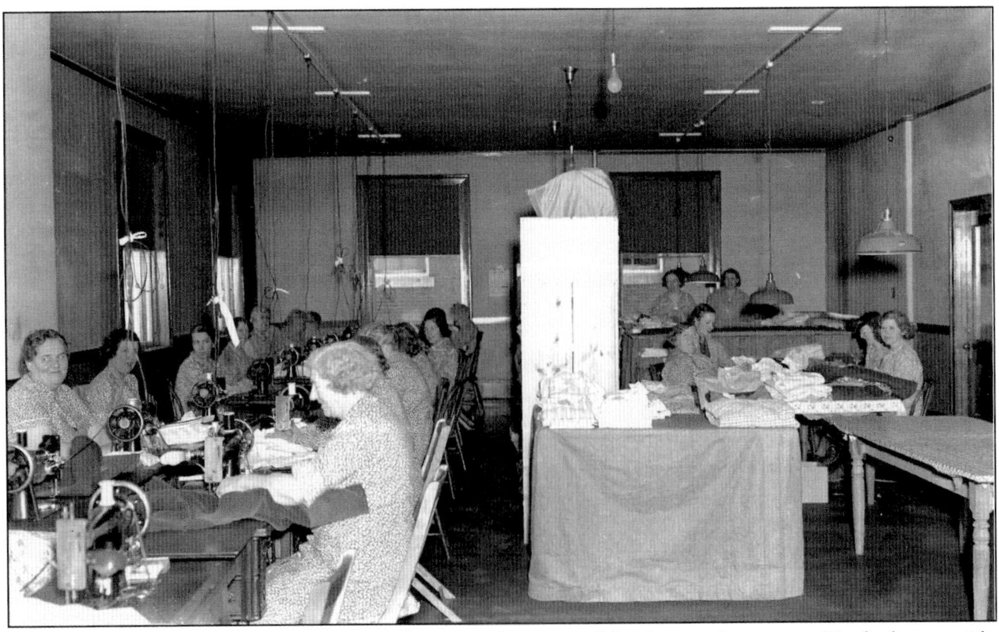

During the Great Depression, unemployment hit record highs in the town. To help provide employment, in 1940 the Works Progress Administration opened a sewing room in the second story of a building on Broadway. The government provided the sewing machines, cloth, and patterns, and paid women to sew hospital garb.

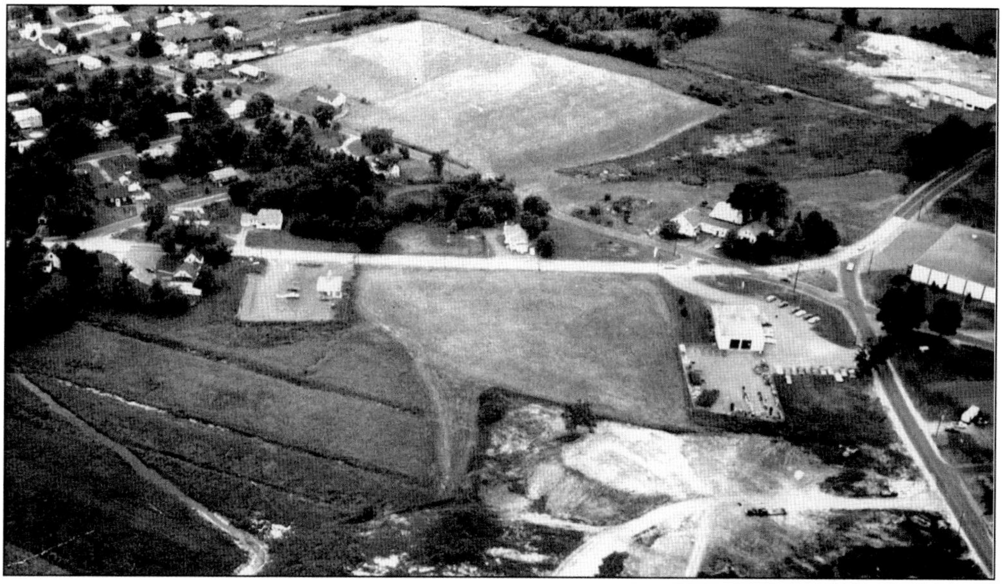

District judge George Grinnell flew over Ross' Corner in 1969 to chronicle the start of Hood Plaza's construction. The road entering on the left is Crystal Avenue. On the far right, the Derry Shoe Company building (now the site of the FireEye Corporation) can be seen. Just above the intersection in this view is the Ross Farm; the area is now occupied by the police department. At the bottom of the image are signs of the first work being done on the new shopping mall.

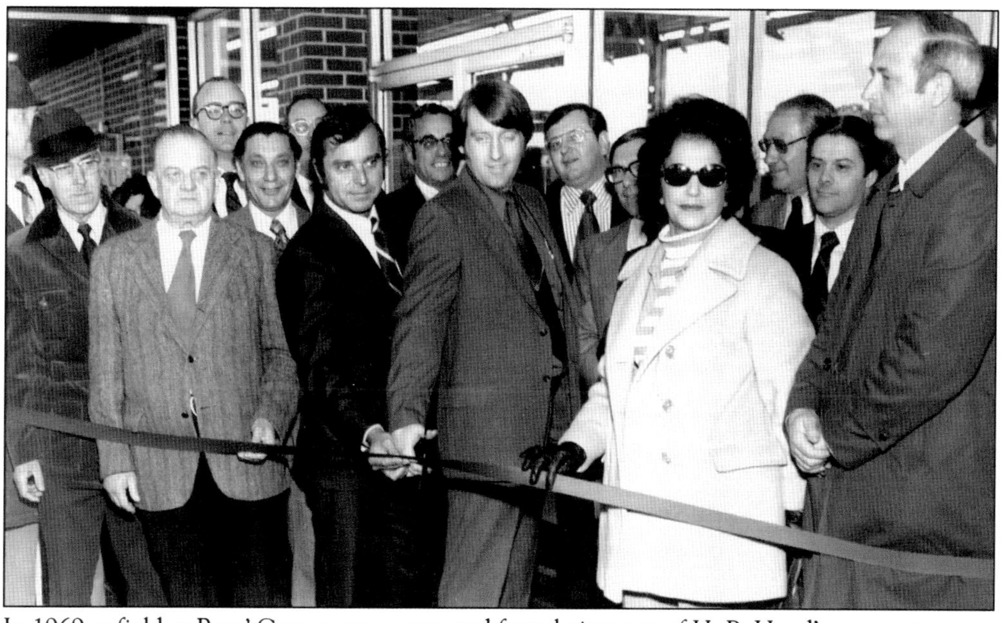

In 1969, a field at Ross' Corner was converted from being one of H. P. Hood's cow pastures to become the site of Derry's first shopping mall. Seen here is the ribbon-cutting for the Ames Department Store at the new Hood Plaza. At the ribbon are, from left to right, selectman Ernie Gaines, state representative Kenneth Senter, two representatives of the Ames corporation, realtor Millie DiMarzio, and selectman Scott Gerrish. The store closed 30 years later. (*Derry News* photograph.)

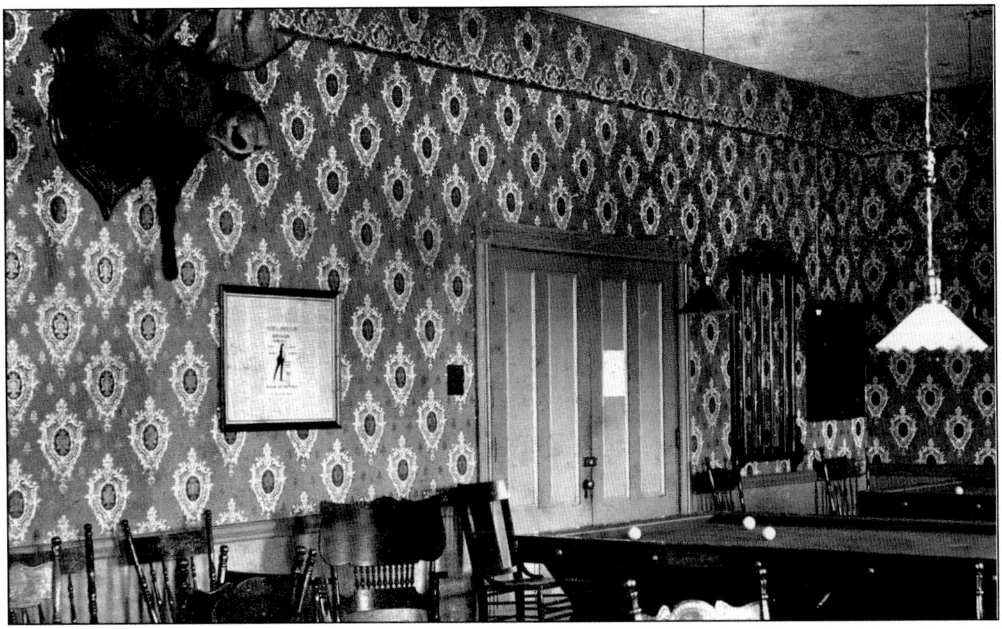

The Derry Athletic Association (DAA) was founded in 1904 to promote exercise and social contact. For decades the group rented this suite of rooms located over the First National Bank on Broadway. The DAA sponsored the town's semi-professional baseball team and the annual winter carnival. Its sports field on South Avenue is still used by the town.

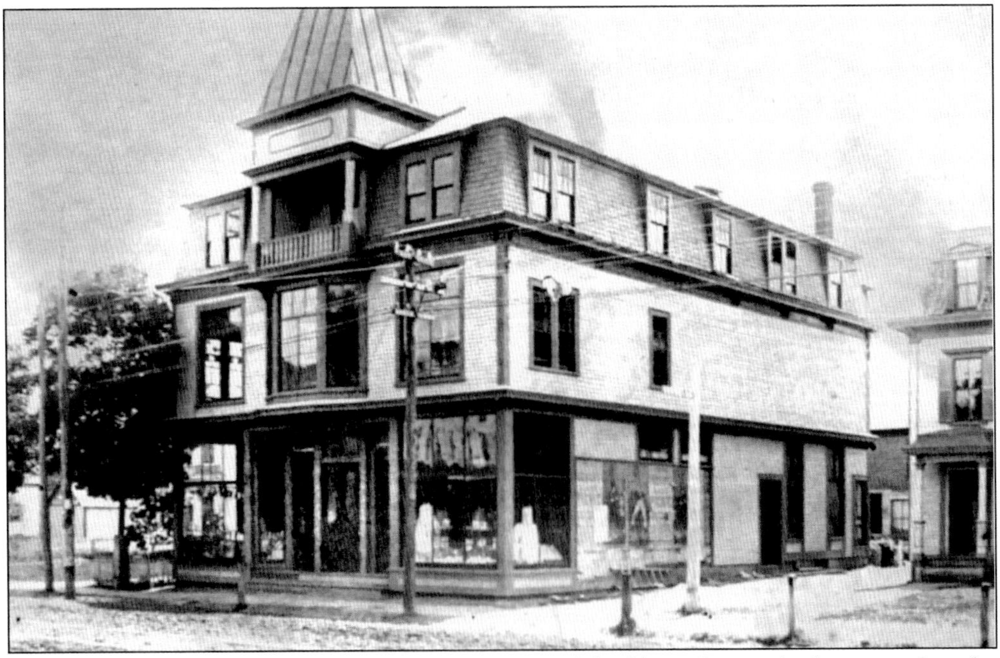

The Central Block was Broadway's first commercial building. It was built soon after the Manchester and Lawrence Railroad first came through the area in 1849. The structure survived the Great Fire of 1882, which destroyed most of downtown Derry. In December 1934, the building was home to Steele's Furniture when it was leveled in an early-morning fire. The lot is now occupied by D & J Automotive.

Ten

SOCIAL ACTIVITIES

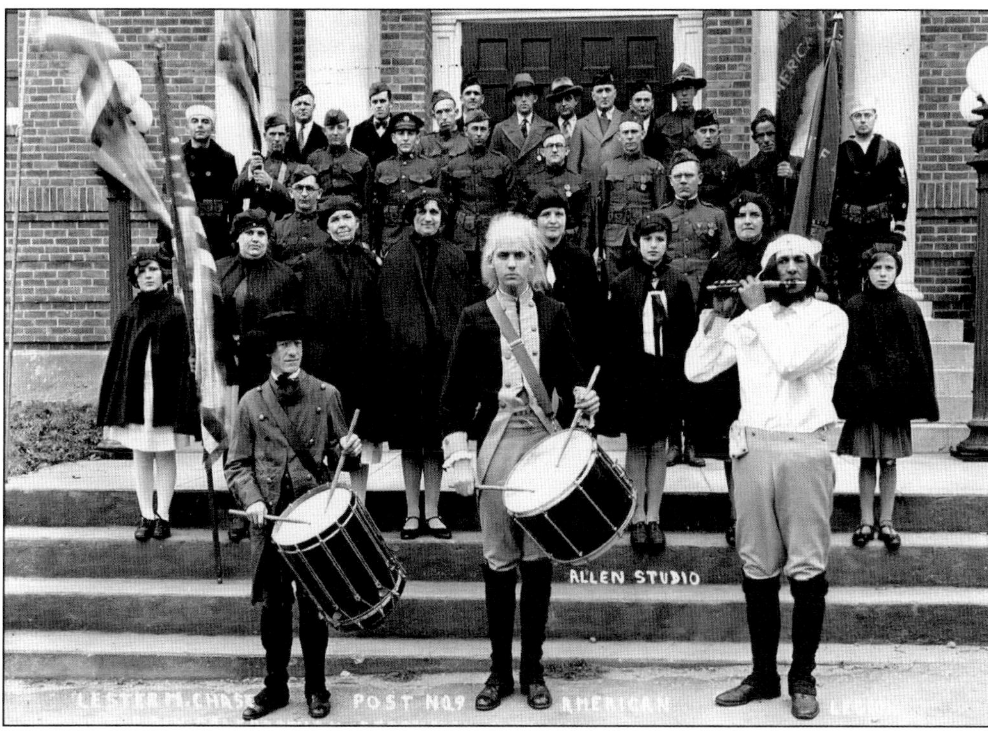

The Armistice Day Parade in 1929 was sponsored by the Lester W. Chase American Legion Post. This fife and drum group led the parade as it marched from Maple Street along Broadway to the present Alexander-Carr Park. On the steps behind the musicians are members of the Derry American Legion and the Ladies Auxiliary. (Allen photograph.)

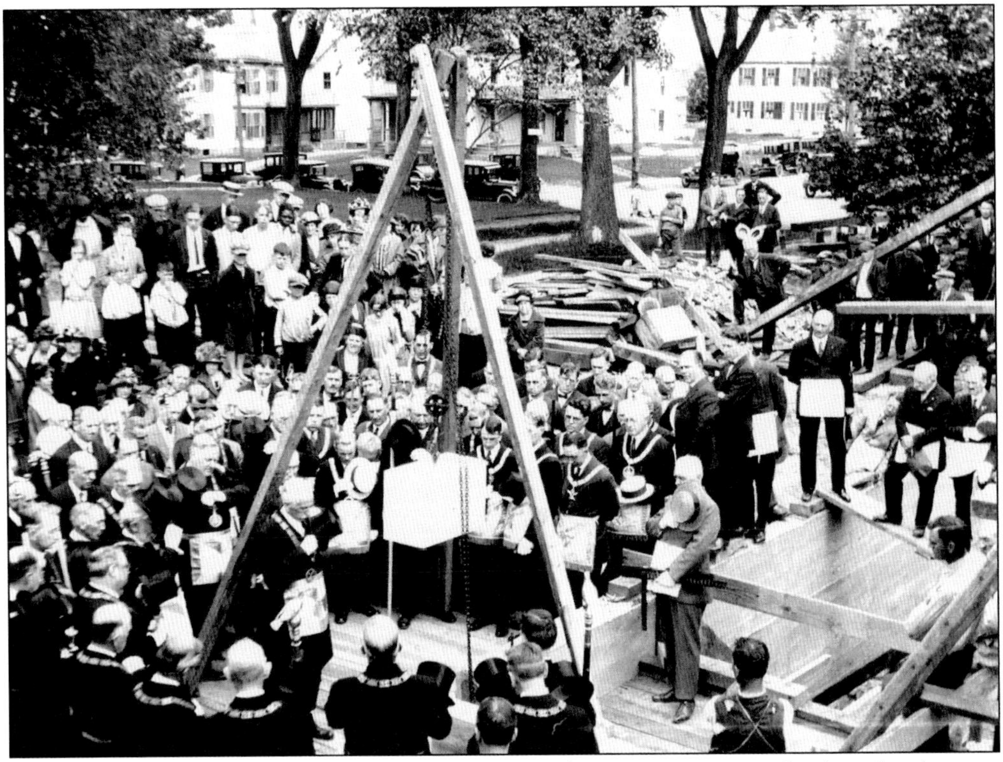

On June 9, 1924, the Masonic temple cornerstone-laying ceremony took place for the new home of St. Mark's Lodge No. 44, F. and A.M. The local Masonic group was chartered in 1826. In 1921, through the generosity of Dr. Charles Newell and his wife, Harriett, funds were secured to buy the property at 58 East Broadway.

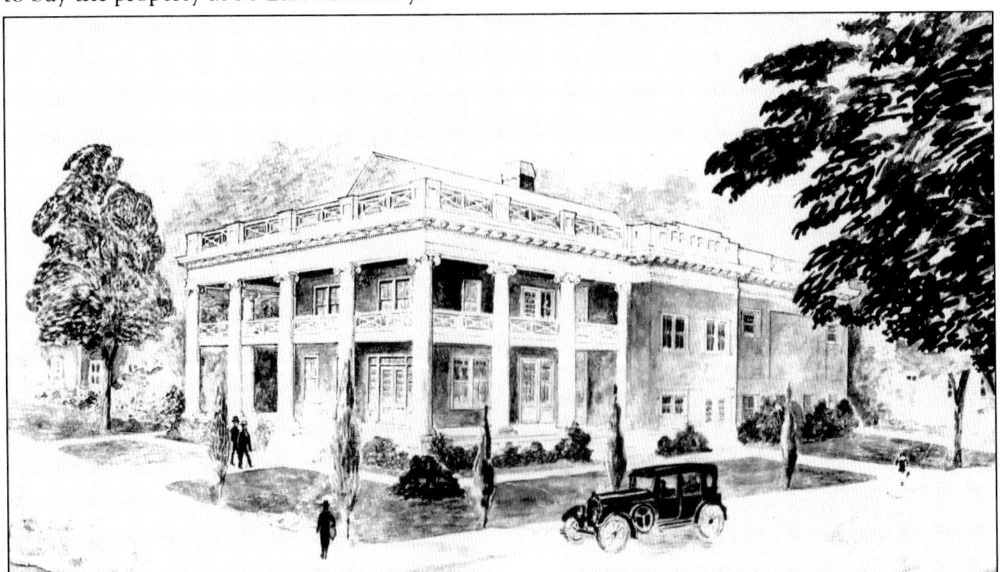

In 1921, the local Masonic Lodge hired architect James Rogers to draw up plans to remodel Dr. Charles Newell's Broadway residence into a proper temple. The work cost $40,000, a huge sum in those days, and the building was dedicated on December 15, 1924.

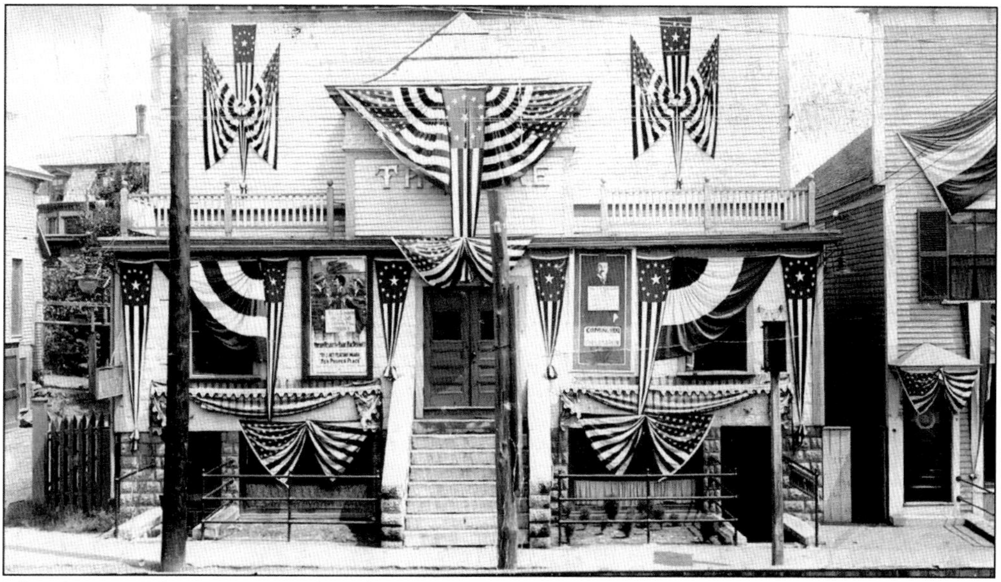

The Scenic Theater on Railroad Avenue was Derry's first movie theater. Originally the building was a roller-skating rink; it was converted for movie shows in 1909. The Scenic offered a new movie every day. The building was purchased by the Eagle Club in 1925 and renovated to become the group's clubhouse. It was destroyed in 1945 and replaced by the present Eagle Club building.

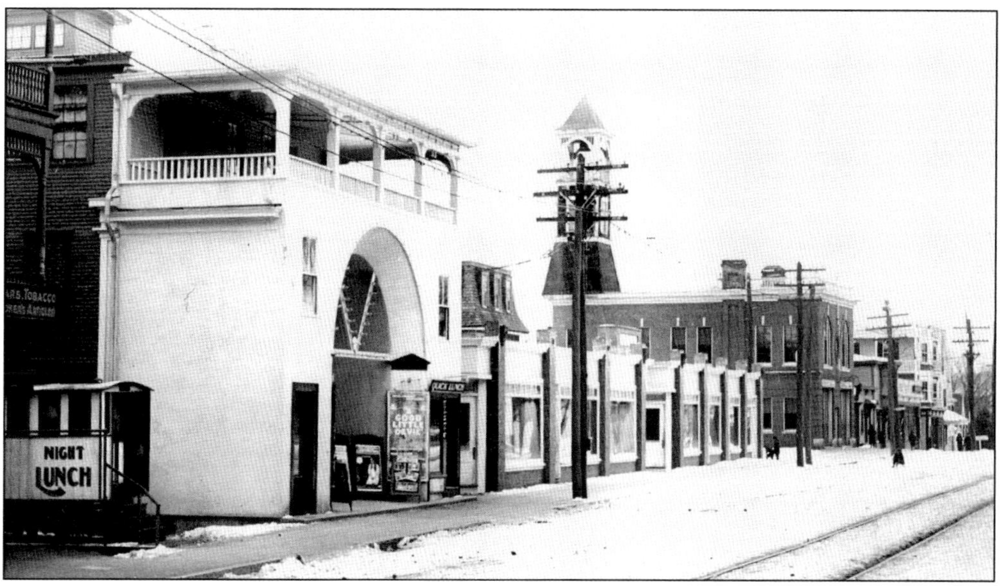

The Broadway Theater (the large building on the left) first opened around 1913 and soon became the entertainment center for the town. The door to the left of the arch led to a poolroom and bowling alleys. At the time of this photograph, the featured film was *Good Little Devil*, with Mary Pickford. The theater could hold up to 400 customers. The name was changed to the Derry Theater in 1938 and to the Plaza Cinema in 1965. The building was destroyed in a 1979 fire.

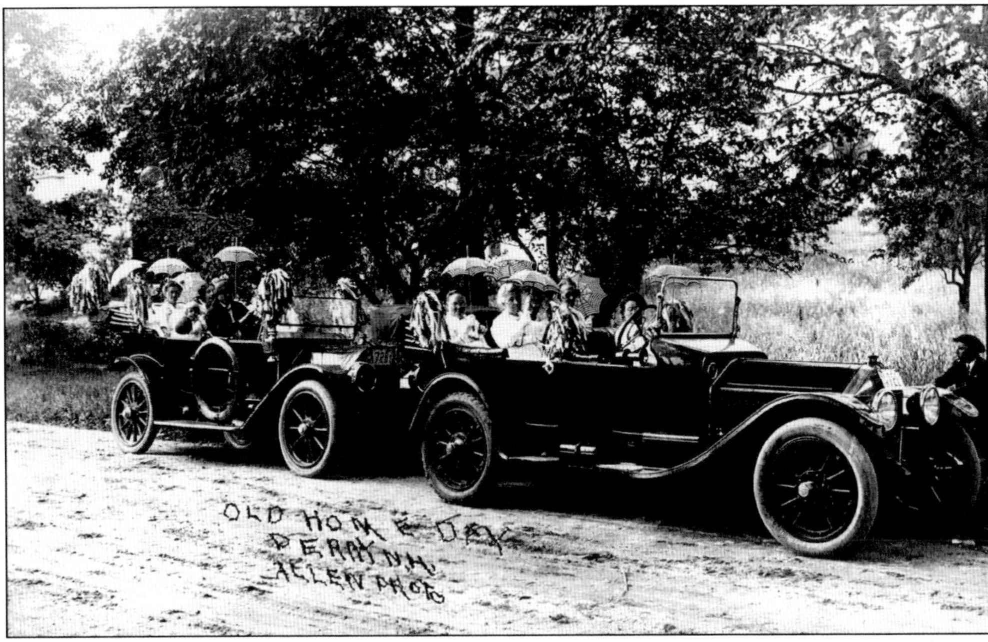

In 1915, former town residents returned to Derry for Old Home Week. There were days of parades, sporting contests, and picnics. Festivities included band concerts, fireworks, and motorcycle races. As many as 10,000 spectators watched a grand parade, which included these two cars. The automobile on the right is probably an English-made Morris-Oxford. The parade was filmed to be shown in area movie theaters. (Allen photograph.)

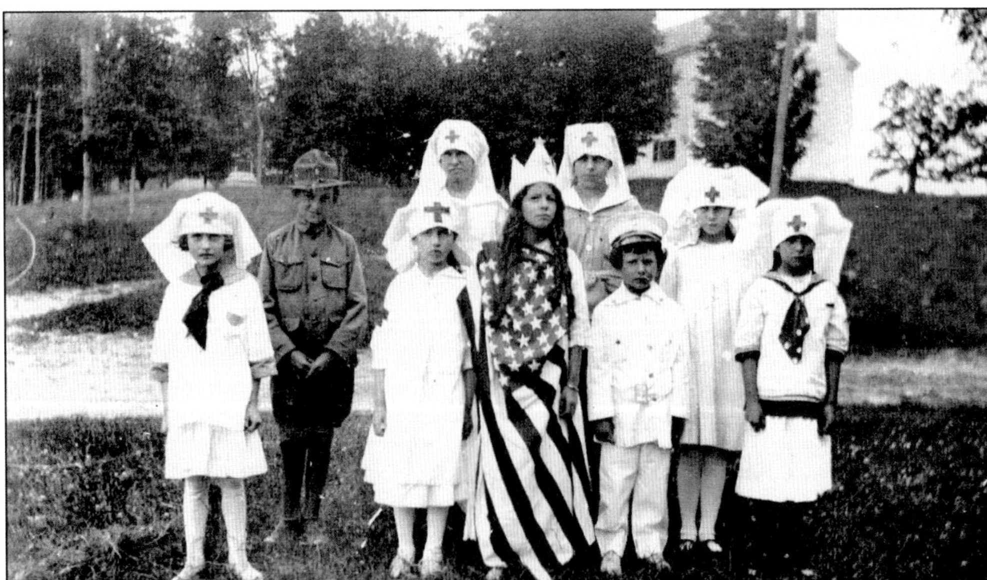

On the home front during World War I, volunteers helped the war effort by collecting scrap metal, milkweed pods, and fats. The local bank offered to make loans to children so they could buy pigs to help feed the fighting men. In 1917, these young children of East Derry put on a patriotic tableau to raise funds for the troops.

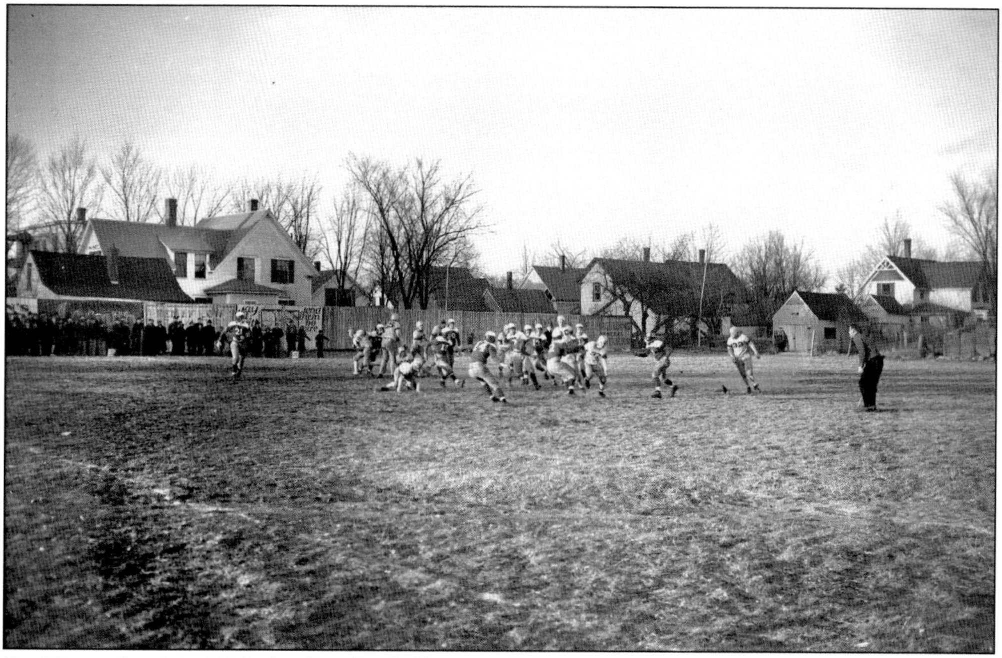

On November 11, 1939, the first football team of the Derry Junior High School, on Oak Street, played its first home game. Teacher Neal Sullivan coached the squad. The blocking of George Kachavos and the field running of Albert Booky were singled out for praise. The team lost to Catholic Central School of Lawrence, 14-0. (Arthur Lear photograph.)

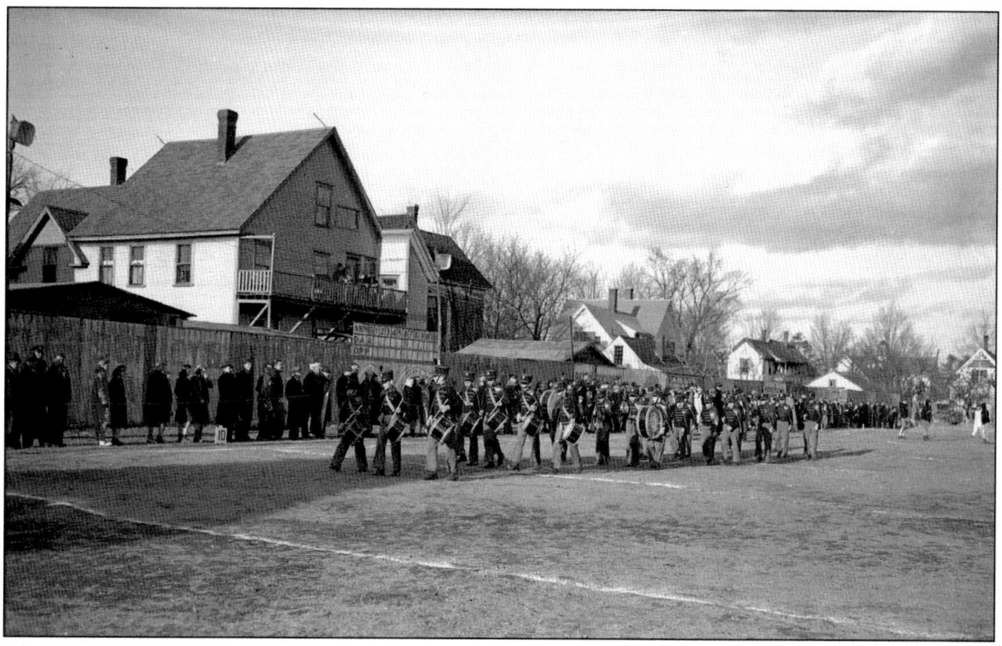

The half-time show at Derry Junior High School's first home football game was performed by the St. Thomas Aquinas Junior Drum Corps. The field is the DAA field off South Avenue. Note the lights installed for use during night games. (Arthur Lear photograph.)

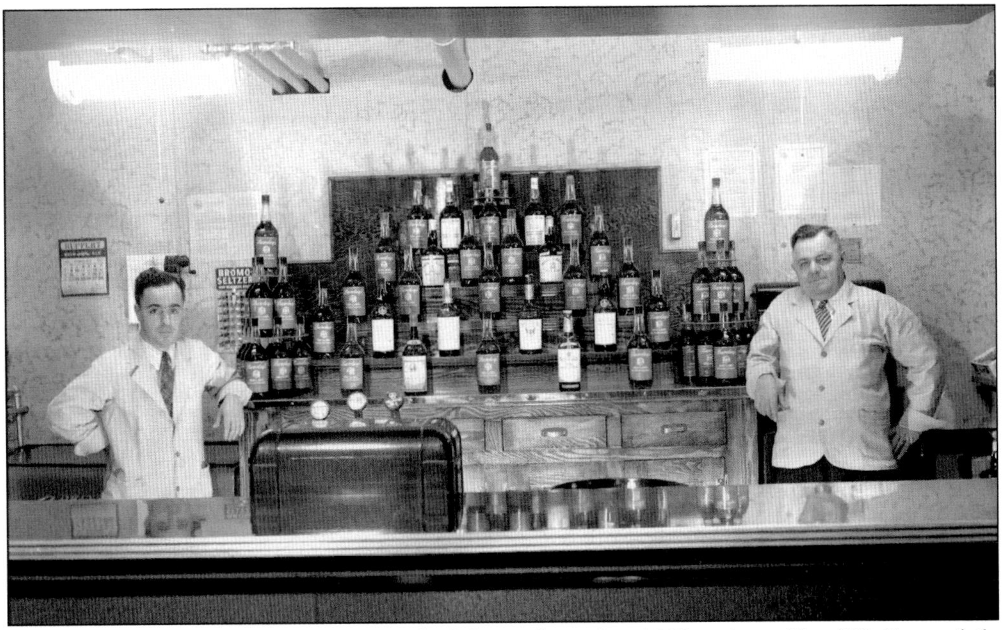

The local chapter of the Eagles Fraternal Club was formed in 1902 as Aerie No. 663. For a while the club owned the Whitney home next to the Adams Memorial Building. The Eagles moved to their present location on Railroad Avenue around 1925. The building was destroyed in a 1945 fire, and the present clubhouse was built soon after. This photograph was taken in 1942.

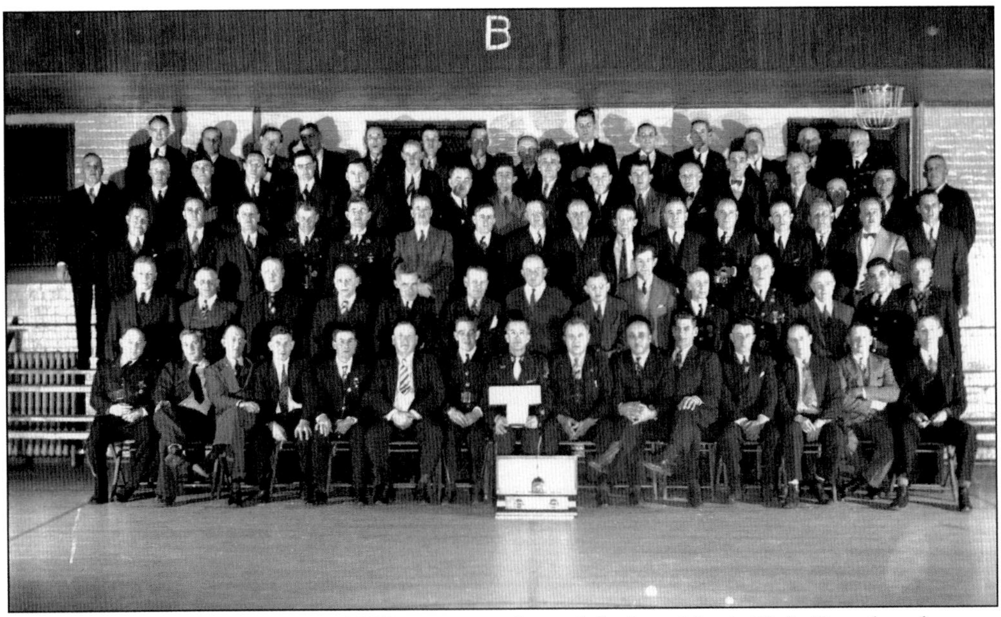

In 1919, a group of 98 Derry World War veterans formed the Last Man's Club. Together the men owned a fine bottle of brandy that would remain sealed until only a single member remained living. That man would then make a toast to the memory of his departed comrades. However, in 1975, the last 10 surviving members decided to open the bottle, perform their obligations, and disband the club.

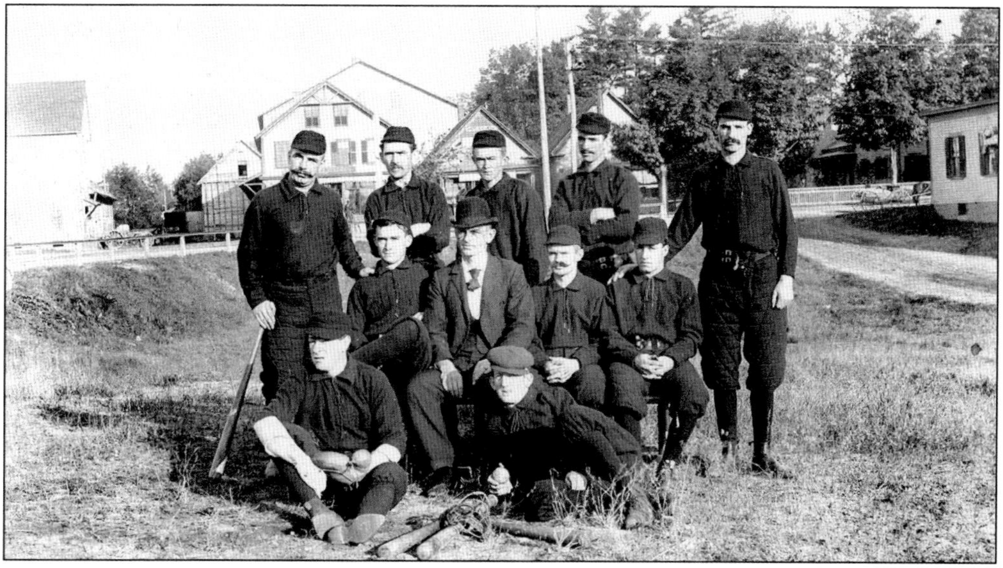

In September 1895, the Derry Baseball team practiced in a vacant lot next to the depot on Broadway. They were the town's first semi-pro ball team. They had just defeated the highly respected Maple Leafs of Lawrence, Massachusetts, in a double-header: 15-8 and 12-4. The Derry players split a victor's purse of $20 for each game.

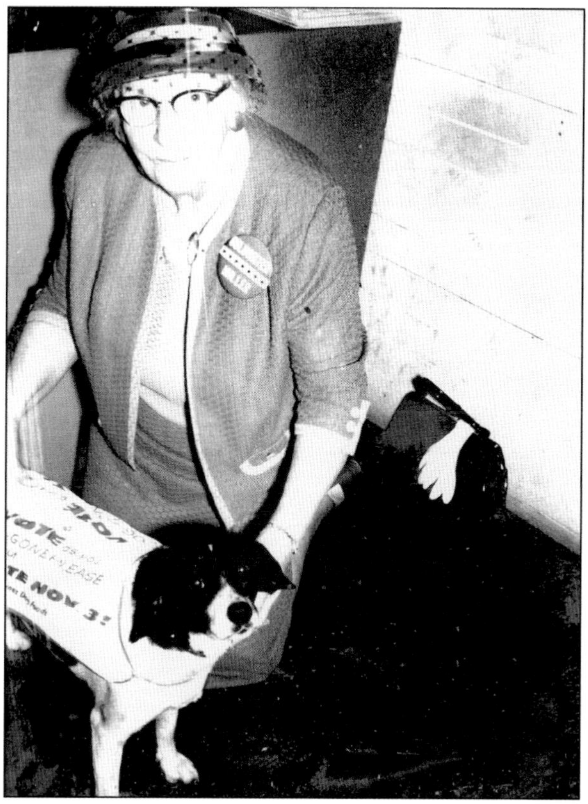

Caroline M. White (1887–1981) was considered by many to be the heart of the Republican Party in Derry. Here she is in November 1964, with her dog Spotty. While she is wearing a "Goldwater for President" pin, her dog is carrying a sign that says, "Vote as you dog-gone please but vote Nov. 3!" (*Derry News* photograph.)

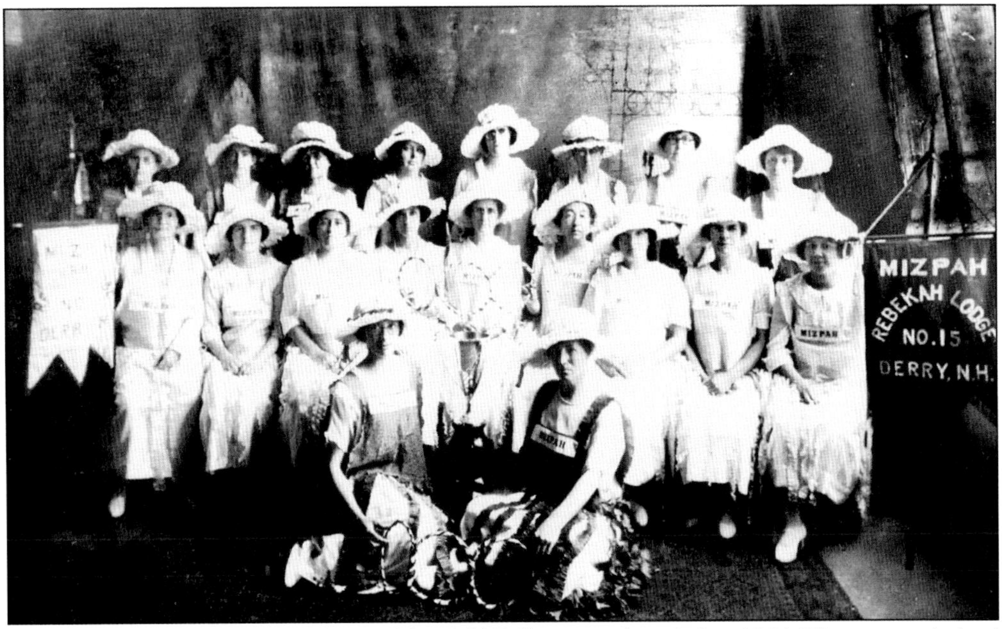

The Rebekah's Women's Auxiliary of the Odd Fellows was founded in 1881. They were pledged to care for the elderly, sick, widows, and orphans. The ladies are shown c. 1910 in their summer-best dresses and picture hats. The significance of the trophy in front is unknown.

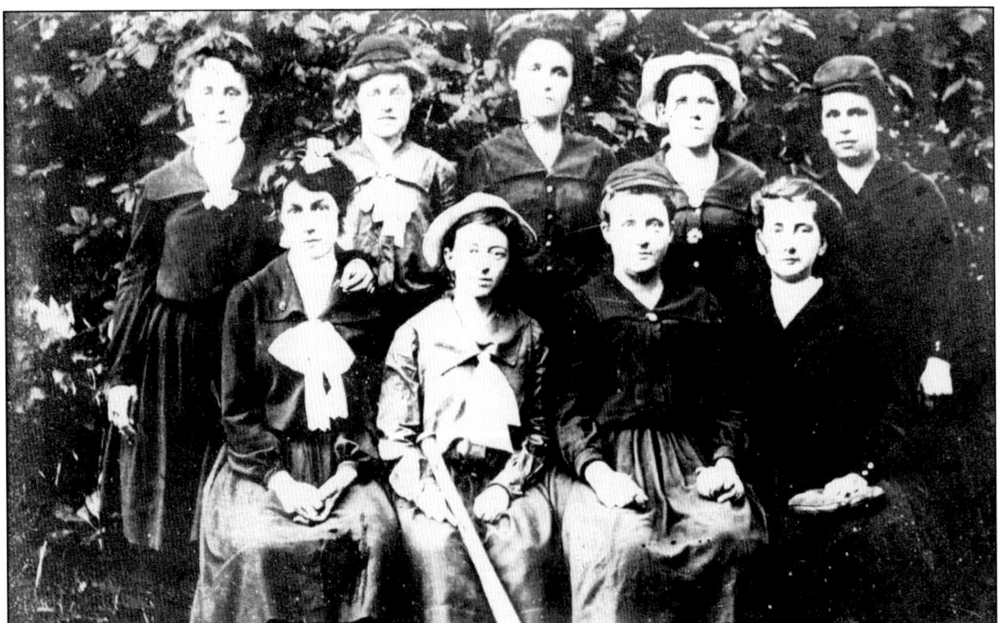
It is believed this group is the local Rebekah's baseball team of 1903. Some of these ladies seem to be well past their high school years in age. This image helps to dispel the stereotype that all club ladies were either at tea parties or organizing fund-raising events for missionaries in Africa.

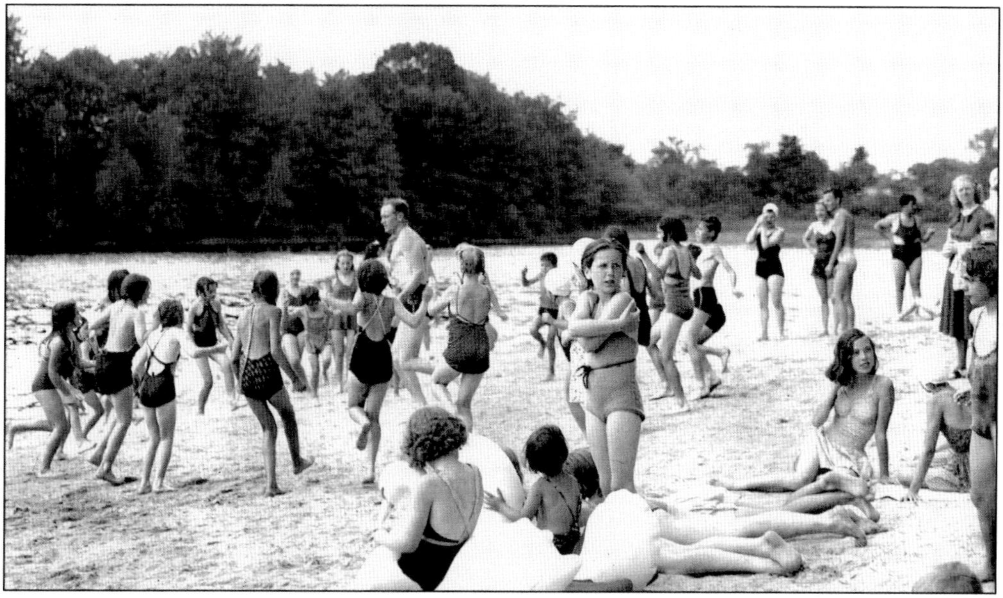

In 1940, Helen Hood (1866–1958) gave the land for Hood Park to the town. Local WPA workers did the construction work. The original plans called for sledding hills, tennis courts, horseshoe pitches, camping grounds, and two swimming areas. This photograph was likely taken at the 1940 grand opening of the park.

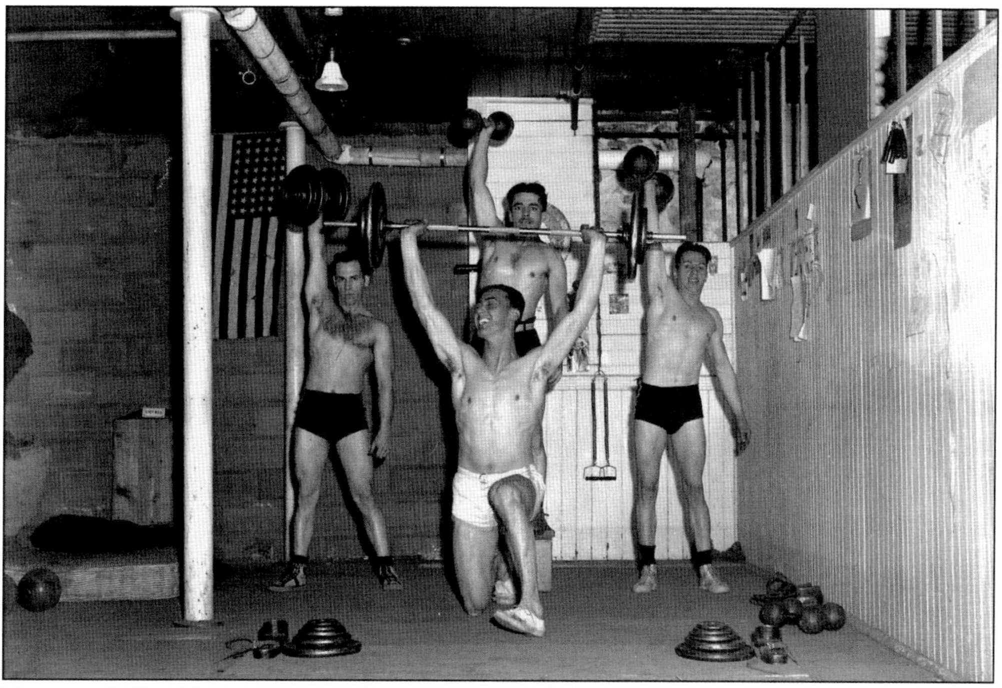

Henry and Harold Lauzon formed the Derry Weightlifters Club in 1939. Here, unidentified members of the club are seen in their practice room in the basement of the American House on Broadway. In meets against teams from other towns, the Derry club competed in three events: the military press, the clean and jerk, and the two-handed snatch. The club disbanded in 1941. (Arthur Lear photograph.)

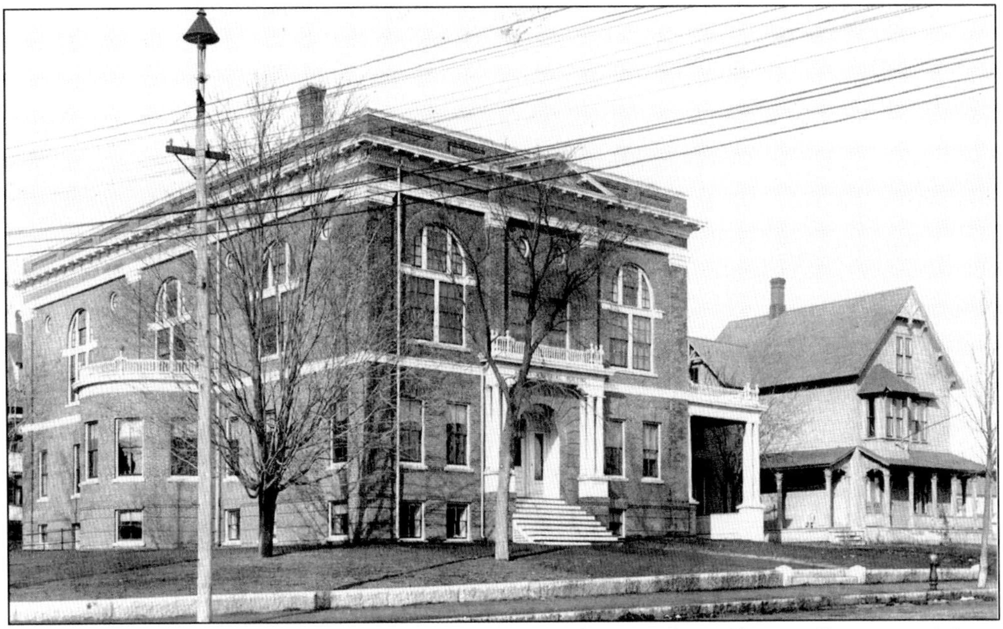

The 29 West Broadway building (on left) was given to the town by mill owner Benjamin Adams (1824–1901), and over the years it has served as the town hall (1905–1972), the public library (1905–1926), and the district court (1905–1998). On the right is the Whitney House, which was torn down c. 1988. The Adams Building is currently the home of the Arts Council, the Southern New Hampshire School of the Arts, the Derry Visitors Center, the Derry Chamber of Commerce, and the Derry Museum of History.

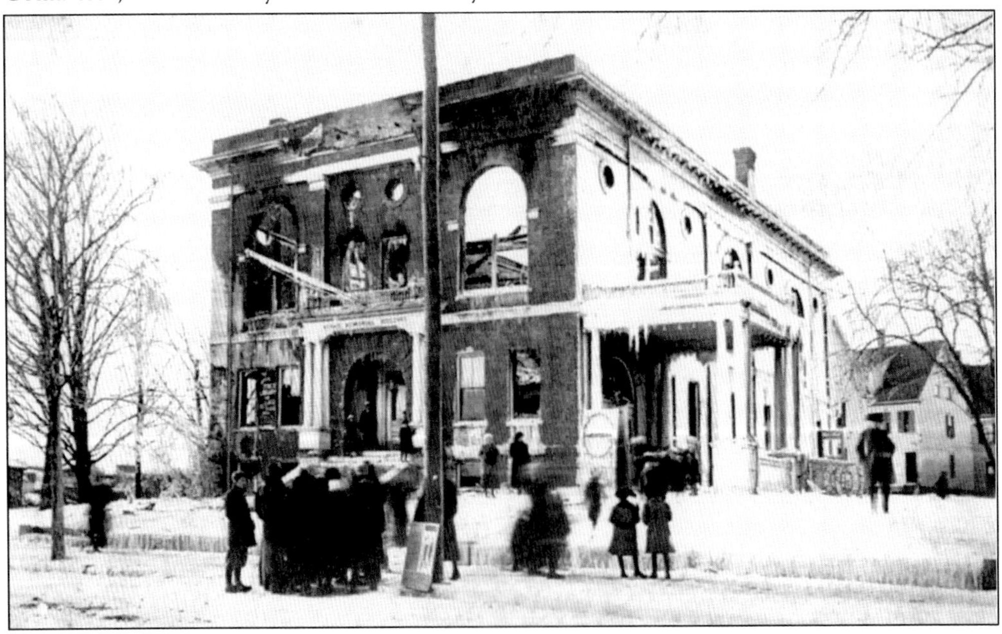

On January 13, 1914, a fire broke out at the Benjamin Adams Memorial Building. Despite the fact that the fire station was located directly across the street, the building was gutted. The thermometer reading that night was minus 25 degrees. Another fire badly damaged the building in 1927. The porte-cochere, or covered porch, seen on the right was enclosed after the first fire.

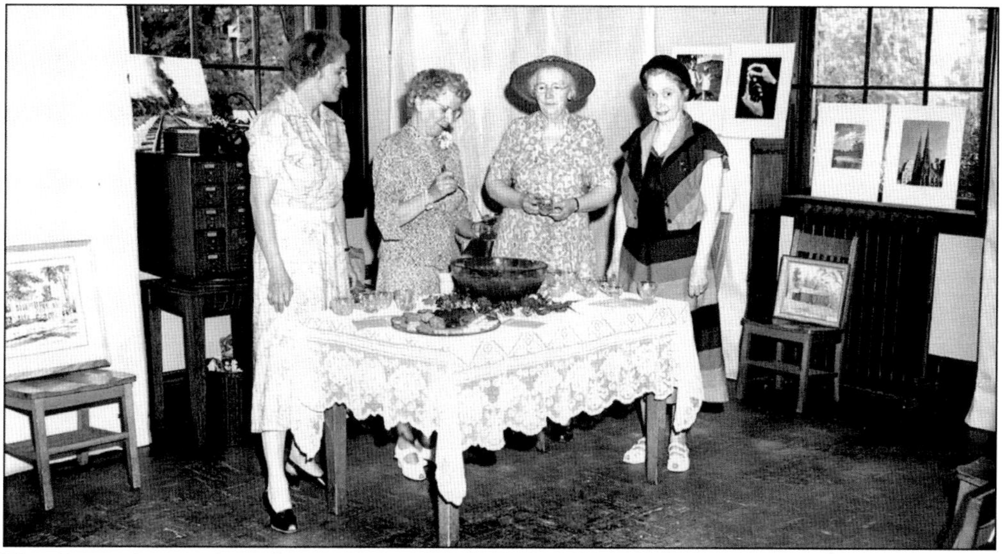

The Derry Arts and Crafts Association was founded in 1950. In this 1952 photograph, the club founders are shown at a reception at the Derry Public Library. They are, from left to right, Grace Scott, Barbara Newell, Carrie White, and Harriet Morrison. The club adopted the thistle and weaver's shuttle as its symbol. The group offered classes to the public in many arts and crafts areas. It disbanded in 1965. (F. J. Sullivan photograph.)

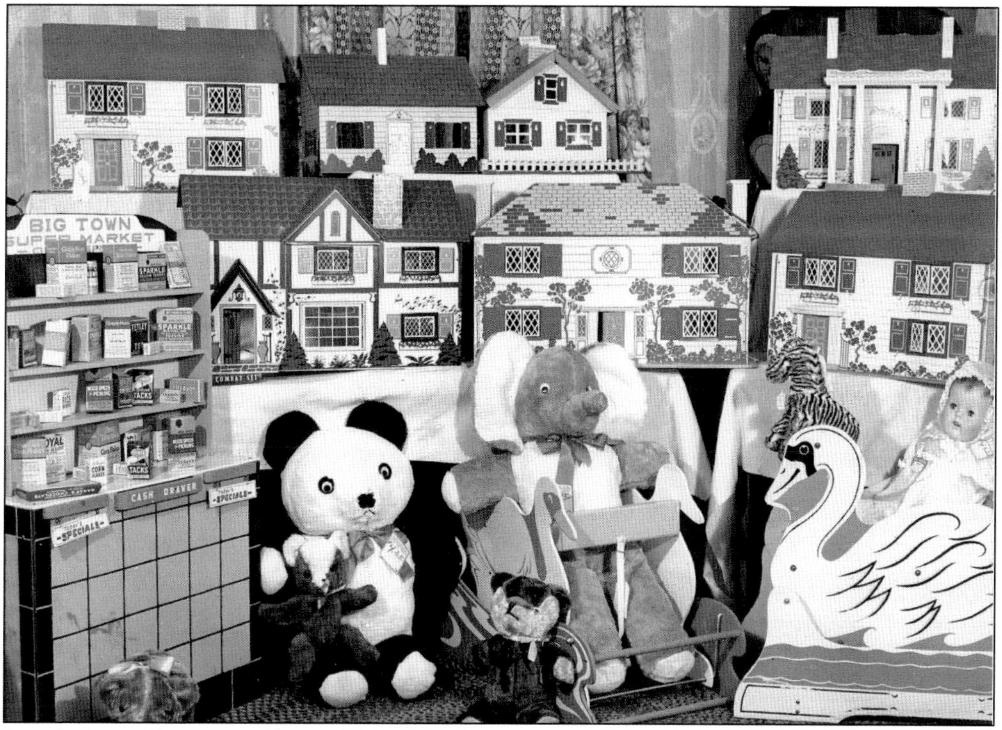

Just before Christmas 1941, Clement's Department Store, at 25 East Broadway, hired photographer Arthur Lear to record its holiday toy display. Shown here is a child's dreamland of dollhouses and teddy bears. This photograph was taken only a couple weeks before the attack at Pearl Harbor, which put a four-year damper on most holiday celebrations.

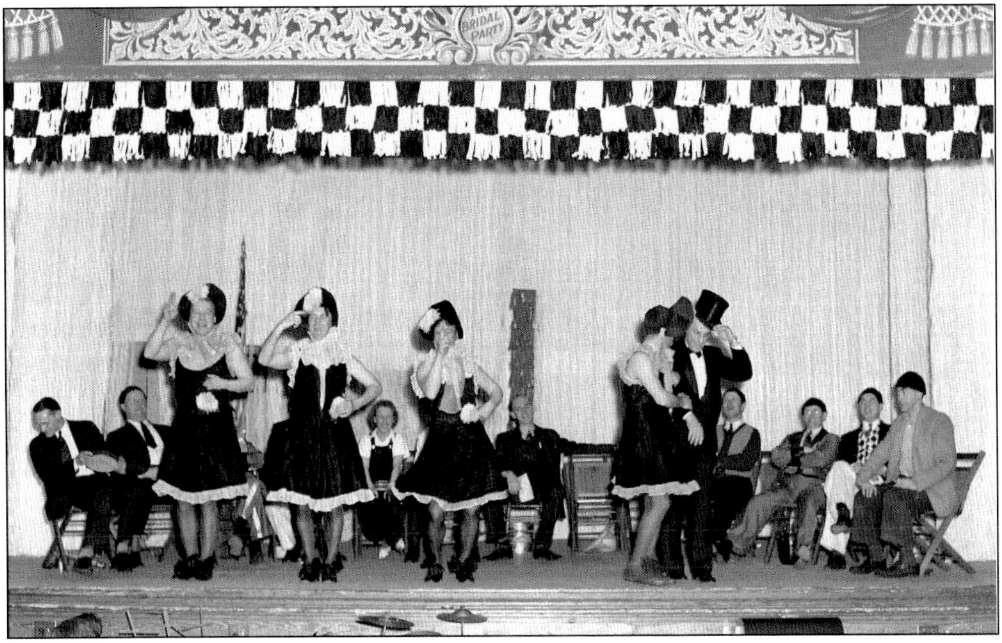

During World War II, the local Red Cross put on the Merry Makers Minstrel Show at the Adams Memorial Building. Mavis Monkley directed the show, with artwork by Ruth Pillsbury, and an orchestra led by Everett Stone. The show was a sellout and raised hundreds of dollars for the war effort. The identity of the dancing men in drag is unrecorded.

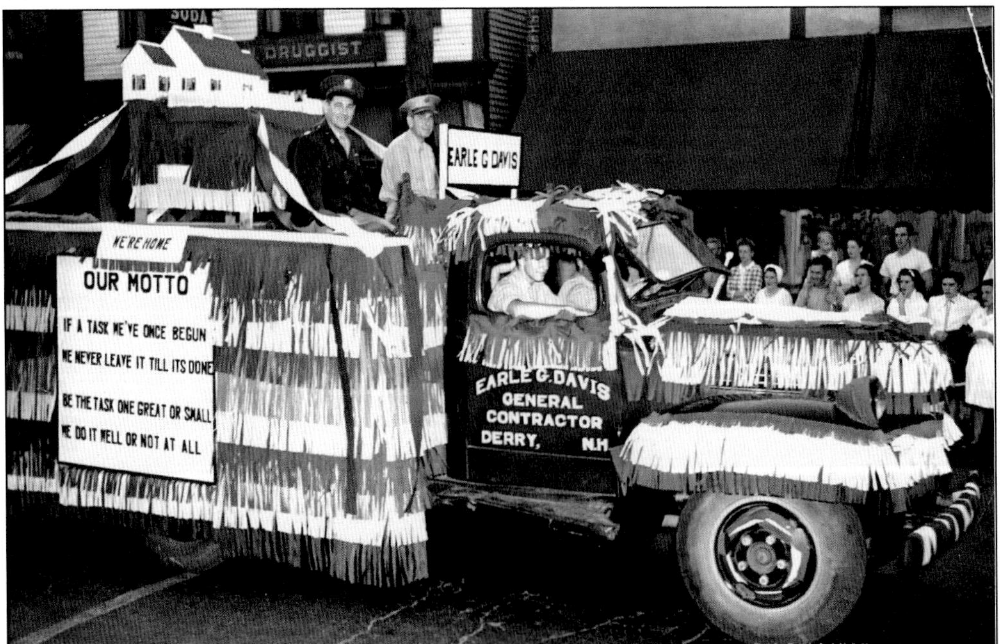

The annual observance of the U.S./Allied victory over Japan in 1945 used to be a major celebration in Derry. The 1946 parade consisted of 50 units and lasted for hours. An estimated 5,000 spectators watched the parade. At night, Maple Street was closed off for a block dance that lasted until midnight. (F. J. Sullivan photograph.)

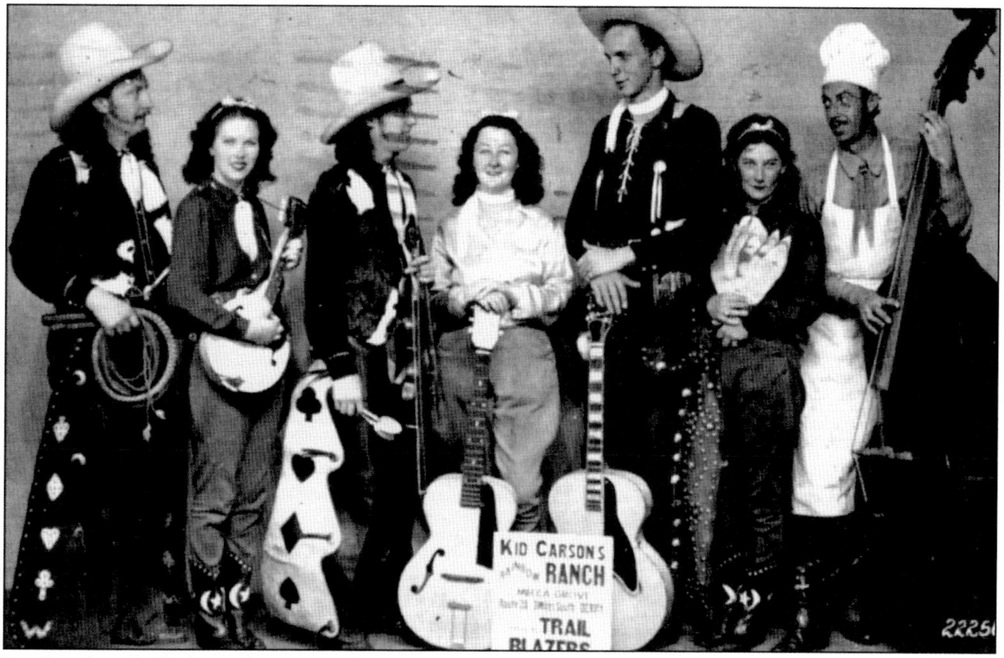

In the decade before the Second World War, there were many locals who sought fame and fortune through show business. In 1941, Kid Carson's Trailblazers (pictured) performed every Sunday at the Rainbow Ranch, on the top of Ryan's Hill. During the week, the roadhouse was called Mecca Grove. The group also had a daily show on a Lawrence radio station.

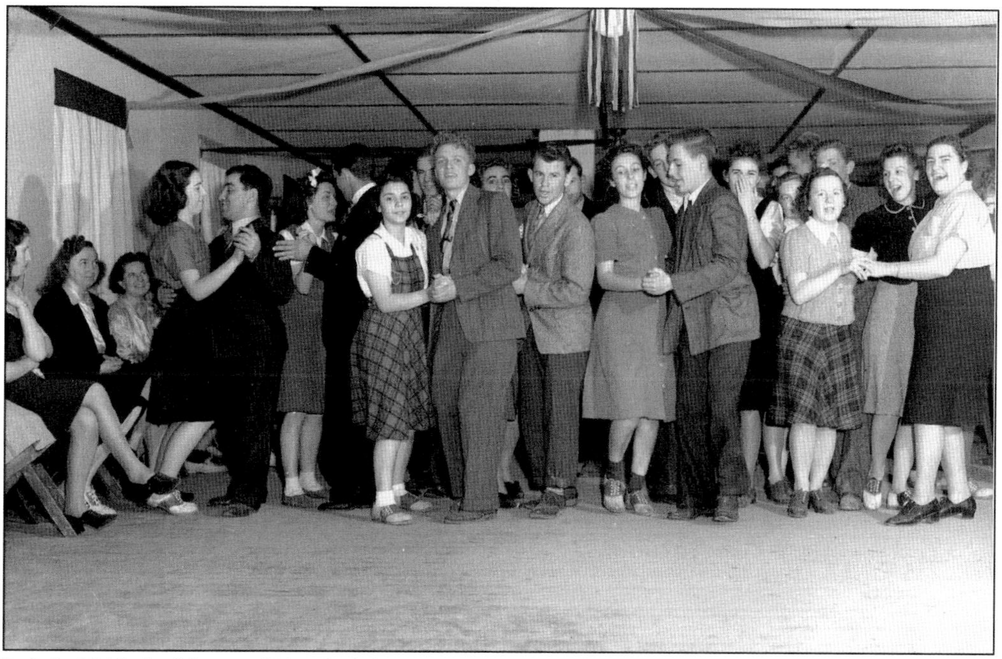

In July 1940, the National Youth Administration opened a third-floor office in the bank building on Broadway. There, young adults, ages 18 to 25, could learn work-related skills. Boys could learn welding or carpentry; girls could learn home economics or secretarial skills. In October, the office sponsored this Halloween dance. (Arthur Lear photograph.)

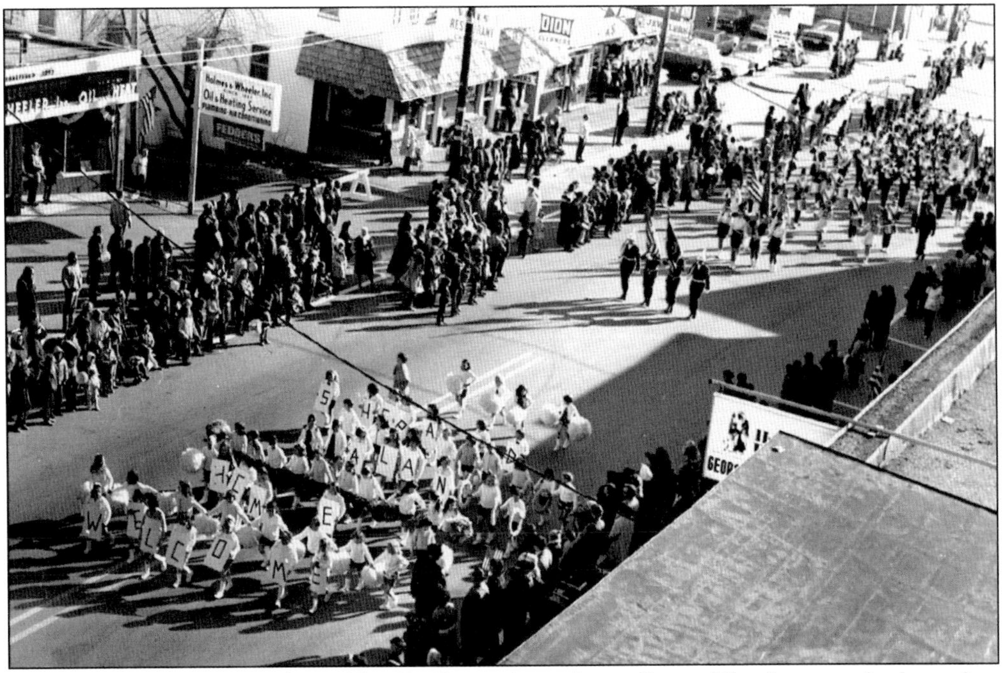

In total, there have been three Alan B. Shepard parades in Derry. The first was the legendary "parade that just happened," on May 5, 1961: the day Shepard first went into space. On June 9, 1962, there was the first Shepard parade with the astronaut in attendance. On April 5, 1971, this parade honored Shepard's walk on the moon.

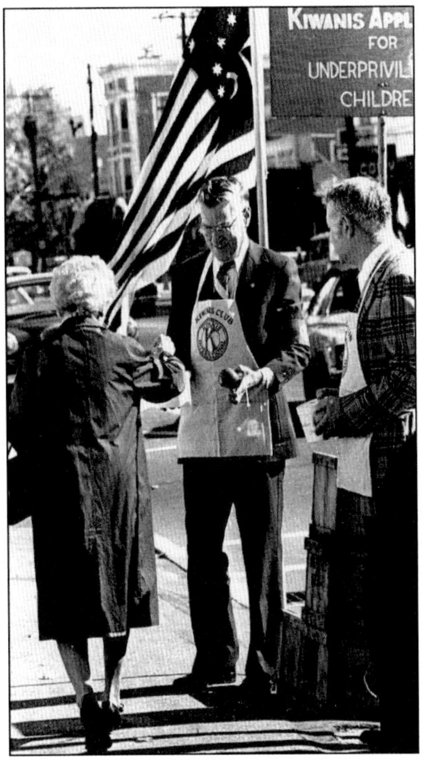

For several decades, the Kiwanis Club of Derry re-created a common scene from the Great Depression: people selling apples on street corners. In this 1965 photograph, bank president Fred Manning and shoe store owner George Kachavos stand in front of the First National Bank (now the Sovereign Bank) as they sell apples to raise funds to help underprivileged children. (*Derry News* photograph.)

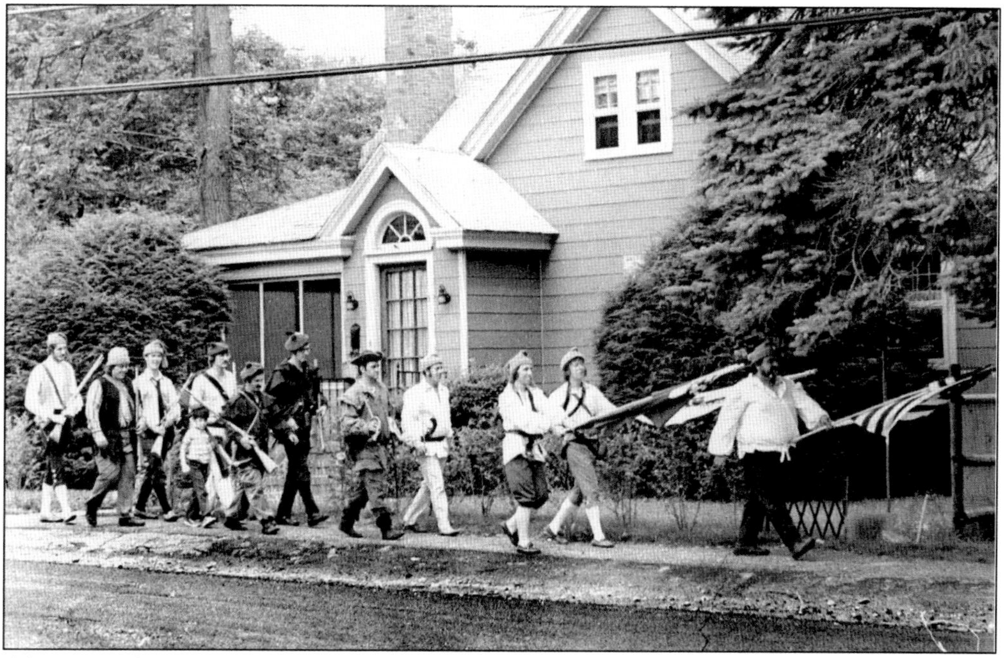

After a 1975 ceremony at the Stark Road birthplace of Gen. John Stark, the Derry Militia marched to the Molly Reid DAR chapter house in Derry Village for a luncheon. Leading the march and holding the American flag is Capt. Jerry Cox, the town's recreation director.

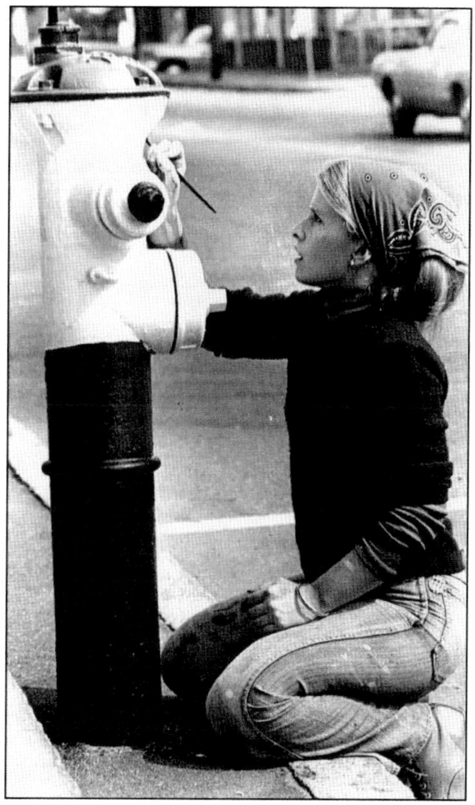

Here is Mary Garvey of the Derry Junior Women's Club, painting the fire hydrants on Broadway for the bicentennial celebration of 1976. The fireplugs were made to resemble miniature Colonial soldiers, painted red, white, and blue. Each little man guarded downtown Derry for several years before being repainted the more traditional red color. (*Derry News* photograph.)

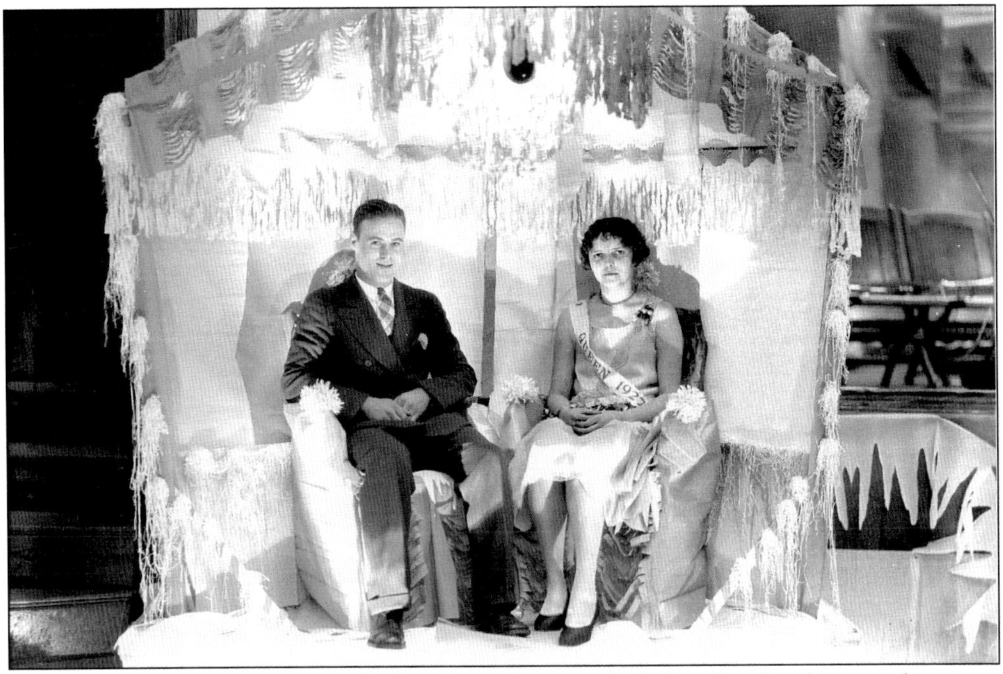

The queen of the Winter Carnival of 1927 was 22-year-old Arline Smith, who won the crown by receiving more than 10,000 votes. She was a bookkeeper at the First National Bank. She selected as her king local star athlete Thomas Steward. The coronation ball was held at the Adams Memorial Building, which was decorated in green and white: the colors of the carnival sponsor, the Derry Athletic Association.

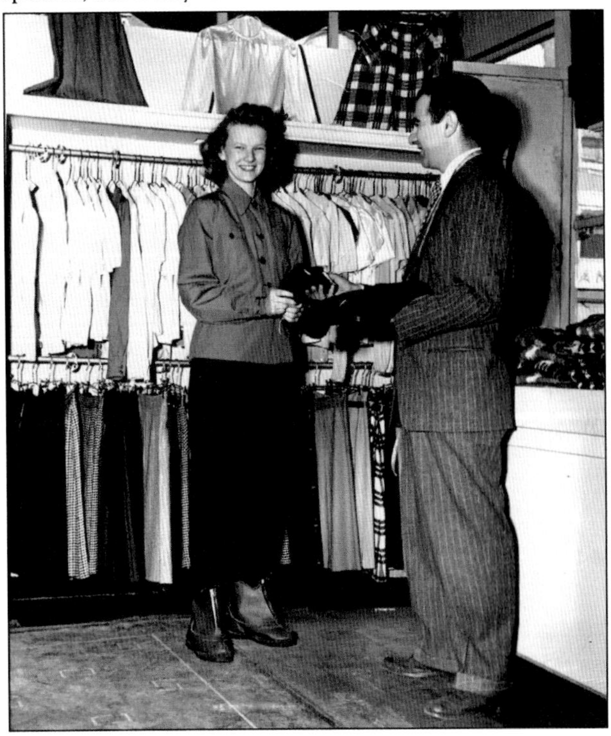

The queen of the 1947 Winter Carnival, Geraldine Traintor, is shown accepting one of her prizes. Edward Semara of Semara's Department Store on Broadway is presenting her with a complete ski outfit worth $50. She also received an official photograph from photographer Francis J. Sullivan. (F. J. Sullivan photograph.)

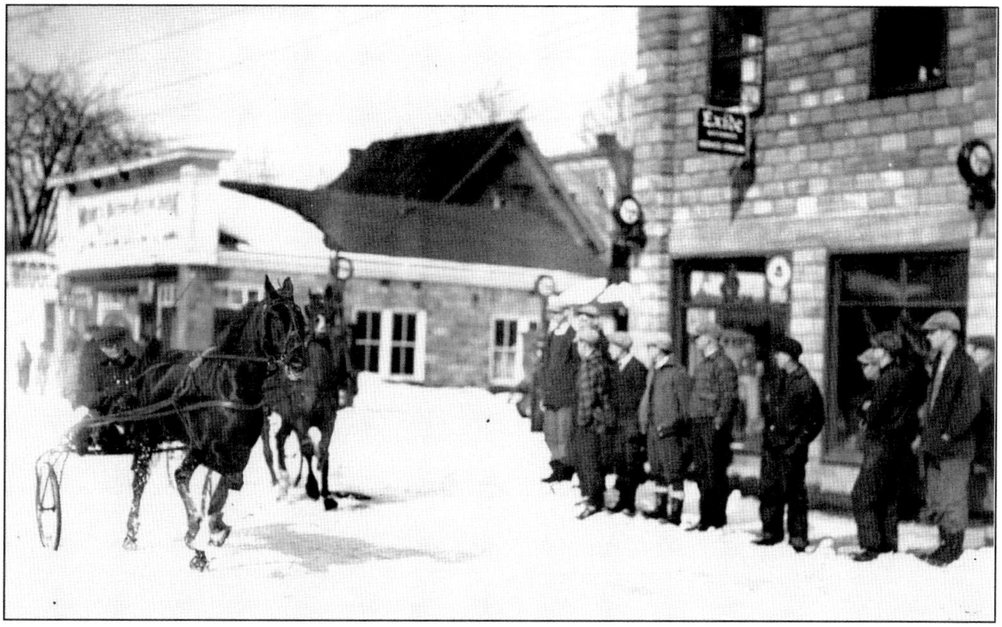

For many years, horse racing was a major event at the Winter Carnival. Pictured here is the 1927 sulky race along a course that ran from Birch Street to East Broadway to Wilson Street. At the upper left is the home of the *Derry News*. In later years, the horse racing was moved to Beaver Lake, where it would continue for decades.

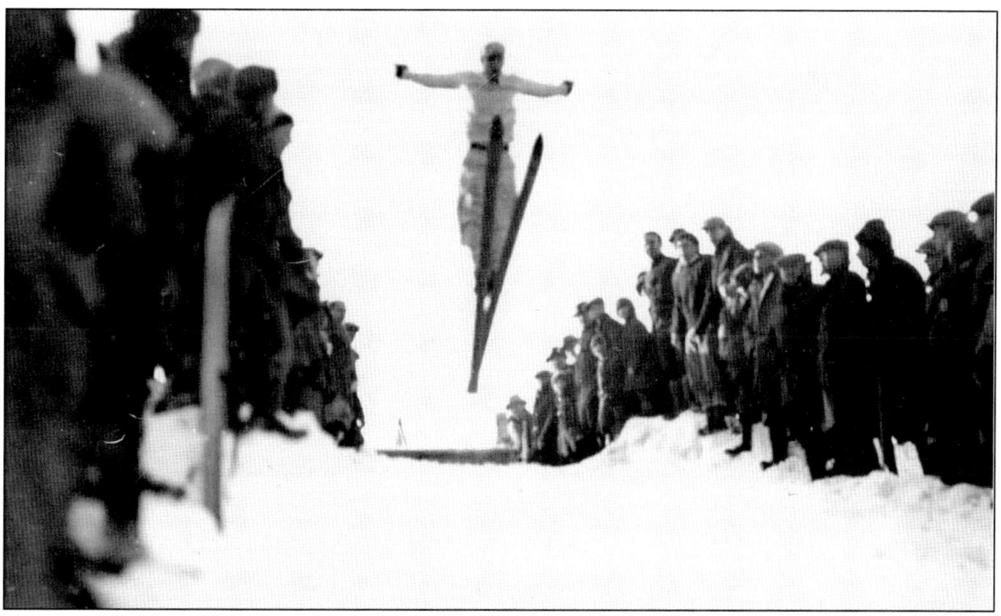

Among the crowd-pleasing events at the annual Winter Carnival were ski-jumping contests. The jumps were usually made at Ela's Hill, just over the border into Londonderry. This hill is now occupied by Exit 4 on Route 93. This photograph was taken during the Winter Carnival of 1927.

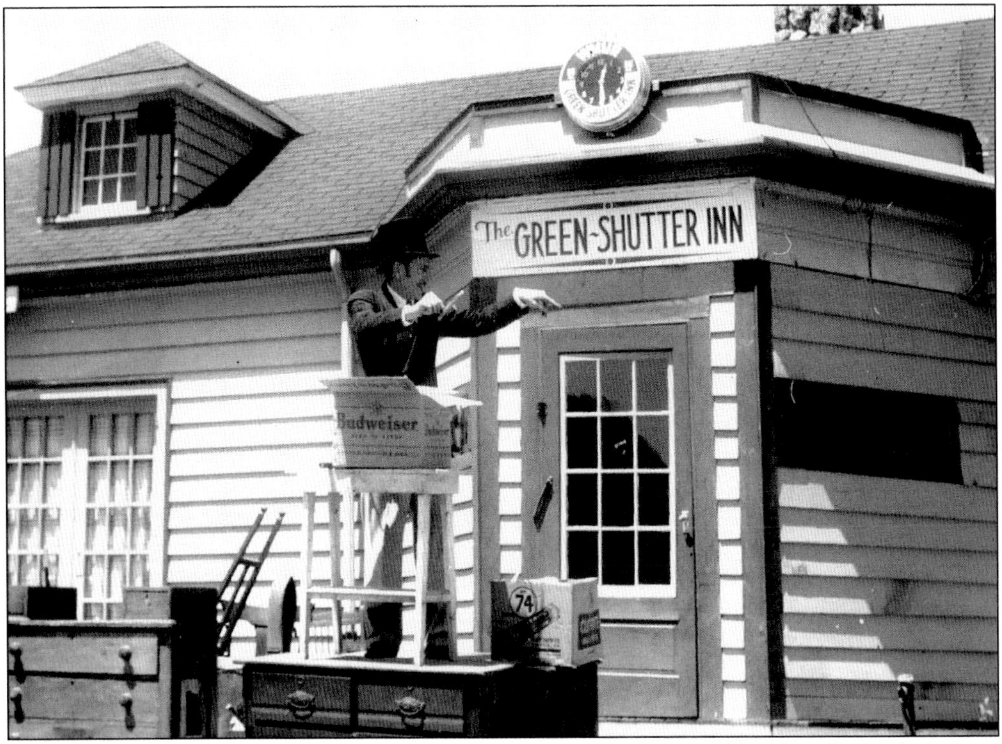

One of the most popular of the local auctioneers was Otis "Topper" Hamblett (1915–2004). Around 1950, he became a full-time auctioneer; it was a career he followed for nearly 40 years. Hamblett always conducted sales while wearing a tall silk hat as a way of identification. He is shown at an auction c. 1953 at the Green-Shutter Inn, now the Yard Restaurant, in Londonderry.

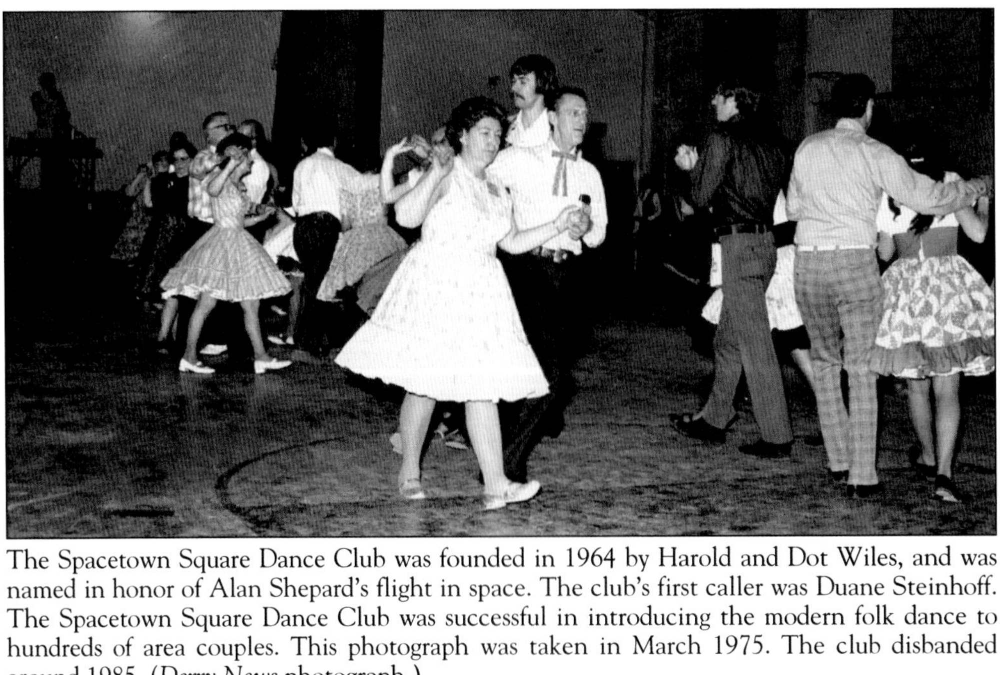

The Spacetown Square Dance Club was founded in 1964 by Harold and Dot Wiles, and was named in honor of Alan Shepard's flight in space. The club's first caller was Duane Steinhoff. The Spacetown Square Dance Club was successful in introducing the modern folk dance to hundreds of area couples. This photograph was taken in March 1975. The club disbanded around 1985. (*Derry News* photograph.)

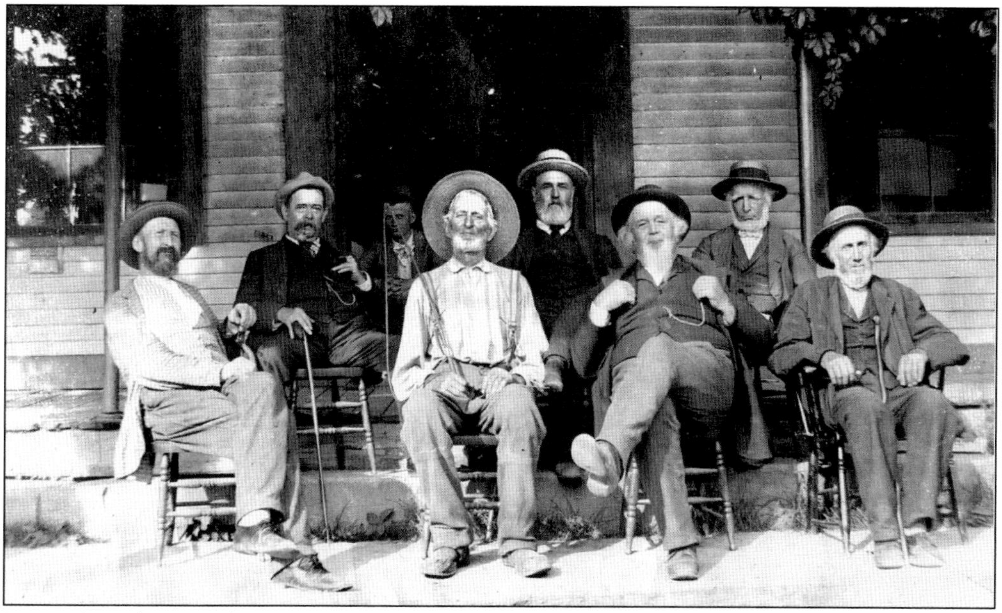

In 1885, a photographer was passing through Derry Village when he spotted a group of men ruminating in front of Couch's Store. This picture was reprinted by newspapers all over the country as being a true representation of New England characters. These village elders are, from left to right, as follows: (first row) Jacob Couch, Isuae Butterfield, Charles Adams, and Benjamin Barker; (second row) unidentified traveling salesman, Elwin Robie, Charles Wilson, and Ebenezer Upton.

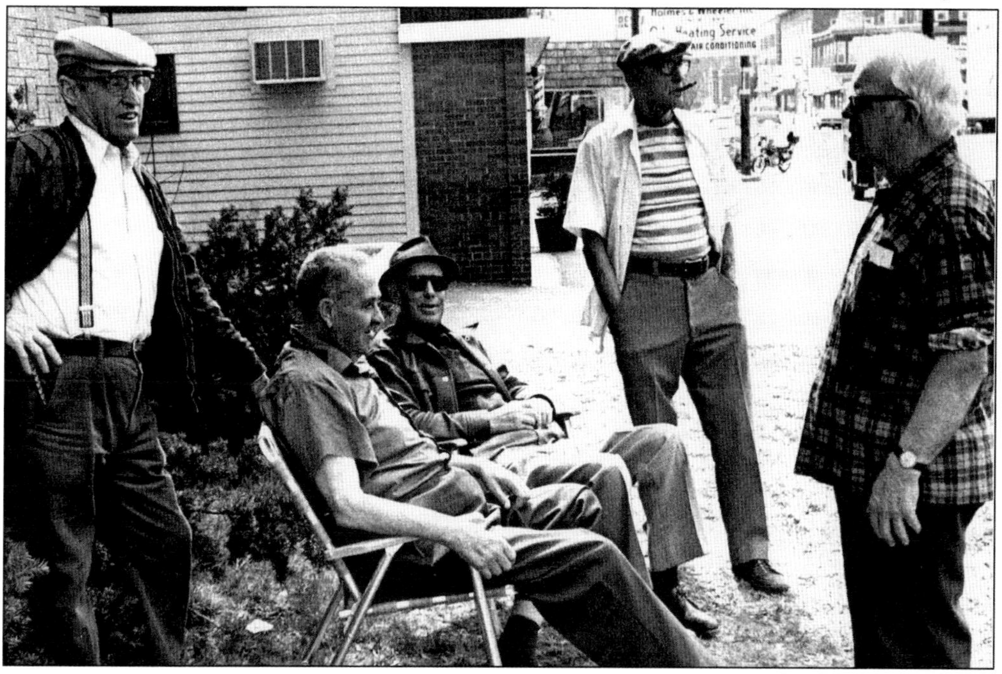

In early April 1976, a group of village elders found a patch of sunshine on the first warm day of spring. Here talking and joking in front of the American Legion on Broadway are, from left to right, Ed Holm Sr., Arthur Hepworth, James Gallien, Joseph Pelky, and Alexander "Shine" Bogle. (*Derry News* photograph.)

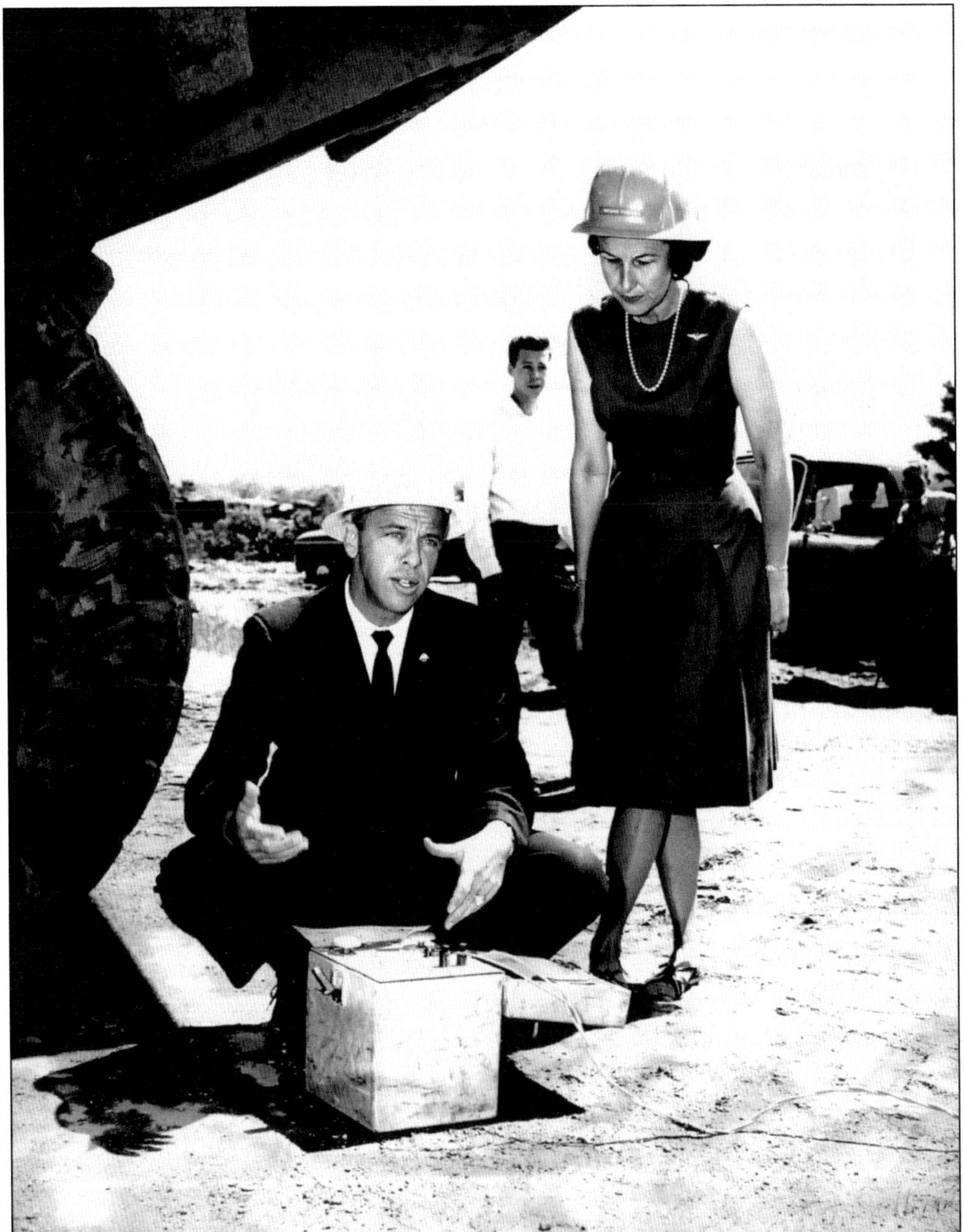

In June 1962, astronaut Alan B. Shepard Jr. (accompanied by wife Louise) prepares to set off the dynamite charge that will begin the construction of Exit 4 from Route 93. The 12-mile-long road was named in honor of Shepard. The new road made it easy for people to commute from Derry to jobs in Massachusetts. Within a decade, Derry's population doubled, and then doubled again. Apartment complexes, housing developments, shopping malls, and new schools sprung up all over the town. In 2005, Derry is New Hampshire's largest town. This photograph by Francis Sullivan captures the moment in history when the Derry way of life changed forever. (*Derry News* photograph.)